After the Last Post

After the Last Post

The Lives of Indian Historiography

BENJAMIN ZACHARIAH

OXFORD
UNIVERSITY PRESS

Great Clarendon Street, Oxford, OX2 6DP,
United Kingdom

Oxford University Press is a department of the University of Oxford.
It furthers the University's objective of excellence in research, scholarship,
and education by publishing worldwide. Oxford is a registered trade mark of
Oxford University Press in the UK and in certain other countries

Published in the United States of America by Oxford University Press
198 Madison Avenue, New York, NY 10016, United States of America

British Library Cataloguing in Publication Data

Data available

Library of Congress Control Number: 2023930592

ISBN 978–0–19–286786–5

Printed and bound in India by
Replika Press Pvt. Ltd.

For Subhas Ranjan Chakraborty, who showed us the way; and

in fond memory of Uttara Chakraborty.

Contents

Preface to the South Asia Edition

It must be something of an anomaly that a book whose origins lie within the remit of what, since the Cold War partitioning of the world into area studies, has been referred to as 'South Asian' history, has had something of a career outside South Asia before it has 'returned' home. The tradition of separate South Asia editions of books published outside South Asia has been led mainly by the question of pricing: most currencies are stronger than the Indian rupee, the strongest of the South Asian currencies, now, even if that rupee has in the meantime acquired a peculiar symbol of its own to upgrade itself to an indigenist pride. But the appearance of a book in South Asia three years after its initial publication elsewhere might have a peculiar intellectual history that cannot be subsumed entirely within a material conditions approach, even by the most reductive of Marxists.

'South Asia' has tended to be dominated by India, and India has been beset by a fever of nationalist-particular insularity. As a consequence, writing on India has been unintelligible to most of the outside world, unless it has been framed as 'global history', in which we are supposed to feel surprised or excited every time a subject of the British Empire from the area of that empire then known collectively as India ventured out of his or her designated area, or celebrate each time an 'Indian' idea travelled without a passport to a 'foreign' part of the world. This 'globalization' of South Asian history has had the effect of flattening details in the interests of a (circular) narrative that insists on its own globality: the set of questions that can be asked are increasingly reductive. The last problem could also fit into the ever-growing 'global south'-ism that also explains to us from where we should start perceiving the world, though we are slightly disturbed to learn that even when viewed from the 'global south' we are supposed to be clear exactly where the 'west' is. I shall have more to say on both these themes later, in separate publications; perhaps we could merely note here that destabilizing established geographies by arbitrary signs used in innovative arbitrariness is supposed to disrupt our sense of comfort, but it sometimes does so by refusing to engage with evidence or reason. Now, as Indian universities compete in a race to the bottom, aided or coerced by political moves to the right, Global Southistan is a good ally for the Hindutva boys who want to return to the glorious past.

But what is a poor book to do if it manages to escape the jaws of the twin beasts of the Global and the Global South? Nothing: it ought to disappear without a trace. South Asianists have, in true British fashion, put the telescope to their blind eye. And yet ... here it is.

Benjamin Zachariah
Berlin, August 2022

Preface: Reflections on Reflexivity

This book is about the production and consumption of history. Much of it is framed by the concerns with which my generation (I was born in 1972) had the honour to come of age professionally, and which will probably be remembered as the age of the posts, affectionately known now as postmodernism and postcolonialism. Several parallel themes crosscut the book's central focus on the discipline of history: its intellectual history, its historiography, and its connection to memory, particularly in relation to the need to establish the collective identity of 'nation', 'community', or state through a memorialization process that has much to do with history, or at least with claiming a historicity for collective memory. None of this can be undertaken without an understanding of the roles that history writing and history reading have played in public debates, or perhaps more accurately in public disputes.

If this book seems to some to be obsolete at its moment of publication, this also illustrates the cyclical nature of apparently linear time: we are spiralling downwards along the same vortex as our historical predecessors. 'History' must serve certain instrumental purposes, and if it does not, various people, self-appointed guardians of 'interests' and 'sentiments', reserve the right to get upset. No one questions this right; it is as if the domain of the historian is to provide serviceable histories to diverse people at the expense of an earlier (albeit inflated and arrogant) claim to 'accuracy'. Has this trend now intensified? Are human beings getting more and more hypersensitive about perceived affronts to their collective identities? Or is history being increasingly called upon to provide a 'safe space' in which no one is to be offended without a trigger warning being provided first, shadowing, as it were, classroom practices in North American universities? The past has never been that safe space, but history is not entirely about the past, the past is not all history, nor, as someone might have noticed, is the present a safe space. Then again, the safe space argument is about creating such non-threatening spaces as special zones. Should these special zones be confused with the larger world? Should historians have a role in the creation of such spaces in historical narrative?

In keeping with my formative experiences as a 'South Asianist', a good deal of the material presented here is specific to that area studies framework, but its resonances across the discipline of history should, I think, be apparent. A set of observations emerges from this material: firstly, histories of 'India' (and histories of the 'Global South', the 'Third World', or whatever collective shorthand one claims to historically stand for less privileged spaces) have come to rely inordinately on victimhood narratives for legitimation (and 'victimhood' at a national level seems to be a strange claim to make, especially for a country that purports at the same time to be an economic giant and a major political player on the world stage). Secondly, the collective memory that is sought to be legitimized as history is nation-state-centric; this often closes off other forms of collective memory, or creates ambivalences and tensions among the national and divergent regional, anti- or non-national collective memories. Since the 'nation' is itself a legitimator for the state, the state appropriates and instrumentalizes the victimhood narratives of its 'nation'(s). Thirdly, there appear to be moral positions to defend rather than research questions to answer; concurrently, an apparent collective retreat from the archives leaves historians without a basis for many of their arguments in the discipline of history itself. Fourthly, as histories are increasingly called upon to perform various public functions such as to legitimate collective claims to identity, it is a history-consuming public that gets to set a large part of the agenda for the public life of historiography, and we must ask as a matter of urgency to what extent and how professional historians should respond to these claims. Fifthly (and this probably applies across the humanities and social sciences), there has been a deterioration of professional standards and an anointing of mediocrity and conformity as principles to which to adhere in academic life, where institutional loyalties are often also existential lifelines that provide jobs, patronage, and protection. In a self-regulating 'profession' that seeks to maintain the right of self-regulation, this is a fatal flaw that can only lead to charges of uselessness and redundancy against which it is then impossible to defend the profession. All this sets up a vicious circle, where the purpose and meaning of writing and researching history, and its public purposes and meanings, are up for grabs in a situation of increasing murkiness and indecision.

Much of these reflections hinge on how political agendas are set or subverted within or outside the realms of academia, what the profession now considers 'good practice' (which varies greatly, given that 'historians' are now far from being a unified professional creed), how public uses of history set or curtail academic or political agendas, and the now-ubiquitous question of the identity, and therefore the qualification to make public utterances of the historian (who must be situated in, but often is reduced to, her 'identity'). And if what might have been a series of admonitions to one's own profession has become relevant in a context where 'fact' and 'post-fact' have merged into a world in which we cannot recognize deliberate lies anymore (we had long been sceptical of 'truth'-claims, but we seemed to know a deliberate lie when we saw one), perhaps it is important for us as 'professionals' to avoid condescension when faced with the history reading or history consuming public: to take them into confidence as to how the discipline functions, its crises, and hesitations included. It is important that the process of history writing as much as its results are communicable.

This is not to suggest that a 'public', however, defined, should be empowered to set a research agenda for historians, or else we will have an alleged 'nation' or 'community' demanding that we treat nicely the Maratha King Shivaji, a historical figure appropriated to mythology, or promote the monkey god Hanuman, a mythological figure, to historical materiality, to the puzzlement of a less insular public that might otherwise be interested in histories of India. Nevertheless, a model that imagines a self-satisfied and self-regulating community of professionals versus a less-educated set of outsiders is vulnerable on a number of counts: at least of relevance (historians have not been particularly good at talking to one another at any level of coherence, so why should they exist at all?) and of mystification (if we cannot communicate, no one needs to make an effort to listen). The current model of interface with a public is for historians to self-censor to some extent, and for a 'public' comprising right-wing paramilitary gangs or self-righteous Dalit groups to take offence at something a historian allegedly wrote (which they did not read but they knew they were offended by, or would have been had they read it). The question of the role that a 'public' can or ought to have and that of the autonomy and self-regulation of the 'profession' needs to be honestly and somewhat brutally discussed.

Parts of the material that have made their way into this book were written over a period of time when it was important to engage with and impossible to avoid the themes of identity and self-representation, and although all of the material has been rewritten to a greater or lesser extent, I have resisted the temptation to completely clean up the original essays to represent a position nearer to what I now hold. Written in the context of engagements with historical scholarship in/and public political debates in various parts of the world in which I have lived and/or worked (principally India, Britain, and Germany in the 1990s, 2000s, and 2010s, more or less in that order with some overlaps), each essay bears the traces of those interventions: context, as intellectual historians have always told us, is the key to understanding the nature of an intervention. Over time, the connected nature of the pieces became evident to me, and built up into an urge to gather them together and to make the connections explicit.

The book starts with my discomfort with postcolonial theories in and as history. Following that are essays that examine the state of the discipline, the art of reading and using archives, and practices of tracking the history of ideas, which I see as important to the continuance of a professional discipline of history. In-between are a number of pieces that play with themes of history, memory, and identity in a variety of ways that postmodernism might have called playful and ironic; I am happy to appropriate this description now, though in some cases, I cannot recall the mood of the original. These in-between essays also enable a reading of the extent to which postcolonialism and modernism were and are a part of my own writing. Contextualizing authors is what historians were taught to do; often, it is all they do, as the (il)legitimacy of the voice amplifies or erases the argument that is made in and by that voice. It was a while ago that Roland Barthes informed us of the death of the author, at whose expense, he said, the reader was born; however, 'the reader is without history'.[1] This is an auspicious and facetious starting point; meanwhile, I hope an actual death of the author might lead to a resurrection of the argument. Meanwhile, on the subject of trying to read the author, whose alleged death is often strategically overlooked, I cannot avoid being awarded or subtracted victimhood points in terms of my identity: sexual

---

[1] Roland Barthes, 'The Death of the Author', in *Image-Music-Text*, trans. Stephen Heath (London: Fontana, 1977), 142–148, quote from 148.

orientation, gender, bodily attributes, colour, or hair; in previous publications, I have provided some of the necessary autobiographical material for *ad hominem* arguments to be made. A quick, last word on the title: 'the Last Post' might well mean 'the most recent post'. I cannot predict endings, even as I am not against closure.

Acknowledgements

Intellectual debts are never just intellectual. I would like to pay tribute to the comradeship of a few people who have shared political and intellectual commitments with me over the last few years. Jeff Vernon is in many ways the co-author of this book, though he would never acknowledge this. Subhas Ranjan Chakraborty and Uttara Chakraborty have, in conversations with me and in arguments with each other, shaped my thoughts since I was an undergraduate at Presidency College, Calcutta. I have benefitted greatly from the support and encouragement over many years of Robert S Anderson. Dhruv Raina and S. Irfan Habib have been with me on many journeys and in many disputes. I have shared ideas and political struggles with Kavita Philip in difficult times.

This book would have been far less coherent without the meticulous and patient comments provided by Lutz Raphael and Brigitta Bernet, who, along with Amar Baadj and Debojit Thakur, provided at the University of Trier the best form of intellectual comradeship that I could ever have hoped for. Rachel Lee has shared with me many ideas and experiences that have informed and enriched this book. Sanghita Sen's comments on rhetoric and tone were important to the framing of the argument. Deborshi Chakraborty and Shreyasi Biswas, separately, and on one occasion together, were part of discussions that alerted me to contemporary political resonances. Anna Diem was an essential interlocutor and sometimes brutal critic. So was Satadru Sen, who did not live to read the final version. I have not always taken your advice, comrades, but I have tried to honour the spirit of your commitments.

Introduction

The Instrumentalization of Historiography and the Production of Victimhood

'History' has had a complicated history in India. Disputes about what it is, who or what it should be about, who should write it, for whom it is intended, who has the right to be offended by it, and who has the duty to make sure it doesn't offend anyone have been central to the history of this historiography. Nearly 25 years ago, one of the leading professional historians of India wrote of the 'many worlds of Indian history',[1] and he might well have added more explicitly that there were many worlds of Indian historiography, of Indian historical consumption, or of claims made on history. The varieties of things that are called history in relation to India are many: sophisticated English-language scholarship of the Anglo-American university, drawing upon French philosophical traditions in their American avatars; imperial history 'old' and 'new'; middle-European derivative scholarship living off the talents of graduate students and 'research assistants'; obligatory courses in provincial universities across India that still draw upon textbooks written in British India by colonial apologists; local historians writing in regional languages; literary figures writing historical novels in several languages, film and television versions of historical events and historical romances; and postcolonial intellectuals who see history as Western colonialist conspiracy but still agree to draw their salaries as historians in the Western academy, happily co-exist in this tolerant world.

This of course does not imply a lack of conflict over history, but these conflicts are often not in academic arenas, and have if anything intensified in recent times. To the list of producers of things called history, we

---

[1] Sumit Sarkar, 'The Many Worlds of Indian History', in *Writing Social History*, ed. Sumit Sarkar (Delhi: Oxford University Press, 1997), 1–49.

can (now?) add fascist groups fomenting violence against recalcitrant professionals, paramilitary groups producing their own versions of history, removing a prime minister here, or adding a religion to a revolutionary atheist there. Violence is not merely epistemic or discursive when connected to history: paramilitary groups belonging to political parties can and do destroy property; or attack, kill, or maim actual people; when their puppetmasters proclaim that they have been offended by works of history that they have almost certainly not bothered to read; or are offended by films that purport to depict historical events that do not fictionalize them the way they wish to fictionalize them. On an optimistic note, therefore, it is possible to celebrate the continued importance of history in India, and therefore of historiography, in the public lives of the Indian state. Whereas in some parts of the world, the lack of relevance of history and/or the humanities and social sciences have been the cause of some concern, leading to a series of laments on the death of the humanistic tradition, in India, on the other hand, history, and historians, are not only relevant but are also engaged in matters of life and death.

We might note here that the polite appellation for the region we usually consider India a part of is 'South Asia'—an inheritance of the Cold War 'area studies' tradition. But it has also long been noted that 'South Asia' tends to become a euphemism for 'India', the largest country of that seven (sometimes eight)-country region brought into being by the demands of Eastern and Western Bloc rivalries and the consequent scholarly division of the world.[2] The particular pathologies of Indian historiography require that they be treated in their own right, even as they must be related to trends that are far wider than those particularities and spill out beyond the boundaries of India or South Asia (what applies to 'history' in and of India applies to a large extent to other social sciences: this is both the strength and weakness of the 'area studies' inheritance that 'South Asia' as a field has had to bear). This is a useful reminder when we consider that the last 30-odd years of scholarship have been about a 'South Asian'/Indian exceptionalism—it's different, we have been told. Different from

---

[2] 'South Asia' comprises Afghanistan, Bangladesh, Bhutan, Maldives, Nepal, India, Pakistan, and Sri Lanka. Afghanistan is not always included in the category 'South Asia'. Historiographically, South Asia is dominated by India, with Pakistan and Bangladesh included mostly during the period they were still a part of British India, but Burma (now Myanmar) has found its way into Southeast Asia, despite having been a part of British India until 1937.

what? We don't know, but it's different. *Alag hai*, as the old advertisement on India's national television channel, Doordarshan, told us in the 1980s about a multinational corporation's attempt to inveigle itself into the national mouths of Indians.[3] As it has been about a generation since South Asianists could be persuaded to study more than South Asia, it is hardly surprising that 'different' no longer implies comparison with other places. There is of course that non-place with which all things Third Worldly can be compared, as if standing in constant juxtaposition and angry confrontation with one another: the 'West'. Where is this West? We're not told any longer, if we ever were. That traditional juxtaposition is so well-worn as to be completely debilitating by now. The comparator has had no historical existence: it's the moral and political *Platzhalter* that is the conceptual child of Edward Said's Orientalism.[4]

The primary imperative for a history of India is that it be compatible with an Indian nationalism. This nationalism is itself now more than ever a matter of dispute: whom does it include or exclude? Historiography perpetually carries us back to the so-called nationalist movement for independence from British rule, where nationalism can be seen as a normative category without any necessary descriptive content. But the normative category has been extremely important. It remains ambiguous to what extent the ongoing rewriting of officially acceptable or state-sponsored histories produce the different versions of nationalism that its protagonists dispute. Since this is a theme we cannot get around, we must plough our way through that rather barren field to get to something that might be more fertile ground, in the process mixing far more than metaphors. And as various claims have been made recently to the obsolescence of national historiography worldwide (something that has had limited resonances in the historiography of India), it might be worth considering what this has meant. Two framing narratives that stand out in importance are addressed below, as their meanings and effects are interpenetrated and overlapping: the imperatives of nationalism, and the imperatives of indigenism.

---

[3] Maggi Tomato Chilli Sauce, 'It's different': advertisement archived on YouTube, accessed 21 July 2018, https://www.youtube.com/watch?v=98Plt4lK7V4.

[4] Edward W. Said, *Orientalism* (New York: Pantheon, 1978).

I.1. Nationalism(')s Without

Why is it so difficult to conceive of post-national narratives? It is easy enough to speak of *pre*-national narratives: of worlds before nationalism, although nationalists' retrospective tendency to project their national-isms into the past can sometimes lead to awkwardly anachronistic histories. Is this merely a belated acknowledgement that nationalisms have specific times and places, rather than projecting nationalisms and nations back into times immemorial? If so, we have surely been here before. We know that 'medieval Sweden' or 'ancient India' has no necessary corres-pondence with modern nation-states; that periodization is retrospective and relatively arbitrary; that the names that stand for the territories are approximations and historical shorthand; and that no one need have much of a stake in whether Charlemagne was French or German. We know, too, that in the age of nationalism, any actual or potential state that seeks legitimation must claim to be a nation; it is not necessary for us to take this circular claim seriously. We know, further, that nationalisms must all claim to be authentic expressions of the indigenous genius of a people: a central problem of nationalism is that it has to be both universal (everybody has them, and in recognizable form) and particular (they must be different from one another's, but in predictable ways)—rather like genitalia.[5]

The questions, at some level, boil down to what stories to tell, how to tell them—and what to call them. Taking the last point first: the candidates for post- (or non-)national histories have now been lining up to make their presence felt. 'Transnational' histories often merely reify the national by marking every border crossing as somehow transgressive rather than every day. 'Cosmopolitanism' has caused some anxieties among postcolonial theorists with a stake in claiming cultural victim-hood: they demand to know on whose terms the cosmopolis operates;[6] among them are those who believe that without being 'rooted' in the

---

[5] See Benjamin Zachariah, *Playing the Nation Game: The Ambiguities of Nationalism in India* (Delhi: Yoda Press, 2011), for elaborations of these points; for the genitalia argument, see p. 11.

[6] Sheldon Pollock, Homi K. Bhabha, Carol A. Breckenridge, and Dipesh Chakrabarty, 'Cosmopolitanisms', in *Cosmopolitanism*, ed. Carol A. Breckenridge et al. (Durham: Duke University Press, 2002), 1–14.

'national', cosmopolitanism can only be disruptive and dangerous.[7] This is a position they share with Josef Stalin,[8] which is ironic given their strong aversion to 'communism' of all kinds (and it is relatively easy nowadays, when there are no communists around to speak of, to get called a communist by retrospective anti-communists). 'Global' histories are neither experientially plausible nor professionally achievable by historians whose movements, scope, and (language?) skills mostly do not match those of the trends or people they are in search of. 'International', today, has been appropriated by states and refers to relations between and among states; 'international NGOs' and other international entities operate in more than one state, and the term seldom, if ever, refers to movements, solidarities, or elective affinities that refuse to base themselves on the principle of the separateness of nations and states.

An attempt to separate our frameworks of analysis, heuristic devices and interested bases for asking questions, from the worlds, world views, and experiences of the historical actors we struggle to interrogate might, however, be of some assistance. In so doing, we can begin to narrate the lives of persons whose worlds transcend the limits of nationalisms or nation-states—without prejudice to the possibility that it might have been nationalism(s) that in part or largely structured their lives or motivated their movements and goals. 'Post-national', then, would refer to us as historians: 'tis a consummation devoutly to be wished. It should be possible to write histories of nationalism and nationalists that are not nationalist histories (or histories of 'Europe' that are not Eurocentric, to use a parallel example): whether this is post-nationalist (or post-Eurocentric) or not depends, of course, on the ideological persuasion of the historian. The point, from the perspective of the post-national historian, is to keep nationalisms without.

---

[7] Benedict Anderson, *The Spectre of Comparisons: Nationalism, Southeast Asia and the World* (London: Verso, 1998), 360–368.

[8] 'Rootless cosmopolitan' was a Stalinist euphemism for Jews; but on the nationalities within the Soviet Union as a deliberate invention of the young Soviet state, and then a change to an essentialized Great Russian chauvinism, see Bert G. Fragner, 'Soviet Nationalism: An Ideological Legacy to the Independent Republics of Central Asia', in *Identity Politics in Central Asia and the Muslim World: Nationalism, Ethnicity and Labour in the Twentieth Century*, ed. Willem van Schendel and Erik J Zürcher (London: IB Tauris, 2001), 13–34.

The first question, then—on what stories to tell—might seem the most trivial. For we can well ask whether we are insisting that the wheels we reinvent are not really the wheels we knew before ('it's a wheel, Jim, but not as we know it'). Is it that historians have not told non-national stories before? Not so. Then why do we consider this non-question at all? For there are plenty of histories to be written, and that have been written, populated by characters or movements that were not interested in national questions, and that do not take national entities as their subject of study. Rather than agonizing about how to write post-national narratives, we could just write a non-national one. Then we avoid adding yet another category to the candidates for newness that peddle their wares in the historian's marketplace today.

But perhaps it isn't so obvious. There appears to be some kind of panic that sets in when a historian leaves behind the safety of the 'national': 'By now it is paradoxically axiomatic that obituaries of the nation are premature'.[9] Do we then wear our mind-forg'd manacles lightly or self-righteously? Do we collapse the question of not writing national histories into one of backing the less-than-national or the more-than-national, thereby forgetting the dependence of both on a stable concept of the 'national'? Do we reject existing culturalist or statist nationalisms, moving instead towards 'anticolonial nationalisms', 'national liberation movements', or eventually 'socially radical and internationalist values appropriate to our vastly transformed times'?[10] Do we adopt a stageist view of nationalism as a necessary phase of our development, through which we must all pass, either in a Marxist-internationalist manner[11] or psychoanalytically (as Julia Kristeva puts it, we all need a 'transitional object' before we can free ourselves from the mother/nation)?[12]

---

[9] Antoinette Burton, 'Introduction: On the Inadequacy and the Indispensability of the Nation', in *After the Imperial Turn: Thinking with and through the Nation*, ed. Antoinette Burton (Durham: Duke University Press, 2003), 1–23; quote from p. 1.

[10] Sumit Sarkar, *Beyond Nationalist Frames: Relocating Postmodernism, Hindutva, History* (Delhi: Peranent Black, 2004), 8.

[11] The stageist interpretation is perhaps a crude interpretation of VI Lenin, *The Right of Nations to Self-Determination* (1914), available online at http://www.marxists.org/archive/lenin/works/1914/self-det/index.htm, accessed 24 December 2018.

[12] Julia Kristeva, *Nations without Nationalism* (New York: Columbia University Press, 1993).

I.2. Indigenism and Authenticity

Hovering about, contained in or enveloping these 'national' arguments is a sense of the importance of indigenism and authenticity in identifying those who truly belong and separating them from those who do not. If you look at the structure of a book that was once extremely important and became a sort of handbook of slogans for right-wing policymakers across the world, Samuel Huntington's *The Clash of Civilizations*, we might note a few implications of the argument (and we can read the *Clash* here as symptomatic of a trend rather than as a particularly original text).[13] Firstly, civilizations act as states and so have to be backed, like states, by violence; therefore, 'the West' is defended and stood for by the United States (or potentially by any other 'Western' power or conglomeration of powers, such as NATO). Secondly, but more importantly for our story in this book, the claim to the universalism of the values that should then be spread and diffused all over the world by the so-called West has now been abandoned. This makes Huntington structure an argument we have come to know well: it is a postcolonial argument. Huntington insists on the subjectivities of the West, unlike earlier claims to the Western origins of all desirable, and therefore exportable, values. The 'West' is now as *alag*, as 'different', as any other different place. To be Western, Huntington assures us, one does not have to actually come from the West, one simply has to accept Western values. This is not a locational but a culturalist argument. Thirdly, and this is what completes the postcolonial argument, the 'West' now lays claim to a victimhood of its own. Huntington is clear that if 'we' do not watch out, 'we' will be victims too. In the structure that distinguishes a postcolonial sensibility of a victim people from the postcolonial sensibility of a 'perpetrator' people, the road is now laid open for a people who could formerly only hope to be considered perpetrators to now claim victimhood status as well.[14]

As postcolonial arguments move out of the rarefied realms of obscure academic jargon and begin to leach into everyday communication, it might be worth considering whether they have, in fact, been destroyed by

---

[13] Samuel P. Huntington, *The Clash of Civilizations and the Remaking of World Order* (New York: Simon & Schuster, 1996).
[14] See Chapter 1.

their own success—or perhaps have found their own ineluctable equilibrium. Relying as they do on identitarian essentialisms that were once the realm of *völkisch* thinking, and on addressing the origins and legitimacy of the speaking voice rather than the argument itself, such approaches are in danger of abolishing the idea of the individual as a dangerous post-enlightenment plot to oppress the downtrodden. And as right-wing movements the world over become adept at using the language of identity and victimhood, those who thought of themselves as morally on the side of the downtrodden, and of identitarian redress as the key to the meaningful transformation of the world, might at least be encouraged to think again.

We can go back to several instances in history where whole peoples have tried to move their status from perpetrator to victim to (re)gain legitimacy, after a period in history where they had been collectively reviled. A case in point is the rights of the so-called *Vertriebenen* in the former Nazi-occupied areas of the Second World War world order: German-speaking peoples from the Europe that had been occupied by the Nazis were expelled after the war, lest (in the rationale of the states expelling them) they became the basis of another territorial claim by a future German state. *Die Vertriebenen* found a constituency in Germany—which was important at a time when 'the Germans' were seen by much of the world as the archetypical villains—able to say that there were victim peoples even among Germans, which was an important softener to the conditions of the post-war world, initially creating a broad consensus in West German politics in the post-war period, and with time providing a resource for right-wing politics in the 'new' (West) Germany.[15] The fallacy of thinking in terms of nationalities as indelible collective entities might be noted in passing here. Anti-racist groups the world over reproduce this fallacy even as much of what we now call 'postcolonialism' encourages the reification of pre-given subjectivities. The difference is, somewhat tautologically, that only 'we' can stereotype ourselves (for which purpose 'we' must already be a 'we'), though now, to a certain extent, we are supposed to claim that stereotyped 'we' as a collective good.

---

[15] Pertti Ahonen, *After the Expulsion: West Germany and Eastern Europe 1945–1990* (Oxford: Oxford University Press, 2003).

Once upon a time, then, essentializing people was considered offensive, somewhat stupid, anti-liberal, and anti-progressive, but now this is only so when it is done by other people. Self-essentializing and self-stereotyping are not only allowed but also considered empowering. In the spirit of coining neologisms that have become good and proper in our inhabited word games, let us call the self-essentializing step 'identity', and the essentializing by others 'youdentity', both pronounced with a softened first 't' in conformity with North American usage[16] (whether a 'wedentity' can create a new universal and/or reaffirm individualism remains an open question). Identity is a cultural right, 'youdentity' is of course still oppression.

The move from the culturalism of a 'people' who claim (or have that claim made on their behalf by their self-appointed spokespersons) that their subjectivities need recognizing to an indigenism which claims a value in and of itself, to claiming the cultural uniqueness of that people and their right to inhabit and defend it against 'outsiders', is something that we need to note. There are at least two routes to understanding the term 'indigenous' when applied to knowledge.[17] There is the attempt to recognize indigenous knowledge which is not in the possession of a state but is publicly accepted as 'culturally authentic': a 'first nation's' knowledge, held in common by people who were formerly considered primitive, knowledge that has not been given the recognition which it deserves, 'folk' practices formerly denigrated as superstition or witchcraft, indigenous knowledge held by aboriginal or *adivasi* societies. The second route maps the kind of indigenism which is claimed as a 'national' culture and which allegedly dates back many millennia civilizationally—the kind of primordialist claim that Jawaharlal Nehru once wrote presciently was constantly being claimed by national chauvinists in India and China.[18] The former move—which was widely considered a 'progressive' one—has given way to the latter move and has even in some ways enabled it.[19] This then becomes the basis for thinking about 'the indigenous' in national

---

[16] I am indebted to Anna Diem for this felicitous word, and to her and Jeff Vernon for discussions thereon: London, November 2017.

[17] Dhruv Raina, 'Afterword: Mainstreaming Indigenous Knowledge: Genealogies of a Meta-Concept', in *Public Health and Private Wealth: Stem Cells, Surrogates, and Other Strategic Bodies*, ed. Sarah Hodges and Mohan Rao (Delhi: Oxford University Press, 2016), 252–268.

[18] Jawaharlal Nehru, *The Discovery of India* (London: Meridien, 1946), 144.

[19] Raina, 'Mainstreaming Indigenous Knowledge'.

categories, and as a quality possessed by the nation-state as a whole (with the obvious implication that the state disciplines its subjects into seeing themselves in terms of these categories, in collective memory and therefore in state-ideology-compatible *ISI-Chhaap* histories).[20] What this indigenism achieves in terms of labelling and human significance is the centring of the positionality of the speaker who speaks for 'her own' group. In scholarship, as in politics, the identity and origin of the speaker is also a source of legitimacy or illegitimacy, but it is increasingly the only source of legitimacy or illegitimacy.

Who is entitled to speak for whom? And who delivers to the entitled their sense of entitlement? A certain set of assumptions here can be traced in tangible historical projects: symptomatically, in this book, we could take the Subaltern Studies project, which moves from the left to a theoretical self-absorption and self-anointing to an implicit and somewhat caste-bound conservatism among some of its (former) members. One of their starting assumptions was that a history from below must be told from reading sources in 'the colonial archive' and therefore 'against the grain'.[21] Then we have possibly the most famous intervention in the history of any historiographical trend: Gayatri Chakravorty Spivak's statement that the subaltern cannot speak on her own.[22] She uses a line from Karl Marx's *The Eighteenth Brumaire of Louis Bonaparte*, 'they cannot represent themselves, they must be represented', as her key citation.[23] Spivak renders it in the German, and then makes a slight pun on the words *treten* and *vertreten*, namely 'to tread on' and 'to represent'. What this enables is that if the subalternist must speak for the subaltern, then the subalternist is treading upon the subaltern to gain a voice in academia. Attempts to recover authorial meaning in retrospect, or to disavow some of the implications of this statement, have faltered on post-structural nothing-outside-the-text theories: if we think that's what she said, it's irrelevant

---

[20] The ISI *chhaap* (or stamp) was a certification provided by the Indian Standards Institute as a guarantee against adulteration of goods and as an indication of acceptable quality.

[21] Ranajit Guha, 'The Prose of Counter-Insurgency', in *Subaltern Studies II*, ed. Ranajit Guha (Delhi: Oxford University Press, 1983), 45–88.

[22] Gayatri Chakraborty Spivak, 'Can the Subaltern Speak?', in *Marxism and the Interpretation of Culture*, ed. Cary Nelson and Lawrence Grossberg (Basingstoke: Macmillan, 1988), 271–313.

[23] Karl Marx, *The 18th Brumaire of Louis Bonaparte* (1852), accessed 1 July 2018, http://www.marxists.org/archive/marx/works/1852/18th-brumaire/index.htm.

how often she or other people on her behalf say that she didn't mean it in that way.[24]

I.3. Who Will Historicize the Historians? The 1980s as a Good Time to Be Brown

The rise of what we now might call a postcolonial sensibility is conjunctural in the sense that the 1980s was a moment of academic guilt that enabled the rise of 'the brown voice'. The colonial, racist, patriarchal, or homophobic (add your victimhood categories of choice here) realities of the outside world were allegedly to be redressed, and in some accounts reversed, in the academic world. This politics of academia was disconnected from the world outside: being a brown person meant that one could still have no voice in a fundamentally racist society (in North America? The United States? The 'West'?) where Eurocentric or white supremacist assumptions still operated, whereas one had a more legitimate space within academia, where one had to be listened to because one's force of legitimacy was indeed that which excluded one from society outside academia: a form of underprivileged or oppressed identity. Colour, gender, sexuality, disability, and other identities also then became the clichés of the backlash against these purported claims to victimhood— arguably, and paradoxically, making 'class', the old metacategory of the left, a resource available more to the right than the left, as identitarian ressentiment. But identity as a link to the legitimate voice was also challenged in different ways (and I do not claim intentionality here). When you claim the right to speak for an entire people, you must claim to be of that people; therefore, the 'nationality' of those who must speak for the underprivileged comes to the fore. Strangely, therefore, in a move that was enabled by the argument that somebody must speak for the subaltern, what we had was a group of rather privileged, perhaps well-meaning, relatively well-educated, middle-class, upper-caste men and women speaking for entire civilizations. In this way, 'South Asian' historiography was a good metonymy for postcolonial studies, its hegemonic

---

[24] Spivak, 'Can the Subaltern Speak?'.

voice, despite the fact that many of its arguments owed a lot to Edward Said's intervention in 1978, *Orientalism*.[25]

Said's 'Orient' was a counter-image to the Occident in order to show the Occident in a better light. In the commonly accepted version of this argument, it would now seem that if 'the Orient' was a creation of the Occident, then that Occident needs to be said to exist. For Said's broader argument to function, the Occident does not need to exist; it has to reify itself but it does not need to be a place or a set of beings. But that was not entirely a consistent position for Said or for his followers; as 'West versus East' was replayed by reversing the earlier hierarchy, that 'Occident' started taking shape and acquiring (different) characteristics, even as the ('constructed') Orient was recovered in ways unforeseen: the self-Orientalizing (in the Saidian sense of 'Orientalism') of the postcolonial subject by exceptionalist arguments. There is a logic to this inconsistency which is already evident in Orientalism, in that the Occident of Said goes back to the Greeks, a point paradoxically used in Said's text to cast the Persians as the original or earlier 'Oriental' to match the self-appointed 'Occidental' Greeks.[26] But in order to make the point about the 'Orient' as a 'construction' that has no corresponding 'reality', there is no need to acknowledge continuity from the ancient Greeks to the present-day 'West' as conservative celebrants of Europeanness or German National Socialists before them had been fond of doing (this would be a case of 'identity' reinforced by 'youdentity' despite the different normative significance given to them in different cases). If one takes the retrospectively constructed nature of these categories as important, and even if one takes a stand well short of Martin Bernal's position,[27] the Greeks have nothing intrinsically to do with the history of the 'West', except for the fact that in the 'West's' own created subjectivity, Greece was the past of Europe that Europeans wished to claim, indeed insisted on claiming. One did not have to be a National Socialist to claim this. The conventions of (European or Anglo-American) political philosophy, such as (symptomatically again) Jurgen Habermas' *Structural Transformation of the Public Sphere*, require, for an argument that 'goes back very far', a reaching

[25] Said, *Orientalism*.
[26] Said, *Orientalism*.
[27] Martin Bernal, *Black Athena* (2 vols, London: Vintage, 1991).

for the Greeks.[28] The ancient past, therefore, is made available; however, this is a kind of unacknowledged indigenist move on the part of Europeans, more or less the same as many moves in the so-called Indic world (the word 'Indic' has come into prominence in the age of the Hindu right) which reach back in a similarly knee-jerk manner to something Vedic or Puranic. There is no real indication that any of this is either operational or available.

The attempt to think of collectivities either directly or by default as national or indigenous collectivities moves us away from any understanding of fractures within a given society. Certainly, this move coincided with the decline of Marxism as a frame of understanding. There were two routes to this (again, for the purposes of this argument, we can take a group like Subaltern Studies as axiomatic but we can also find these two routes in historical thinking elsewhere). One is a Marxian way away from Marxism, via E. P. Thompson, in whose writing there is a certain inherent culturalism (this is something that he would not have acknowledged; but if there is an English working class and there are many practices of which he writes and which appropriates to a left cause of describing the actual development of collective consciousness among people, which could equally be appropriate to describe a community consciousness and a parochialism of a collectivity that is well short of a universal class).[29] The other is the Saidian route away from Marx, from a few stray and ill-considered remarks in Edward Said's writing about Marx's journalistic output as correspondent for the *New York Daily Tribune*, where Marx becomes an Orientalist in the Saidian sense,[30] and then being a Saidian becomes a way of not reading Marx. Some scholars of postcolonial studies had actually read and had taken their Marxism very seriously; hence there seems to be a genuine point of conflict there. In drawing its own genealogy, too, 'postcolonialism' would find it hard to disavow the Marxian lineage that was self-evident for many writers who are now claimed in retrospect as postcolonial: Antonio Gramsci, of course,[31] but also Frantz Fanon—the title of *The Wretched of the*

---

[28] Jürgen Habermas, *Strukturwandel der Öffentlichkeit* (Darmstadt: Hermann Luchterhand, 1962).
[29] E. P. Thompson, *The Making of the English Working Class* (New York: Pantheon Books, 1964).
[30] Said, *Orientalism*.
[31] Antonio Gramsci, *Selections from the Prison Notebooks*, ed. and transl. Quintin Hoare and Geoffrey Nowell Smith (London: Lawrence and Wishart, 1971).

Earth is not exactly unconsciously drawn from the Internationale, both in the French and in the English version, and Fanon does not have to mention it in the text; it is part of the everyday consciousness of his readership. When we read Fanon talking about the 'national' from our 'postcolonial' perspective of reducing everything to the narrowness of the authentic and indigenous, we might well be unable to read any longer that while he is using the term 'national', he is talking about a social transformation from below that carries the bourgeoisie away from its collaboration with the metropole into a genuine solidarity with the people. He may call this 'nationalism' because he is defending the stageist position of a national-revolution-before-socialism of a classical Comintern-era Marxism, but this is not actually 'national' in the sense of the indigenous-authentic that many wish now to read, and though of course we have no clear grasp of authorial intention, it is indeed possible to argue that a cultural authenticity argument was difficult to make from Fanon's contextual position.[32]

I.4. At Home in India: The Unity of Left and Right Culturalism

Outside the rarefied field of historical scholarship, but not entirely without its effects in that field of scholarship, the 1980s saw the beginnings of the emergence of a strong Hindu right in Indian politics. This was now an organized group of people who had already identified 'authentic' belonging to the nation as Hindu, and of course as upper-caste as well. But given that they needed the strength of numbers, they had to reclaim lower-caste Hindus at least provisionally for electoral purposes. It was thus claimed that caste had been highly misunderstood. Caste could be variously a form of social division of labour, a form of organization of non-hierarchical hierarchy—'separate but equal', to borrow the slogan of apartheid. There were various ways of representing caste as either actually rational but by now distorted (an argument in consonance with Gandhi's

---

[32] Frantz Fanon, *The Wretched of the Earth* (Harmondsworth: Penguin 1967) [1961]; see Zachariah, *Playing the Nation Game* (Chapter 1) for the longer version of this argument.

views on the subject),[33] or as a contemporary distortion that had not existed at all in the pristine ancient texts (helped along by 'constructionist'
texts that in strategic readings could be seen to support an argument that
caste itself was a British invention).[34] In all cases which saw the rise of a
Hindu right, first in electoral terms, there was also a movement in forms
of legitimation to forms of assertive culturalism.

This culturalism emerged together in the 1980s in various separate
spaces. Official communist parties in India in the 1980s also had a form
of culturalist understanding of authenticity, which they then more or less
shared with the right. Therefore, they propounded the idea that 'Western'
culture was consumerist, capitalist, and bad. The moralism of these positions was in consonance with the repressive practices of 'Indian' family,
community, and state in all its avatars: sexual freedoms were considered
outrageous insults to the cultural fabric of the nation. The arguments
were that consumerism and individualism and sexual liberation (and
homosexuality) were all 'Western'. This range of arguments was made in
respectable journals, including the *Economic and Political Weekly*, and
not just in the rants of elderly male Party comrades.[35]

The shorthand of how the left came to this form of culturalism can be
said to be a consequence of the old stageist argument: that the national
goal is primary. After the first goal has been reached, it is said that national independence is not enough and that we need to move towards socialism. But in order to justify the national frame, in order to justify how
generations of comrades are trained in the rhetoric of nationalism, the
national frame cannot altogether be abandoned, and by the time it is allegedly obsolete, everyone has become so acclimatized to it that they can
only make nationalist arguments.[36] The question of the separation of the

---

[33] For an accessible summary, see Arundhati Roy, *The Doctor and the Saint: Caste, Race, and Annihilation of Caste, the Debate Between B.R. Ambedkar and M.K. Gandhi* (London: Haymarket, 2017). This was originally a long introduction to a critical edition of B. R. Ambedkar, *The Annihilation of Caste* (Delhi: Navayana, 2014), which became an identitarian dispute about whether Roy, not a Dalit herself, was entitled to write anything about Ambedkar at all.

[34] Paradigmatically, see Nicholas B. Dirks, *Castes of Mind: Colonialism and the Making of Modern India* (Princeton: Princeton University Press, 2001).

[35] H. Srikanth, 'Natural Is Not Always Rational', *Economic and Political Weekly* 31, no. 15 (April 13, 1996): 975–976; H. Srikanth, 'Marxism, Radical Feminism and Homosexuality', *Economic and Political Weekly* 32, no. 44/45 (November 8–14, 1997): 2900–2904.

[36] Such forms of historical consciousness have now become common sense for historical reasons: in the period of the premiership of Jawaharlal Nehru, the actual coalition of political forces was not the Congress versus the rest as we are often given to understand, but was more or less the left wing of Congress allied with socialists and communists outside Congress against a

communist movement from crude forms of nationalism remained open; there were any number of people who thought subtly about these issues, but there were party lines to follow. By the 1980s, the communists had come upon a mobilizing strategy that seemed to rely upon an appeal to cultural chauvinism rather than an appeal to reason, class struggle, or any of the standard moves of communism. The Communist Party was most important then for the longest period of time in West Bengal and Tripura. But it was remarkably silent on forms of discrimination such as caste, except to some extent in Kerala.[37]

The question of caste brings both forms of indigenism into play: the indigenism, which claims the authenticity or the legitimacy of a local practice, and the legitimacy of the authentic 'national'. But it can also be suggested that the separation of these two forms of indigenism was never complete, because the lineage of indigenism stems from early assertions of what makes up the unity of the so-called nation, and in almost all cases, one also goes back to the so-called folk. If we are to draw other lineages of right-wing nationalist thought, folk would be translated as *Volk*, a translation that was self-evident to the protagonists of folk revivalism the world over, and of course therefore, also in India[38]: Indian protagonists of the *völkisch* nation were certainly not ignorant of contemporaneous German debates, just as they were not ignorant of contemporaneous British debates which tried to distinguish between Aryan and non-Aryan. We can here belabour the point that even when the 'indigenous' is sought to be used as an empowering category, it is not as revolutionary as it has been made out to be. Also, the indigenous is foreign.

right-wing conglomeration of forces which were both inside the Congress and outside it to the right. In this coalitional situation, there was one problematic moment when the communists were called upon explicitly to defend the 'nation' under attack from (Communist) China. The 1962 border dispute, as is well known, was the cause of the split in the Communist Party of India. The pro-Chinese group then took what was considered an anti-national line, but both sides of the Communist Party began to claim that they were not anti-national, with the result that tendencies towards cultural-essentialist arguments were built into both of them. For the larger argument about the actual 'Nehruvian' coalition, see Zachariah, *Playing the Nation Game*, Chapter 5.

[37] For a recent retrospective look at the 1980s and the communist movement in West Bengal and India, see Debraj Bhattacharya, *Exploring Marxist Bengal, c. 1971–2011: Memory, History and Irony* (Calcutta: KP Bagchi, 2016).

[38] Benjamin Zachariah, 'At the Fuzzy Edges of Fascism: Framing the *Volk* in India', *Völkisch and Fascist Movements in South Asia*, special issue of the journal *South Asia* (December 2015): 639–655.

In the 1980s and 1990s, as the developmental state came to be dismantled, the culturalism of left and right shared a space. In ordinary public discourse, there was a sense that what was Western and individualistic was illegitimate and had to be combated by a deepening of indigenous culture. The indigenist factor was always central to the argument that forms of individualism were immoral and Western: Indian public debate has continuously refused sustained engagement with the idea of the rights of the individual, who apparently only has any rights when comfortably imprisoned in family, community, or nation. The communists had a version of this, which said that there were some forms of 'Western' culture that were acceptable: the folk revival movement in the United States in the 1960s, or the songs of the Popular Front. The communists could therefore claim their invented tradition by specific moments in which they tried to disavow the charge that they were pro-indigenist. But in practise, it was often very difficult to distinguish between the concepts of 'cultural' authenticity of the right and the left.[39] That this was considered anomalous at the time is in our living memory; what is less clear, given the anti-communist polemic of the Sangh Parivar, was that the cultural politics of anti-'Western' complaint was shared across left and right, and it was only the 'centre' at the time that appeared not to worry so much about how 'Western' or 'indigenous' its members appeared.

I.5. Feedback Loops

These wider worlds might seem disconnected from the academic self-contained systems that we like to imagine. All too often, historiographical production is seen as a world in which abstract intellectual choices are made by historians, professional, or otherwise, making history in circumstances of their own choosing. The precise interactions of historians and their worlds may elude us, for no one's writing is determined by their origins or contexts, despite all the identitarian arguments that function as if this were so. But the influence of political and social worlds on historical

---

[39] Again, symptomatically, there was at least one coalition government at the centre which was supported from the outside by both the communists and the emergent fascist BJP, that of the short-lived Prime Minister Vishwanath Pratap Singh (1989–1990).

production, communication, mediation, and consumption needs to be brought to the forefront of historical writing on historiography. The feedback loops of historical thinking, or of thinking with history, depending on how one prefers to put it, are more important than we think.

The chapters put together in this book are divided, like Caesar's Gaul, into three parts. The first, 'Marking the Posts', puts forward my argument about the political and intellectual consequences of the historiographical trends that mark the last 30-odd years of historical scholarship in and about South Asia. It comprises a chapter on the political consequences of postcolonial thinking, and another longer one that tries to historically situate the growth and development of postcolonial history. Neither is intrinsically or only about South Asia, but as much of my work has been done in South Asianist contexts, it is important to make transparent the antecedents of the material I draw upon. Both chapters are in the spirit of what I call destructive criticism, or to use a now disused paradigm of developmental thinking, an attempt to provide the advantages of backwardness to late entrants into these debates: they need not follow the dead ends that others have already followed.[40]

The third part, 'Postdiscursive Possibilities', comprises two chapters of methodological reflections, on how to track moving ideas, and on reading archives at the same time as one reads in archives. The two chapters address the importance and difficulties of returning to nuanced historical thinking after a long period of abstinence from both non-essentialist thinking and archival research.

The second part, which conventionally enough comes between the first and the third, is entitled 'Instrumentalisations'. This section provides three chapters by way of analogy and disanalogy with subjectivist, identitarian, or victimhood histories. The first is on the difficulties of finding a usable national narrative in histories of the events of 1857 and 1858, the 'Revolt' or 'First War of Independence'. The second is about defending the British Empire in the course of attacking its rationale, celebrating its impending end as the end of empire (in the sense of its purpose) and the use of national stereotypes in a set of arguments in which the self-justification of imperial civil servants and the needs of wartime propaganda can live in

---

[40] Alexander Gerschenkron, *Economic Backwardness in Historical Perspective* (Cambridge, MA: Belknap Press, 1962).

perfect harmony. The third is about the uses and misuses of history in cinema and the disputes and anxieties created among imperial officials, Indian interest groups and private commercial interests in an atmosphere of protecting the 'sentiments' of the population, which were allegedly of preeminent interest. Analogies with postcolonial or present-day situations have not been drawn out explicitly in this section, but the resemblances to present-day events or characters are not coincidental.

PART I
MARKING THE POSTS

1

Identifying the Beast Within

Postcolonial Theory and History

One of the central difficulties in writing about 'postcolonial history' is that no one is sure what it is, or when it is. 'Postcolonial*ism*' is a label worn uneasily by practitioners of 'postcolonial theory', of 'postcolonial history', 'postcolonial criticism', or (more non-committally) of 'postcolonial studies'. The 'ism' maintains (in some uses) pejorative connotations, as does the 'theory', especially for some critics whose commitment to the discipline of 'history' is construed as a practical rather than an abstract one, with 'theory' being construed as necessarily abstract (not too much space will be given in this chapter to the anti-theorists' false dichotomy). The 'history' part is in some readings also problematic, given that history as a discipline is itself seen as complicit in 'Western' power/knowledge constellations[1] (this may be a matter of naming rather than of something essential to the discipline of history itself, which is far from the monolithic entity that some practitioners of postcolonial criticism sometimes make it out to be). Terminological embarrassments, therefore, make for the first set of engagements and difficulties with 'the postcolonial', another label that belongs in the cluster of terms.

For purposes of initial (and artificial) clarity, we can treat 'postcolonial history' as a subset of 'postcolonial studies'. What, then, is postcolonial studies? There is no coherent set of positions or theoretical engagements that can define it as a field. It refers, in a most general sense, to the consequences of empire, in and for the (former) colonies, and also, in a broader reading, in and for the (former) metropolitan countries, in the latter instance in the form of diasporas, diasporic identities, 'multicultural'

---

[1] Dipesh Chakrabarty, 'Postcolonialism and the Artifice of History: Who Speaks for "Indian" Pasts?' *Representations* 37, *Special Issue: Imperial Fantasies and Postcolonial Histories* (Winter 1992): 1–26.

societies, or more generally the presences of the colonies in the metro-poles. It has been extended to include parts of the world that were not subject to formal colonialism but had experiences that could be con-sidered related to colonialism: areas of informal empire such as China or Latin America after the formal independence of many of its states had been achieved; then, as 'postcolonial' became a more theorized and self-conscious set of positions, this justified its expansion and application to unlikely times, places, and peoples. The prefix 'post', in a word which has gradually lost its hyphen, does not refer necessarily to a chronological period after (formal) colonialism (this it has in common with 'the post-modern', from which it borrows much); it refers also to 'going beyond' colonial modes of power/knowledge relations, in which 'the tension between the epistemological and the chronological is not disabling but productive'.[2] It seeks to 'deconstruct' Eurocentric modes of reading and writing history, whether explicit or implicit.[3] Its engagements tend to be 'cultural', related to the sensibilities and subjectivities of the colonized in their encounter with colonialism; 'identity' and 'difference' are thus central themes to be studied. Some commentators nevertheless claim, standing against the 'cultural turn', that the term 'postcolonial' grew out of an engagement with the problems of conceptualizing the economic and political aftermath of formal colonialism that nonetheless saw a continu-ation of imperial control by other means. This is part of a longer debate within postcolonial history of the place of Marxist and materialist read-ings of history within the concerns of postcolonialism;[4] an earlier gen-eration of scholars, such as Stuart Hall and Benita Parry, was centrally involved in political struggles and engaged closely with Marxism, with socialist theory and politics, and only ambivalently (if at all) embraced the increasingly decontextualized 'culturalism' of 'postcolonalism'.[5]

---

[2] Stuart Hall, 'When Was "the Post-Colonial"? Thinking at the Limit', in *The Post-Colonial Question: Common Skies, Divided Horizons*, ed. Iain Chambers and Lidia Curti (London: Routledge, 1996), 242–260: 254.

[3] 'Deconstruction' came into postcolonial theory from Jacques Derrida, *De la Grammatologie*, translated into English by Gayatri Spivak, considered one of the main theorists of 'the postco-lonial'. Jacques Derrida, *Of Grammatology*, transl. Gayatri Chakravarty Spivak (London: Johns Hopkins University Press, 1976).

[4] See Aijaz Ahmad, 'Postcolonialism: What's in a Name?' in *Late Imperial Culture*, ed. Roman de la Campa, E. Ann Kaplan, and Michael Sprinker (London: Verso, 1995), 11–32.

[5] Benita Parry, *Delusions and Discoveries: Studies on India in the British Imagination, 1880–1930* (London: Allen Lane, 1972) was a pioneering work in focusing on British imperial attitudes to Empire; criticisms of her by (among others) the emerging heroes of 'postcolonial theory'

Postcolonialism draws upon an eclectic series of theoretical interventions in the social sciences and in philosophy, and it often does so unsystematically, in an allusive and elusive manner. At its best, it engages politically where it discerns a need, using theory to legitimately claim an academic space from which to make a political intervention. Here, postcolonialism needs to distinguish itself from postmodernism, which is generally seen as being in favour of a multiplicity of readings of 'texts', and is often agnostic about truth claims.[6] Postcolonialism, as it uses many of the tools of postmodernism to expose the complicity of dominant discourses with oppressive (power/knowledge or political) regimes, but being interested in making interventions with political implications, cannot afford quite the same level of agnosticism. Hence, postcolonialism often needs to fall back upon what Gayatri Spivak has called 'strategic essentialisms' as first premises upon which to ground an argument.[7]

Postcolonial history, then, is not fully separable from postcolonial studies except as a matter of relative emphasis and of the need to engage with the disciplinary rules of the historian's profession—the renegotiation of these rules remains one of its central concerns. It is interdisciplinary, but this is an indisciplined interdisciplinarity; its borrowings are eclectic, sometimes playful. It uses poststructuralism via Foucault, Derrida, Lacan; anthropology, critical theory, literary criticism, heterodox Marxism (somewhat guiltily), psychoanalysis, semiotics, feminist theory. It is often difficult to ground the theoretical basis of a particular intervention in specific statements by any particular thinkers. The mood

---

led to a first round of polemics. For a contextualization of some of these debates, see Michael Sprinker, 'Foreword' to Benita Parry, in *Delusions and Discoveries* (new edition, London: Verso, 1998), vii–xiii; Benita Parry, 'Preface' to the new edition, 1–28.

[6] Thus, the contention by Michel Foucault that there are always contending 'regimes of truth' is inadequate for the purposes of postcolonialism—see Michel Foucault, 'Truth and Power', in *Power/Knowledge: Selected Interviews and Other Writings 1972–1977*, ed. Colin Gordon (New York: Pantheon, 1980), 109–133. Again, there is no consensus on what 'postmodernism' really is, and the label is often disavowed by thinkers associated with it. But there is by now a readily recognized set of characteristics attributed to it by outsiders who know they are outside.

[7] Gayatri Chakravarty Spivak, 'Introduction: Subaltern Studies: Deconstructing Historiography', in *Selected Subaltern Studies*, ed. Ranajit Guha and Gayatri Chakravarty Spivak (New York: Oxford University Press, 1988), 3–24; Sara Danius, Stefan Jonsson, and Gayatri Chakravorty Spivak, 'An Interview with Gayatri Chakravorty Spivak', *boundary 2* 20, no. 2 (Summer 1993): 24–50, in which Spivak says she no longer wants to use the term.

is what counts, and the theory is often a kind of received common sense, for which the sources are by now forgotten.

Critiques of postcolonialism are inherent in the field of postcolonialism, and critics who engage with the field are, whether they like it or not, incorporated into the field. Postcolonialism is therefore, to some extent, the victim of its own success: if we are all postcolonial now, a counter-hegemonic project has succeeded, at least within academia; outside academia is quite another matter.[8] Thus, sceptics or opponents find themselves implicated in the terminological constellations of the 'postcolonial', with the consequence that they are part of the legitimating frameworks they seek to problematize. Central debates often hinge upon the nature of one's political engagement, with the result that positioning oneself politically sometimes becomes central to an argument. There is, however, also a tendency for the structure of arguments to reduce speakers or writers to their origins, in a manner reminiscent of forms of stereotyping and essentialization that, it has been argued, are a feature of colonial thought.

At its best, postcolonialism's political project is to change the ways in which colonialism and its consequences are thought about and written about. One could argue that the partial successes of postcolonialism in achieving recognition in public arenas outside the academic world are based on a formulaic engagement with the more academic debates, and make their appearance mainly as various politically correct formulations—which is still an improvement, as it has discredited certain explicit forms of racism, sexism, and cultural discrimination as forms of publicly acceptable behaviour. The question of whether postcolonialism has replaced some forms of discrimination with the axiomatic privileging of the subjectivities of 'victim communities', historically defined and with self-proclaimed inheritors of that victimhood taking centre stage as their retrospective spokespersons, needs to be kept in mind. It must also be said that postcolonial theorists are very keen on writing their own histories and their own genealogies, in a kind of self-monumentalization as sites of memory for the downtrodden.[9] Since no one person holds any of

---

[8] On the potential divergences, see Edward W. Said, *Covering Islam: How the Media and the Experts Determine How We See the Rest of the World* (revised edition, London: Vintage, 1997) [1981], still quite relevant today.

[9] Gyan Prakash, 'Writing Post-Orientalist Histories of the Third World: Perspectives from Indian Historiography', *Comparative Studies in Society and History* 32, no. 2 (April 1990): 383–408; Gyan Prakash, 'Subaltern Studies as Postcolonial Criticism', *American Historical Review* 99,

the positions that can be attributed to a mood, the denials and rejoinders retreat from some of the corollaries of their theories with which they are no longer entirely comfortable. Equally problematically, a good deal of debate takes place at a meta-theoretical level: much energy is expended on a critique of 'modernity' (in some versions, 'Western modernity' or 'post-Enlightenment modernity'), but there is little agreement and little coherent theorization on what these categories might mean.

1.1. Themes, Concerns, Locations: A Partial Inventory

'The postcolonial' is too large to be a unified field, as it is evident that it could take in the world as a whole as its geographical area of concern, though it tends not to.[10] As it retrospectively defined itself, it claimed a set of solidarities with the marginalized, the victimized, and the downtrodden[11]—which are solidarities by intuitive analogy rather than academic engagements. Some versions of postcolonial history run the risk of creating pure victims, as in Ashis Nandy's claim to defend the 'innocence' of the colonized.[12]

It was the Anglo-(North) American (and in the first instance North American) academic world that was integral to the development of postcolonialism, although ostensibly the subject matter was about areas

---

no. 5 (December 1994): 1475–1490; Dipesh Chakrabarty, 'A Small History of Subaltern Studies', in *Habitations of Modernity: Essays in the Wake of Subaltern Studies* (Chicago: University of Chicago Press, 2002), 3–19, etc. Rosalind C. Morris, ed., *Can the Subaltern Speak? Reflections on the History of an Idea* (New York: Columbia University Press, 2010) is among the latest monumentalizing efforts.

[10] That which is referred to as postcolonial history is now so large a set of fields that it is impossible for any one individual to treat it as a whole. It is therefore necessary for me as an author to declare my perspective as, in the first instance, a historian of South Asia, interested in intellectual histories and the movements of ideas. The case studies selected for the purposes of this chapter are intended to be illustrative rather than comprehensive, and far longer works treating postcolonialism(s) are readily available should a reader be interested in fields or sub-fields not adequately treated here. See for instance Robert J. C. Young, *Postcolonialism: An Historical Introduction* (Oxford: Blackwell, 2001).

[11] Gyan Prakash, 'Can the Subaltern Ride? A Reply to O'Hanlon and Washbrook', *Comparative Studies in Society and History* 34 (1992): 168–184; Homi K. Bhabha, 'Introduction: Locations of Culture', in *The Location of Culture* (London: Routledge, 1994), 1–18.

[12] Ashis Nandy, *The Intimate Enemy: Loss and Recovery of Self Under Colonialism* (Delhi: Oxford University Press, 1983), ix.

in the periphery. Postcolonialism found a good reception at a time of the exploring of subjectivities and the decentring of 'mainstream' history that followed feminist histories, 'history from below', histories of homosexuality, of native Americans, and so on, from the 1960s through to the early 1980s, although in some instances, the institutional bases were not North American in the first instance: for example, the Subaltern Studies group operated for a while out of the Australian National University, Canberra, and later Sussex University, when its founder, Ranajit Guha, taught and worked there. In many ways, it remains a phenomenon of the Anglo-American world, although adopted in some centres of intellectual activity in the periphery, the former colonial world. Despite postcolonialism's use of much French theory, its reception in France has been frosty; the belief in France's civilizing mission in the colonies has proved remarkably resilient. It was, at least until recently, more American than British; Britain was a reluctant latecomer, having followed the American lead. 'Imperial history' was resolutely old-fashioned and resilient, surviving the need for self-reflexivity in its bases in Oxford and Cambridge, resisting, or sometimes merely ignoring, the onslaught of the 'new imperial history'—which, to a large extent, is British domestic history projected onto a larger backdrop, and arguably defeats the purpose of its alleged 'newness'.[13]

Much of the theory and many of the debates on postcolonialism originated in departments of literature, most often in metropolitan or North American universities; however, this literary endeavour took hold in departments of English literature in the former colonies, which had a particular need to justify or rethink their existence if they were not simply to reify a canonical set of English (in a national sense) texts rather than texts in English; the study of writing in English by writers from the colonial and former colonial world then provided a route into understanding the sensibilities of the colonial imagination. From this starting point, comparative transnational studies of colonial literature, both in English and in translation, led to the highlighting of certain common themes in the literature of colonies and former colonies, and came to be compared with the literature of subordinated groups elsewhere (native Americans,

---

[13] See for instance Kathleen Wilson, ed., *A New Imperial History: Culture, Identity and Modernity in Britain and the Empire, 1660–1840* (Cambridge: Cambridge University Press, 2004); the appearance of such metanarratives can be seen as an important step towards the creation of a (counter?-)canon.

African-Americans, homosexuals); departments of English literature thus increasingly became departments of literature.

This genesis of postcolonialism in literary criticism is important to note. The issues that postcolonial history addresses are most elusive in traditional archival sources, which are dominated by institutional, and particularly statist, imperatives. The legitimacy of the jumps in imagination that the literary critic is permitted to make then provides certain insights that a historian might then be encouraged to substantiate in terms of the methodology of that discipline. But this crossover also changed the rules of historical writing—forcing it to acknowledge the point that history is a genre that makes truth claims, but is in fact not very different from other literary pursuits that frankly acknowledge the role of imagination and arbitrary reconstruction.[14] This insight has been around since at least the beginning of the 1960s;[15] postcolonialism cannot do without it, as it relies so often on exposing the hidden assumptions behind a 'discourse' and asking whether these assumptions are legitimate.

It is also, therefore, to be noted that disciplinary boundaries are consequently weakened; some would argue that rules of evidence according to the demands of the historian's profession have consequently also been weakened. But these 'rules of evidence' have also been subject to renegotiation within the 'historian's profession'; the counterargument would be either that postcolonialism is an important attempt at such a renegotiation, or that history itself is tyrannical, tainted with 'Western' 'hegemonic' assumptions and teleologies, and must be abandoned in favour of other ways of seeing the past.[16]

Postcolonialism contains much theory that is variously taken from European thinkers in translation, often pertaining in the first instance to the metropolis, but subjected to decentred and sometimes

---

[14] The work of Hayden White is influential in this regard: see for example Hayden White, 'The Value of Narrativity in the Representation of Reality', *Critical Inquiry* 7, no. 1 (Autumn 1980): 5–27; 'The Question of Narrative in Contemporary Historical Theory', *History and Theory* 23, no. 1 (February 1984): 1–33; and other essays collected in Hayden White, *The Content of the Form: Narrative Discourse and Historical Representation* (Baltimore: Johns Hopkins University Press, 1987).

[15] See for example E. H. Carr, *What Is History?* (2nd edn, reprint, Harmondsworth: Penguin, 1990) [1961], esp. pp. 22–25.

[16] Dipesh Chakrabarty, *Provincializing Europe: Postcolonial Thought and Historical Difference* (Princeton: Princeton University Press, 2000).

eclectic readings.[17] It is possible to argue that this theoretical basis robs postcolonialism of its claim to provide alternatives to Eurocentric models, and that it merely provides a critique of the limitations of some of this theory. For instance, the claims to universalism of what has been referred to as 'the Enlightenment' were exposed as particularistic and often oppressive. Romantic reactions to the Enlightenment, however, were subsumed within the term 'post-Enlightenment', a term that appeared often in 1980s and 1990s writing. This discursive violence done to 'Western' thinking was not considered carefully; after Edward W. Said's powerful critique of 'Orientalism'—arguing that the 'Orient' did not actually exist but was the necessary Other in the 'Western' imagination that confirmed the self-congratulatory narrative of the 'West'[18]—it ought to have been clear that 'West' and 'East', if rhetorically operational historical categories, cannot afford to be the analytical categories of academic writing.

An unanswered set of questions waits in the wings. What is the place within postcolonial history of aspirations to universal frameworks of understanding? Can there be a critique of the pretensions to the universality of certain frameworks of understanding that lead to a more universal framework, the qualifier 'more' then establishing that the 'universal' is an absolute abstraction that is not achievable but is nevertheless an aspirational category? There are tendencies now manifesting themselves, in what we can tentatively call a post-postcolonial moment, where the polarities 'universal' and 'local' have given way to a concern with interconnected histories, and with the co-constitution of subjectivities of the colonizer and colonized, rather than with a Europe versus non-Europe, East and West, universalist-tyranny-versus-particularist-liberationist-subjectivity set of frameworks. Some of this runs the risk of inventing a new triumphalist narrative of 'transnational history', 'global history' for an age of 'globalization', and of 'cosmopolitan sensibilities' projected backwards in time.[19]

---

[17] See for instance Ranajit Guha on Asia, and India, being outside Hegel's Universal History: Ranajit Guha, *History at the Limit of World History* (New York: Columbia University Press, 2002).

[18] Edward W. Said, *Orientalism* (New York: Pantheon, 1978).

[19] See Benjamin Zachariah, *Playing the Nation Game: The Ambiguities of Nationalism in India* (Delhi: Yoda Press, 2011), 'Conclusion', for an earlier discussion of this. Recent trends appear to confirm the misgivings expressed therein.

An inventory of important influences on postcolonial history would have to include Michel Foucault, Jacques Derrida, and Jacques Lacan, as thinkers who can assist in the study of representations of colonized subjects, of their 'Othering', 'deconstructing' 'colonial discourse'. These theorists are often the presiding deities that no longer need to be explicitly cited. At its reductionist minimum, what this amounts to is the borrowing of the idea of a 'discourse' from Foucault, in the sense of a set of implicit assumptions that structure ways in which the world is seen, but which remain powerful by remaining implicit. Edward Said famously borrowed 'discourse' from Foucault and twinned it with the Italian Marxist and anti-Fascist Antonio Gramsci's concept of 'hegemony',[20] 'hegemony' being a state of affairs where people are ruled with their apparent consent because an explicit resort to coercion is not required: people have internalized the disciplinary regime.[21] This internalized disciplinary regime is an aspect of 'biopower', to re-translate to a Foucauldian idiom: a form of political control that encompasses everyday practices and even bodily practices of a population.[22] And it becomes necessary to speak of Foucault's conception of 'governmentality' or 'governmental rationality',[23] as a result of which a concern with 'colonial governmentality' has now become part of a concern with 'colonial discourse'. Does this run the risk of too static and structuralist a view of 'colonialism'? From Derrida, postcolonialism chiefly uses 'deconstruction' and the slogan 'there is nothing outside the text', the latter being used to justify the reading of texts to render history, and to read all things as text.[24] From Lacan, 'the Other' makes its continuous and mostly unacknowledged appearance, often in conjunction with an attempt to understand the vicissitudes and dynamics of 'race'.[25]

[20] Said, Orientalism.

[21] Antonio Gramsci, Selections from the Prison Notebooks, ed. and transl. Quintin Hoare and Geoffrey Nowell Smith (London: Lawrence and Wishart, 1971).

[22] Michel Foucault, The History of Sexuality, vol. 1: An Introduction (New York: Pantheon, 1978); Thomas Lemke, ' "The Birth of Bio-politics": Michel Foucault's Lecture at the Collège de France on Neo-liberal Governmentality', Economy and Society 30, no. 2 (May 2001): 190–207.

[23] Michel Foucault, 'Governmentality', in The Foucault Effect: Studies in Governmentality, ed. Graham Burchell, Colin Gordon, and Peter Miller (Chicago: University of Chicago Press, 1991), 87–104.

[24] Derrida, Of Grammatology.

[25] Jacques Lacan, The Four Fundamental Principles of Psychoanalysis (London: Hogarth Press, 1977).

Then there are postcolonialism's very own theorists—Edward Said, of course, but also perhaps Gayatri Chakravarty Spivak and Homi K Bhabha, who Robert J. C. Young called the 'Holy Trinity' of postcolonial critics.[26]

The recovery of earlier generations of anticolonial thinkers (Frantz Fanon, Aimé Césaire, Amilcar Cabral, Albert Memmi, perhaps also Steve Biko), though often stripped of much of their political radicalism, has also come to be part of postcolonial history and theory (thus we have Homi K. Bhabha's Fanon as opposed to Fanon the Marxist).[27] Postcolonialism is particularly ambivalent about Marxism, which often makes its appearance as a rigid system of thought that 'imposes closure' and is, after Edward Said, an 'orientalist' framework.[28] But there is still a concern with Marxism running through postcolonialism in some respects, sometimes explicit, often disavowed, and sometimes in dialogue with the earlier selves of the writers who disavow it.

Much of the early work that has (retrospectively, at least) been incorporated into the genealogy of postcolonialism, for instance, Subaltern Studies (of which, more below), was part of a cluster of concerns with peasant societies, with which left-wing intellectuals engaged closely in the 1960s and 1970s. Not a long time later (and it is tempting to connect this explicitly with the so-called fall of communism c.1989–1992), Marxism was seen in many ways to be another European and Eurocentric metanarrative. This highlights another potential problem of postcolonial history: anachronistic readings based on the (often moral) values of a different context in space and time are projected onto the past, according to which standards the past is always deficient (and in this sense, postcolonial history, despite its denials, is a theory of 'progress'). Karl Marx, listening to the debates in Parliament on the East India Company's Charter, should somehow have anticipated late twentieth-century critiques

---

[26] Robert J. C. Young, *Colonial Desire: Hybridity in Culture, Theory and Race* (London: Routledge, 1995), 163.

[27] Homi K. Bhabha, 'Foreword: Remembering Fanon', in Frantz Fanon, *Black Skin, White Masks,* (London: Pluto Press, 1986); Cedric Robinson, 'The Appropriation of Frantz Fanon', *Race and Class,* 35, no. 1 (July 1993): 79–91.

[28] Said, *Orientalism,* 155–157.

of Eurocentrism[29]—later Marxist theory that rejected, for instance, the 'Asiatic mode of production' does not recover Marxism for a non-Eurocentric reading as a result.[30]

Postcolonial history is counter-canonical, but it increasingly operates without a canon to counter, content with decentring that which is no longer at the centre. Arguably this is itself a result of the success of post-colonial histories: the (neo)colonial attitudes that (once) underpinned the writing of (some) history are no longer legitimate. However, this can also be attributed to the larger set of contemporaneous trends that challenged mainstream histories from the 1960s: feminist histories, histories from below, postmodernism, and to some extent, gay and lesbian histories (though these have been relatively little used in postcolonial fields, for reasons that we shall not have space to enter into). There is now a danger of the creation of a canon from the counter-canon of 'postcolonial thinkers', whose self-referentiality and collusive footnoting of one another have much to do with this.

Lest it be imagined that these sets of characterizations and criticisms are merely external and hostile, a clarification is in order. The field of postcolonialism has been, as befits its concerns, quite relentlessly engaged in self-criticism; its agenda changes with time, and it reorients its engagements. All of the difficulties outlined above have been to a greater or lesser extent acknowledged among the practitioners of postcolonialism, and have been the subject of vigorous internal debates. However, these have also been the lines of external criticism to postcolonialism. Hostility of this kind has been expressed very often in the periphery itself, often in terms of the location of the postcolonial strongholds (North America) and a perceived lack of political engagement on the part of the anointed theorists of postcolonialism with important issues at a local level (geographically and temperamentally distanced as they are from the peripheral country that their scholarship is ostensibly concerned with).

---

[29] Shlomo Avineri, ed., *Karl Marx on Colonialism and Modernization* (New York: Doubleday, 1969).

[30] Stephen P. Dunn, *The Rise and Fall of the Asiatic Mode of Production* (Boston: Routledge and Kegan Paul, 1982).

1.2.   (Post)Marxism and the Lost Histories
of Liberation: The Case of Subaltern Studies

It is now so ingrained in hearts and minds that *Subaltern Studies* (*SS* for short) was at the vanguard of the postcolonialism wave that it comes as a surprise for those who came in late to learn that *SS* in its origins was actually a late wave of the 'history from below' movement of the 1960s and 1970s. Its models were the British Marxist historians, notably E. P. Thompson, a man quite hostile to 'theory'.[31] *SS*'s main theoretical engagement was with a heterodox Marxism, in particular following Antonio Gramsci. Gramsci's lament, following the Fascist seizure of power in Italy, was that the left had not really bothered to understand the Italian peasantry, which had seemingly betrayed its own interests by siding with the Fascists; the *SS* group similarly sought the basis of 'subaltern consciousness'.[32] Of particular importance was Gramsci's idea of a 'passive revolution', in which major social changes do not accompany the transition from (the remnants of) a feudal order to capitalism: an older elite assists in the transition with minimal or limited support from a working class, thereby presiding over its own continuity as an old aristocracy merges with and identifies with an emergent bourgeoisie, who in turn do not need to invoke solidarities (through the 'national' idea) with classes lower down the social order. The resultant political order is devoid of the experience of popular participation in revolutionary change, in contradistinction to the 'classical' revolutionary trajectory of the French Revolution, hence the 'passive revolution'.[33] This model was important in that it explained the top-down nature of the transition to 'modernity' in India (castes and estates rather than classes, a strong state, state capitalism, 'pre-capitalist' survivals, and so on, although the debate on 'modernity in India/ Indian modernity' is an ongoing one). An attempt to 'recover the voices' of the 'subaltern', a term that loosely meant 'non-elite' and therefore was the

---

[31] See E. P. Thompson, *The Poverty of Theory* (London: Merlin Press, 1995) [1978], his long polemic against Louis Althusser. On Thompson's importance to *SS*, see Sumit Sarkar, 'The Relevance of EP Thompson', and 'The Decline of the Subaltern in Subaltern Studies', for his understanding of the changes—for the worse—in the *SS* project, both in Sumit Sarkar, *Writing Social History* (Delhi: Oxford University Press, 1997), 50–81 and 82–108, respectively.

[32] David Arnold, 'Gramsci and Peasant Subalternity in India', *Journal of Peasant Studies* 11, no. 4 (1984): 155–177; Gramsci, *Selections from the Prison Notebooks*.

[33] Antonio Gramsci, *Selections from the Prison Notebooks*, 106..

acknowledged Other or stranger to the historian's alleged Self, was later to give way to a reduction of the 'subaltern', to a cultural symbol that legitimated the historian as its cultural spokesman, even as 'the subaltern' ceased to be considered by its self-appointed representatives as a real person.

Among the important work to come out of the early period of SS was a set of critiques of 'the colonial archive', notably on how subsequent historians of divergent ideological persuasion were in danger of reproducing the assumptions of the colonial state.[34] SS quickly had to face the problem of sources for non-elite voices, as with most histories from below. The 'colonial archive', often the only written source available, was according to Ranajit Guha to be 'read against the grain', but this was only possible with a jump into the historian's imagination taking the place of 'hard' evidence, by altering or reversing the assumptions of the ruling elite whose reports, written in the 'prose of counter-insurgency', filled these archives.[35] One could, of course, argue that a rather static view of 'the archive' dominated such writing, where the active role of the historian in constituting the relevant archives for particular questions was not taken into account.[36] The models, however, for the forms of social history reconstructed painstakingly from difficult archives, are not difficult to recognize: they are Carlo Ginzburg's *The Cheese and the Worms*, Emmanuel Le Roy Ladurie's *Montaillou*, and Natalie Zemon Davis's *The Return of Martin Guerre*.[37]

SS worked with conceptions of class from a quasi-anthropological perspective: class and caste were regarded as akin to each other, and class and religious affiliation tended to be difficult to separate, with distinctions not

---

[34] Ranajit Guha, 'The Prose of Counter-Insurgency', in *Subaltern Studies II*, ed. Ranajit Guha (Delhi: Oxford University Press, 1983), 45–88; Shahid Amin, 'Approver's Testimony, Judicial Discourse: The Case of Chauri Chaura', in *Subaltern Studies V*, ed. Ranajit Guha (Delhi: Oxford University Press, 1987), 166–202; Gyanendra Pandey, 'The Bigoted Julaha', in *The Construction of Communalism in Colonial North India* (Delhi: Oxford University Press, 1990), 66–108.

[35] Guha, 'The Prose of Counter-Insurgency', 45–88.

[36] See Chapter 7.

[37] Carlo Ginzburg, *The Cheese and the Worms: The Cosmos of a Sixteenth-Century Miller* (London: Routledge & Kegan Paul, 1980) [1976]; Emmanuel Le Roy Ladurie, *Montaillou: Cathars and Catholics in a French Village, 1294–1334* (Harmondsworth: Penguin, 1980) [1975]; Natalie Zemon Davis, *The Return of Martin Guerre* (Cambridge, MA: Harvard University Press, 1983). These became central to the project of teaching students how to write social history with problematic sources; they formed models for work such as Shahid Amin, *Event, Metaphor, Memory: Chauri Chaura, 1922–1992* (Delhi: Oxford University Press, 1995) and, later, in a book that sits awkwardly with the theoretical directions of SS, Partha Chatterjee, *A Princely Impostor? The Strange and Universal History of the Kumar of Bhawal* (Princeton: Princeton University Press, 2002).

easy to draw from an emic perspective.[38] Bernard Cohn, historical anthropologist from Chicago, who made a contribution to *SS* in Volume IV, was largely responsible for the insight that colonial social dynamics created the very units of society in the colony that were apparently ancient and long-standing (a variation on the 'invention of tradition' argument, a volume in which Cohn had a contribution).[39] Cohn was not a long-term member of *SS*, and had been writing since the 1950s; Nicholas Dirks later claimed that Cohn had anticipated Michel Foucault by several years in showing the impact of colonial discourse in the power/knowledge constellations within which political and social life was lived.[40]

There was also a strong set of interventions on the allegedly incomplete development of the Indian working class[41]—in part emerging from the 'mode of production debate' of the 1970s that had taken place outside and before *SS*: was there an incomplete transition to capitalism in a colony or an ex-colony, contrary to Karl Marx's formulation that colonial rule would inadvertently be progressive, because it would destroy the 'Asiatic mode of production', static, and village-based? Was there indeed an 'Asiatic mode of production' that survived?[42] These were part of a cluster of concerns with the potential of peasants to become the social basis for revolutionary or socialist regimes that emerged around and during the Vietnam War and the Chinese Cultural Revolution;[43] they thus amounted

---

[38] Partha Chatterjee, 'Agrarian Relations and Communalism in Bengal, 1920–1935', in *Subaltern Studies I*, ed. Ranajit Guha (Delhi: Oxford University Press, 1982), 9–38.

[39] Bernard S. Cohn, 'The Command of Language and the Language of Command', in *Subaltern Studies IV*, ed. Ranajit Guha (Delhi: Oxford University Press, 1985), 276–329.

[40] Nicholas Dirks, 'Foreword' to Bernard Cohn, *Colonialism and Its Forms of Knowledge: The British in India* (Princeton: Princeton University Press, 1996), ix–xvii.

[41] Dipesh Chakrabarty, *Rethinking Working Class History: Bengal 1890–1940* (Princeton: Princeton University Press, 1989).

[42] Dunn, *The Rise and Fall of the Asiatic Mode of Production*.

[43] For the genealogy of these concerns, see Henry Bernstein and Terence J. Byres, 'From Peasant Studies to Agrarian Change', *Journal of Agrarian Change* 1, no. 1 (January 2001): 1–56. Thus, Friedrich Engels, *The Peasant War in Germany* (1850) was a key text, as was the 1966 translation of A. V. Chayanov, *The Theory of Peasant Economy* (Homewood, IL: The American Economic Association, 1966) (first published in 1920); in Ranajit Guha, *Elementary Aspects of Peasant Insurgency in Colonial India* (Delhi: Oxford University Press, 1983), a breathtakingly wide array of examples from across the world, in different times and spaces, are brought into play; the influence of Eric Wolf's *Peasant Wars of the Twentieth Century* (New York: Harper and Row, 1969); of Teodor Shanin's *Peasants and Peasant Societies* (Harmondsworth: Penguin, 1971); of ongoing debates in the *Journal of Peasant Studies*; of Karl Marx's letters to Vera Zasulich late in his life which talked of the possibility of a radical peasantry as the vanguard class instead of the proletariat, all need to be acknowledged. Much of this could be said to have essentialized 'the peasantry' as broadly comparable worldwide—a point acknowledged in Bernstein and Byres, 'From Peasant Studies to Agrarian Change', p. 7.

to a sort of radical-developmentalism-and-its-alternatives approach (a surprising absence in this set of concerns is Mao Zedong himself, although some members of the SS collective were practising Maoists before they were academics). Dipesh Chakrabarty postulated an 'incomplete transition' to capitalism because the Indian worker's 'mentality' was still pre-capitalist; rural loyalties and 'communal' (religious) consciousness remained central to his being.[44] Chakrabarty was then very much a part of what he would later criticize as the theory of the not-yet, of India and the 'non-West' more generally being seen by the standards of 'Western' history as incomplete, as in the 'waiting room of history'.[45] It is curious that Chakrabarty sought a model of a working class in Karl Marx's theoretical writing, in *Capital* rather than in his historical writings—as his reinvented self ought to have told him. These earlier genealogies of SS's concerns were soon to be repressed, although the repressed returned periodically in strange distorted forms.

One of the points of continuity from this early phase to the later phases of SS can be said to be an investment in the 'national'—although SS claimed to be challenging elite and top-down views of a national elite directing the masses, and of most communist narratives similarly showing the party leading the people. It also challenged what it saw as neo-imperialist readings of imperial rule providing progress and modernity, leading to a modern nation-state. Allegedly following Gramsci, SS sought to understand peasant consciousness; it also set out to find popular versions of the 'nation' and popular contributions to 'nationalism'—expecting to find this.[46] That there was no popular version of the nation was discomforting. Gramsci's idea of a 'passive revolution', however, proved important in that it seemed to explain the top-down nature of the Indian state and the inadequate development of a national-popular consciousness, in which the limited participation of the 'masses' in revolutionary activity led to the continuation of pre-independence institutions and elites rather than their displacement in the new, non-revolutionary

---

[44] Chakrabarty, *Rethinking Working Class History*.

[45] Chakrabarty, 'Postcolonialism and the Artifice of History', recycled eight years later as Chapter 1 of Chakrabarty, *Provincializing Europe*, 27–46, when the argument proposed had few, if any, academic opponents.

[46] Ranajit Guha, 'On Some Aspects of the Historiography of Colonial India', in *Subaltern Studies I*, ed. Ranajit Guha (Delhi: Oxford University Press, 1982), 1–8.

order.[47] As we shall see, this concern with nationalism among SS scholars who never quite succeeded in abandoning national frameworks of analysis provided something of a justification for the subalternists' claim to the right to speak for the subaltern.[48]

Early SS was criticized for not being adequately theoretically oriented—a charge that in retrospect seems strange indeed.[49] Gayatri Spivak entered the project in Volumes IV and V, published in 1985 and 1987.[50] The following year, she published the now iconic 'Can the Subaltern Speak?', addressing the problem of representation as a problem of the historian appropriating the experience of someone else and rendering it in the language of history. Thus the subaltern could not speak—in the language of history—except when spoken for, which mediation made the project of the 'recovery' of subaltern voices impossible. Subalternity, in Spivak's reading, was a pure state of voicelessness, and her ideal-typical subaltern was a woman. Her statement that the speaking for colonized women was a way in which the colonizer legitimated his role was also central to one of her central lines of argument: 'white man saves brown woman from brown man' was her pithy summary of the claim,[51] which of course left open the question why 'brown elite woman' speaking for 'brown subaltern woman' was a more legitimate form of representation.

In Partha Chatterjee's coinage of the possibility of the 'subalternity of an elite', a relational rather than an absolute subalternity was established.[52] The (dis)advantage of this turn of phrase was that it potentially enabled the rendering of elites as victims of colonialism, obscuring their

---

[47] Partha Chatterjee, *Nationalist Thought and the Colonial World: A Derivative Discourse?* (London: Zed Books, 1986).

[48] I have made this argument in more detail elsewhere: see Benjamin Zachariah, 'Residual Nationalism and the Indian (Radical?) Intellectual: On Indigenism, Authenticity and the Coloniser's Presents', in *Of Matters Modern*, ed. Debraj Bhattacharya (Calcutta: Seagull Books, 2008), 330–359.

[49] See for instance Rosalind O'Hanlon, 'Recovering the Subject: Subaltern Studies and Histories of Resistance in Colonial South Asia', *Modern Asian Studies* 22, no. 1 (1988): 189–224, a review article on the first three volumes of SS.

[50] Gayatri Chakravarty Spivak, 'Discussion: Subaltern Studies: Deconstructing Historiography', in *Subaltern Studies IV*, ed. Ranajit Guha (Delhi: Oxford University Press, 1985), 330–363; Gayatri Chakravarty Spivak, 'A Literary Representation of the Subaltern: Mahasweta Devi's *Stanadayini*', in *Subaltern Studies V*, ed. Ranajit Guha (Delhi: Oxford University Press, 1987), 91–134.

[51] Gayatri Chakraborty Spivak, 'Can the Subaltern Speak?' in *Marxism and the Interpretation of Culture*, ed. Cary Nelson and Lawrence Grossberg (Basingstoke: Macmillan, 1988), 271–313.

[52] Partha Chatterjee, *The Nation and Its Fragments: Colonial and Postcolonial Histories* (Princeton: Princeton University Press, 1993), 37.

own role as oppressors (although this is not necessarily the way he meant the phrase). This is a non-problem if one insists on the *relationality* of the category 'subaltern'; but gradually, 'subaltern' as a term seemed to lose anything like a stable meaning as programmatic statement followed programmatic statement among the protagonists of the movement that were prone to programmatic statements, in all of which the 'subaltern' took different shapes.[53] Some critics pointed out that 'subaltern' was Gramsci's term used to avoid the Fascist censors, and it made no sense that SS used it without the need to hide their politics. But the term served them well after their Marxism had been underplayed, disavowed, or forgotten. 'Subaltern' became a shorthand for all the oppressed, for peasants, for non-westerners, and thus was blurred, imprecise, a literary device, a metaphor or metonymy, etc.

> The peasant acts here as a shorthand for all the seemingly nonmodern, rural, nonsecular relationships and life practices that constantly leave their imprint on the lives of even the elites in India and on their institutions of government. The peasant stands for all that is not bourgeois (in a European sense) in Indian capitalism and modernity.[54]

It is unnecessary, for the purposes of this essay, to map the journey of 'subaltern' from peasant to symbol,[55] nor is it necessary to try and trace exactly when the decentring of elite narratives gave way to the centring of the subaltern*ist* as spokesman for the subaltern (variously construed), with the subalternist-symbolic-subaltern combination taking on the 'Western'. It might also be noted in passing that history itself, in some readings, was abandoned as a sort of Western, post-Enlightenment form of discrimination,[56] and other forms of reading the past had been anointed as co-equal ways of seeing: 'I take gods and spirits to be existentially coeval with the human, and think from the assumption that the

---

[53] Reviewers have pointed out that despite SS's claims to being a movement or a school of thought, many writers who have published under its banner have made no programmatic claims.

[54] Chakrabarty, *Provincializing Europe*, 11.

[55] For a non-subalternist narrative of this kind, see David Ludden, 'Introduction: A Brief History of Subalternity', in *Reading Subaltern Studies: Critical History, Contested Meaning, and the Globalisation of South Asia*, ed. David Ludden (London: Anthem Press, 2001), 1–27.

[56] Chakrabarty, 'Postcolonialism and the Artifice of History'.

question of being human involves the question of being with gods and spirits'.[57] It might instead be noted that a project of understanding 'subaltern consciousness'—understanding the subaltern who was, initially, the stranger, the Other—gave way to a self-evident appropriation of the right to represent that Other as a sort of extension of the Self, against a new Other, variously conceived as 'the West', 'the oppressor', or 'History' itself. The implicit subjecthood and nationalization of that new Self against an increasingly 'Western' Other—whether that 'West' lay in 'discourse' or elsewhere—needs to be noted here.

SS's coupling with 'postcolonialism' was announced in a monumentalizing publishing venture a mere six years into the *SS* project: *Selected Subaltern Studies* in 1988, with an introduction by Spivak that had initially been a part of *SS IV*, 'Subaltern Studies: Deconstructing Historiography',[58] and a foreword by Edward W. Said attesting to the importance of the project.[59] Ranajit Guha edited a *Subaltern Studies Reader* in 1997,[60] and subsequent publications by members of the collective have kept the brand name alive. In many ways, *SS* and 'postcolonialism' were separate developments that moved closer in mutual recognition. *SS* had Gramsci; Said himself used Gramsci and Foucault in his similarly iconic *Orientalism* (1978),[61] and *SS* followed.

As *SS* began to epitomize the success and possibilities of a counter-hegemonic project against the tyrannies of an academic establishment, it became somewhat of a model for the historiographies of Other regions. But what part of it? By the 1990s, the divergence between a radical liberationist approach and an increasingly textual one could no longer be ignored or regarded as easily bridgeable. Latin American supporters of *SS*, as they modelled themselves on their Indian colleagues, found themselves faced with this problem of whether to concern themselves with the recovering of the lifeworlds and experiences of the 'subaltern' as a historical figure *à la* Gramsci, or whether to focus on the deconstructing of 'Western' modes of thought relating to Latin America—two projects

---

[57] Chakrabarty, *Provincializing Europe*, 16.

[58] Spivak, 'Introduction: Subaltern Studies: Deconstructing Historiography', 3–24.

[59] Edward W. Said, 'Foreword', in *Selected Subaltern Studies*, ed. Ranajit Guha and Gayatri Chakravarty Spivak (New York: Oxford University Press, 1988), v–x.

[60] Ranajit Guha, ed., *A Subaltern Studies Reader 1986–1995* (Minneapolis: University of Minnesota Press, 1997).

[61] Said, *Orientalism*.

that, it was increasingly apparent, were methodologically and politically incompatible.[62]

1.3. Decolonizing the Self

Edward Said's *Orientalism* described a strategy of representation: the Orient did not exist as such, but was a creation of the 'West' that was in need of a strong Other to define itself; the 'Orient', passive, decadent, feminine, was what the 'Occident', active, vigorous, virile, was not. Thus, orientalism was a form of power/knowledge that enabled the imperial endeavour to succeed.[63] Said chose to use the term despite the fact that it referred already to a set of scholarly endeavours as well as to a political position among colonial administrators in colonial India (i.e. those who opposed the imposition of European principles of governance and society on India and preferred to govern in an 'Oriental' manner); he therefore used the term in an extended way.[64] Said could, as later debates in which he participated confirm, be accused of 'occidentalism' in that he flattened the 'West' into an unproblematic and relatively monolithic set of discourses (it is not really a place).[65] This is nowhere more evident than in his tracing 'Western' discourses about the 'East' back to ancient Greece, which is only possible by accepting European myths of its own origins that make Greece 'Western' and 'European'—as the *Black Athena* debates soon afterwards were to underline.[66]

---

[62] Latin American Subaltern Studies Group, 'Founding Statement', *boundary 2* 20, no. 3 (1993): 110–121; Florencia A. Mallon, 'The Promise and Dilemma of Subaltern Studies: Perspectives from Latin American History', *American Historical Review* 99, no. 5 (December 1994): 1491–1515; Daniel Mato, 'Not "Studying the Subaltern", but Studying *with* "Subaltern" Social Groups, or, at Least, Studying the Hegemonic Articulations of Power', *Nepantla: Views from South* 1, no. 3 (2000): 479–502.

[63] Said, *Orientalism*.

[64] See e.g. S. N. Mukherjee, *Sir William Jones: A Study in Eighteenth-Century British Attitudes to India* (Hyderabad: Orient Longman, 1987); Martin Moir and Lynn Zastoupil, eds., *The Great Indian Education Debate: Documents Relating to the Orientalist-Anglicist Controversy, 1781–1843* (Richmond, Surrey: Curzon, 1999).

[65] Aijaz Ahmad, 'Orientalism and After: Ambivalence and Metropolitan Location in the Work of Edward Said', in Aijaz Ahmad, *In Theory: Classes, Nations, Literatures* (London: Verso, 1992), 159–219, summarizes some of these debates.

[66] Martin Bernal, *Black Athena* (2 vols, London: Vintage, 1991); the debate thereafter is too long to summarize, but see for instance Jacques Berlinerblau, *Heresy in the University: The Black Athena Controversy and the Responsibilities of American Intellectuals* (New Jersey: Rutgers

But Said is symptomatic of a quest for a voice that decentres—'provincializes' in currently fashionable terms—Europe, or at least the Eurocentric imagination. This Eurocentric imagination is not peculiar to Europeans, the argument goes, but could be internalized by the colonized. Said's own work is in many ways a rebellion against his own colonial education—his *Culture and Imperialism* seeks to demonstrate how the classic texts of the European canon are complicit in imperialism.[67] Said's doctoral student, Gauri Vishwanathan, showed how English literature as a discipline that glorified the English and Englishness developed in the colonies rather than in the metropole.[68]

The rediscovery for postcolonialism of earlier anticolonial voices that wrestled with the internalized colonizer was a part of the same dynamic: Frantz Fanon, Aimé Césaire, Léopold Senghor, Steve Biko, or Ngugi wa Thiong'o, the artiste formerly known as James Ngugi.[69] The reference to a period of self-strengthening, of the acquisition of cultural self-confidence among the dispossessed before they can regard themselves as equals, is common to these texts. Among the dangers that attend this process is the risk of seeking the authentically 'indigenous'. And as with many stageist arguments—another one being the Marxist argument that 'national liberation' must precede 'socialism' for the colonies—we all seem to be stuck in the immediate or intermediate stage and never succeed in proceeding to the next one. The discursive contest continues; 'we' wrest the right to write 'our' 'histories' (or to tell our pasts differently) from 'them'; 'they' are no longer the possessors of Universal truths.[70] What happens, then, when there appears a need for a universalism of sorts?

University Press, 1999); Martin Bernal, *Black Athena Writes Back: Martin Bernal Responds to His Critics*, ed. David Chioni Moore (Durham: Duke University Press, 2001).

[67] Edward W. Said, *Culture and Imperialism* (London: Vintage, 1994) [1993].

[68] Gauri Vishwanathan, *Masks of Conquest: Literary Studies and British Rule in India* (London: Faber, 1990).

[69] See for example Frantz Fanon, *Black Skin, White Masks* (New York: Grove Press, 1967) [1952]; Frantz Fanon, *The Wretched of the Earth* (Harmondsworth: Penguin, 1967) [1961]; Aimé Césaire, *Discourse on Colonialism* (New York: Monthly Review Press, 1972) [1955]; Léopold Sédar Senghor, 'Negritude: A Humanism of the Twentieth Century', in *The African Reader: Independent Africa*, ed. Wilfred Carty and Martin Kilson (New York: Vintage, 1970), 179–192 [1964]; James Ngugi, *A Grain of Wheat* (London: Heinemann, 1967); Steve Biko, *I Write What I Like: A Selection of his Writings* (London: Heinemann, 1979) [1969–1978].

[70] See Ranajit Guha, *An Indian Historiography of India: A Nineteenth-Century Agenda and Its Implications* (Calcutta: KP Bagchi, 1988), reprinted with revisions in Guha, Ranajit, *Dominance Without Hegemony: History and Power in Colonial India* (Cambridge, MA: Harvard University

Historians might also wish to note that many of these texts emerge from a rather schematic reading of French colonial rule, for which the myth of the civilizing mission was far more directly important than for other European empires, British, Dutch, Portuguese, or Belgian. Aimé Césaire, for instance, writing in 1955, seeks to demolish precisely this claim: 'colonisation works to *decivilise* the coloniser, to *brutalise* him in the true sense of the word, to degrade him, to awaken him to buried instincts, to covetousness, violence, race hatred and moral relativism.'[71] Furthermore, 'the very distinguished, very humanistic, very Christian bourgeois of the twentieth century' needs to be told that:

> without his being aware of it, he has a Hitler inside him … what he cannot forgive Hitler for is not *crime* in itself, *the crime against man*, it is not *the humiliation of man as such*, it is the crime against the white man, the humiliation of the white man, and the fact that he applied to Europe colonialist procedures which until then had been reserved exclusively for the Arabs of Algeria, the coolies of India, and the blacks of Africa.[72]

In addition, the importance of understanding 'the value of our old societies' was stressed:

> They were communal societies, never societies of the many for the few.
> They were societies that were not only ante-capitalist, as has been said, but also *anti-capitalist*.
> They were democratic societies, always.
> They were cooperative societies, fraternal societies.
> I make a systematic defence of the societies destroyed by imperialism.[73]

This rather romanticized 'defence' of an idealized precolonial society reappears more often in writing in postcolonial mode from the 1980s

---

Press, 1997), 152–214; and Guha, *History at the Limit of World History*, for a remarkable continuity of concerns.

[71] Césaire, *Discourse on Colonialism*, 13.
[72] Césaire, *Discourse on Colonialism*, 14.
[73] Césaire, *Discourse on Colonialism*, 23.

onwards. And although sometimes phrased in a quasi-leftist language, borrowing some of the languages of Marxism, it demonstrates the absence of class, of social stratification, and of power relations in the invocation—rather than analysis—of 'precolonial' societies. As 'precolonial', 'colonial' and 'postcolonial' become the terms of analysis, colonialism becomes the most important set of facts about a society. This is despite the fact that only the first of the terms is unambiguously chronological in its significance.

Such a position tends easily towards a defence of the 'innocence' of the colonized and a search for the 'authentic' 'native' style in a cultural nationalism that is untainted by 'Western' or other 'foreign' influences: Ashis Nandy's Gandhi, for instance, is the authentically national anticolonial in his rejection of things and civilizations 'Western', his alleged use of 'feminine' resources of the self thereby rejecting hypermasculine Western masculinities.[74] The obvious problem with this interpretation is that 'indigenist' readings of colonial rule are responses to colonial rule, and thus reifications or inventions of 'indigenism'.[75] 'It is the colonialist who becomes the defender of the native style', Frantz Fanon wrote perceptively in *The Wretched of the Earth*,[76] and versions of 'tradition' borrowed for anticolonial polemics could easily be the self-Orientalization of the 'native', strategic, or otherwise.

Postcolonial historians themselves run the risk of reproducing such a move in their own recounting of these histories of the 'indigenous'. An awkward or ambivalent relationship to anticolonial or 'Third World' nationalisms marks much anticolonial history writing—the postcolonialists' ability to speak a nationalism at second remove, but also a disavowal of the narrowness of any nationalism and at least a rhetorical identification with national liberation movements elsewhere in the world. That the 'liberation' is legitimated by the 'national' makes it difficult for a consistent disavowal of all nationalisms to be made: an alternative axis of legitimate identity that will serve to justify a place in an international world of nation-states does not materialize.

---

[74] Nandy, *The Intimate Enemy*.
[75] See E. J. Hobsbawm and T. O. Ranger, eds., *The Invention of Tradition* (Cambridge: Cambridge University Press, 1983).
[76] Fanon, *The Wretched of the Earth*, 195–196.

Thus, difficult questions, for instance, of internal colonialism within the boundaries of a 'postcolonial' state, of gender issues (in which women are subordinated to the building of a 'nation'), or indeed of class exploitation do not always get the attention they deserve—which itself becomes a matter of strong (internal) dispute among people who (have been classified as) postcolonial thinkers or historians. By contrast, metropolitan nationalisms have been subject to the criticism that they discount the diversity of culture and identity in their midst, and attempt to discipline identities into rigid, homogeneous, and more or less racially characterized nationalisms. Metropolitan nationalisms are explicitly seen as forms of oppression, and thus intolerant of diversity of human experience and desire. Why such criticisms are far less often levelled at their non-metropolitan versions is not a matter of logical consistency.

The question of who the spokespersons for a 'culture', a people, and a 'nation' are raises itself here, in particular by claiming a privileged position as (post)colonized to (re)present 'Indian pasts', 'African pasts', and so on. It has not gone unrecognized that this, and at times only this, is in danger of becoming the 'project' of postcolonial historiography: 'a certain postcolonial subject had . . . been recoding the colonial subject and appropriating the Native Informant's position'.[77] 'We cannot fight imperialism by perpetuating a "new orientalism" '[78]; these dangers are manifested in the necessity to explicitly distance oneself from the implications of postcolonial argument: to deny the charge of indigenism, and to point out that the postcolonial intellectual writes from within the 'inheritance' of a 'universal and secular vision of the human' that 'is now global'.[79]

That many of the identitarian journeys mapped by postcolonial writers are personal as much as they are historical or political is not denied by them: 'For objective reasons that I had no control over, I grew up as an Arab with a Western education'[80]; 'I have lived all my conscious life in the framework of institutionalised separate development'.[81] Coming to terms with the past and with forms of writing about the past are thus ways of

[77] Gayatri Chakravarty Spivak, *A Critique of Postcolonial Reason: Towards a History of the Vanishing Present* (Cambridge, MA: Harvard University Press, 1999), ix.
[78] Gayatri Chakravarty Spivak, 'The Question of Cultural Studies', in *Outside in the Teaching Machine* (New York: Routledge, 1993), 277.
[79] Dipesh Chakrabarty, *Provincialising Europe*, 4–5.
[80] Edward Said, *Culture and Imperialism*, xxx.
[81] Steve Biko, 'We Blacks', *I Write What I Like*, 27.

coming to terms with oneself: 'the black man has become a shell, a shadow of a man, completely defeated, drowning in his own misery ... The first step therefore is to make the black come to himself; to pump back life into his empty shell; to infuse him with pride and dignity'.[82] A return to universalism can only take place once this vital move has taken place.

1.4. Theme and Variations: Writing History and the (Post)Colonizer

One theorist identified with a new postcolonial canon who has resisted the search for the 'indigenous' has been Homi Bhabha; his insistence on the 'hybridity', the 'ambivalence', the 'in-between-ness' and 'fluidity' of human experiences, and his search for comparable examples in other contexts, however, have still been within the framework of seeking the subjective experiences of fellow victim communities.[83] The ambivalence that Bhabha describes makes its presence felt, for instance, in the 'mimicry' of the colonial subject of the 'post-Enlightenment' norms of the colonizer: 'colonial mimicry is the desire for a reformed, recognisable Other, as *a subject of difference that is almost the same but not quite*'.[84] The colonial subject's mimicry slides easily into mockery, subversive in that the Anglicized native is not, cannot be, English; it is a reminder that the principles articulated for the metropolis, not intended for the colony, are, when appropriated, disruptive of the existing order.

If we were to use this principle to read the writings of postcolonial theorists rather than just postcolonial situations in the historical past (and one of the characteristics of postcolonial theorizing is an anachronistic set of readings that demand the past be read in the light of present perceptions and sensibilities), then we can trace the oscillation between the nativist tendencies of seeking 'authenticity' (in community, culture, 'nation') and the attempt to find standpoints that are generalizable and defensible outside of the subjectivities of the colonized, or of their retrospective interpreters and representatives.

---

[82] Steve Biko, 'We Blacks', *I Write What I Like*, 29.
[83] Bhabha, *The Location of Culture*, especially 'Introduction: Locations of Culture', 1–18, and 'Of Mimicry and Man: The Ambivalence of Colonial Discourse', 85–92.
[84] Bhabha, *The Location of Culture*, 86.

Postcolonial histories are of course many, and to draw an axis of differentiation between the 'colonial difference' theme, which was important earlier on, to the 'entanglements' and 'co-production' of colonial and metropolitan societies theme that has of late been more prevalent might be useful, although the division proposed here is too schematic and presupposes a 'progress' from the former to the latter that is difficult to sustain if one looks at everyday writing in postcolonial mode, now the hegemonic common sense of much well-meaning academic writing. The latter theme is represented in the so-called New Imperial History. The 'new' is a critique of metropolitan nationalisms often implicit in writing 'old' imperial histories, or imperial histories of imperialism, as we might call it.

The trend that has come to be called 'the New Imperial History' (hereafter NIP) provides a strong critique of, for instance, 'Little Englander' histories of Britain, which underestimate or ignore the impact of the empire on British domestic life. An early and programmatic statement of this position was provided by Catherine Hall:

In Britain, the traces of those imperial histories appear everywhere—in the naming of streets, the sugar in tea, the coffee and cocoa that are drunk, the mango chutney that is served, the memorials in cemeteries, the public monuments in parks and squares.[85]

This is not particularly dissimilar to the Manchester revisionism of the 1980s, led by John MacKenzie, who insisted that if empire was not always a central issue in domestic British affairs, this was because its ubiquitous presence made it always visible and therefore invisible[86]—an argument close to Edward Said's in *Culture and Imperialism*,[87] though MacKenzie, an anti-Saidian, might not have appreciated this.[88] That the plea for a 'new' imperial history was made alongside a plea for the relevance of imperial

[85] Catherine Hall, 'Histories, Empires and the Post-Colonial Moment', in *The Post-Colonial Question*, ed. Chambers and Curti (London: Routledge, 1996), 65–77: 66.

[86] See for instance John M Mackenzie, *Propaganda and Empire: The Manipulation of British Public Opinion, 1880–1960* (Manchester: Manchester University Press, 1984); John M. Mackenzie, ed., *Imperialism and Popular Culture* (Manchester: Manchester University Press, 1986).

[87] Said, *Culture and Imperialism*.

[88] John M. Mackenzie, *Orientalism: History, Theory and the Arts* (Manchester: Manchester University Press, 1995).

history in the history of Britain should not blind us to differences: the 'nation' (British? English?), in the 'new' argument was not merely shaped by the experience of empire, but was unthinkable without it. The argument that there was a core 'Englishness' or 'Britishness' at 'home' impervious to the experiences and cross-currents of the perambulations of colonial subjects, diasporas, migration, consumption patterns, etc. was implausible; the myth of the 'national' core, contemporaneously as well as retrospectively among Little-England histories and 'old' imperial historians alike, was a refusal to acknowledge that the Empire was always also at Home.[89] It might be noted in passing that the NIP was more sceptical of a metropolitan national imagination than it was of the 'national liberation movements' that set themselves up in opposition to (but also at least in part on the model of) metropolitan nationalisms, and that NIP was more sceptical of nationalisms, nation-states, or states than SS was.

What this amounted to was a critical approach to British 'national' history, exploring lines of tension. The outsider within; the importance of empire in constructing norms of masculinity and femininity; the similarities of race and class as discursive categories; the imperialism of early (British, imperial) feminist projects; race, sexual anxieties, miscegenation; the exclusions of the liberal imagination all became themes for exploration.[90]

---

[89] For a programmatic statement, see Antoinette Burton, 'Who Needs the Nation? Interrogating 'British' History', *Journal of Historical Sociology* 10, no. 3 (September 1997): 227–248. See also Catherine Hall, *Civilising Subjects: Colony and Metropole in the English imagination, 1830–1867* (Chicago: University of Chicago Press, 2002); Catherine Hall, ed., *Cultures of Empire: Colonizers in Britain and the Empire in the Nineteenth and Twentieth Centuries: A Reader* (London: Routledge, 2000); Catherine Hall and Sonya O. Rose, eds., *At Home with the Empire: Metropolitan Culture and the Imperial World* (Cambridge: Cambridge University Press, 2006).

[90] For instance Frederick Cooper and Anne Laura Stoler, eds., *Tensions of Empire: Colonial Cultures in a Bourgeois World* (Berkeley: University of California Press, 1997); Mrinalini Sinha, *Colonial Masculinity: The 'Manly Englishman' and the 'Effeminate Bengali' in the Late Nineteenth Century* (Manchester: Manchester University Press, 1995); Antoinette Burton, *Burdens of History: British Feminists, Indian Women, and Imperial Culture 1860–1915* (Chapel Hill: University of North Carolina Press, 1994); Antoinette Burton, *At the Heart of Empire: Indians and the Colonial Encounter in Late Victorian Britain* (Berkeley: University of California Press, 1998); Philippa Levine, *Prostitution, Race, and Politics: Policing Venereal Disease in the British Empire* (London: Routledge, 2003); Anne Laura Stoler, *Race and the Education of Desire: Foucault's History of Sexuality and the Colonial Order of Things* (Durham: Duke University Press, 1995); Anne Laura Stoler, *Carnal Knowledge and Imperial Power: Race and the Intimate in Colonial Rule* (Berkeley: University of California Press, 2002); Mary Louise Pratt, *Imperial Eyes: Travel Writing and Transculturation* (London: Routledge, 1992); Sudipta Sen, *Distant Sovereignty: National Imperialism and the Origins of British India* (London: Routledge, 2002); John Marriott, *The Other Empire: Metropolis, India and Progress in the Colonial Imagination*

Paul Gilroy was notable in resisting the trend of opting for a cultural counter-nationalism in opposition to metropolitan nationalism or parochialism:

As a supplement to existing formulations of the diaspora idea, the black Atlantic provides an invitation to move into the contested spaces between the local and the global in ways that do not privilege the modern nation state and its institutional order of the sub-national and supra-national networks and patterns of power, communication and conflict that they work to discipline, regulate and govern.[91]

Gilroy coined the term 'The Black Atlantic' as 'my own provisional attempt to figure a deterritorialized, multiplex and anti-national basis for the affinity or "identity of passions" between diverse black populations'.[92] He thus stands against a counter-nationalism of a black variety,[93] invoking Homi Bhabha's ideas of the 'in-between-ness' and 'hybridity' of cultural forms.[94] Gilroy never loses sight of the fact that the arguments about being a nation were invoked consciously due to the legitimacy of national paradigms on a world stage, rather than treating 'nations' as inevitable entities (even when imagined or invented).

The paradox for NIP is, however, that it needs the nation for its own structure: 'By now it is paradoxically axiomatic that obituaries of the nation are premature'.[95] Thus, identities, subjectivities, and the colonial impact on the production of identities and the control of those identities end up being studied, more often than not, in the context of metropolitan

---

(Manchester: Manchester University Press, 2003); Adele Perry, *On the Edge of Empire: Gender, Race, and the Making of British Columbia 1849–1871* (Toronto: University of Toronto Press, 2001); Alan Lester, *Imperial Networks: Creating Identities in Nineteenth-Century South Africa and Britain* (London: Routledge, 2001).

[91] Paul Gilroy, 'Route Work: The Black Atlantic and the Politics of Exile', in *The Post-Colonial Question*, ed. Chambers and Curti (London: Routledge, 1996), 17–29: 22.

[92] Gilroy, 'Route Work', 18.

[93] Paul Gilroy, *The Black Atlantic: Modernity and Double Consciousness* (Cambridge, MA: Harvard University Press, 1993); also Paul Gilroy, *Between Camps: Nations, Cultures and the Allure of Race* (Harmondsworth: Penguin, 2001).

[94] Bhabha, *The Location of Culture*.

[95] Antoinette Burton, 'Introduction: On the Inadequacy and the Indispensability of the Nation', in *After the Imperial Turn: Thinking With and Through the Nation*, ed. Antoinette Burton (Durham: Duke University Press, 2003), 1–23; quote from 1.

nationalisms. That the tone of writing about such nationalisms is not one of approval makes little difference to the process of reification.

1.5. Some Conclusions

Postcolonial history's sensitivity to 'discourse' and to the cultural dynamics of how colonialism disciplines the Other appears for some years now to have reached a *cul de sac*. At its worst, 'postcolonialism' descends to the politics of comparative victimhood, where an assertion of solidarity with the oppressed, generically, takes the place of rigorous intellectual engagement. At its worst, again, in centring the academic voice that claims the right to speak for the downtrodden, it privileges the identity of the academic speakers themselves. If 'postcolonial history' remains relevant, it can only be by historicizing itself.

No single intellectual or academic would accept the charge that their writing has produced a valorization of 'authenticity', a freezing and reification of identities, an imprisonment of the individual in a pre-defined collectivity, and her surrender to the authority of self-proclaimed custodians of 'culture' and 'tradition', recognized as such by states and governments. But indeed, this is what appears to have happened.

The claiming of a privileged position as (post)colonized to (re)present the subjectivities of one's fellow downtrodden subjects requires an identification that is as uncertain as that of the inheritor of the (historically defined) perpetrator community (the colonizers, the white races) identifying with the victim community (the colonized, 'Indians', 'First Nations', women) and writing from that perspective. A trend set in motion is difficult to arrest—the notoriously autonomous text, perhaps? And is it possible to draw back from the implications of the project without surrendering the cultural authority that has been won for oneself, and is sustained, by that project?

The acknowledgement of diversity, plurality, and a multiplicity of voices is now considered common sense; it is 'difference' rather than similarity that is assumed when two people not of the same 'culture' come face to face. This is differently problematic; it is a semi-coercive assumption of alterity that produces conversations in which one assumes that the 'stranger' does not speak one's language.

And as to the dangers of universalistic claims that yield an oppressive cultural imperialism when left unquestioned: the new 'Western' conservatives operate not by continuing to assert the universality of 'Western' thought and therefore the right of the 'West' to export its values by force to a reluctant world that must be administered the painful cure to an illness it is ignorant of; they operate by acknowledging diversity and difference and by fighting that diversity in the name of the right of the 'West', self-proclaimed as particular rather than universal, to impose itself on its Others—as a matter of its survival.

Samuel Huntington's notorious 'clash of civilizations' argument identifies several 'cultures', among them the 'Western', whose contending subjectivities must battle for survival, and he therefore argues that the 'West' must defend itself or be destroyed.[96] So the decentring of the 'Western' claim to universalism and to a monopoly of standards of 'progress', 'modernity', 'rationality', etc. have arguably created a new situation in which, shorn of such universalist pretensions, 'Western man' must defend his subjectivity—and his potential loss of power and therefore his own (potential) victimhood—in the same way as the Native American (or the First Nations), or the Chinese, or the 'Islamic', civilizations, have to. In another book, Huntington argued that 'Western' culture did not require being born 'Western', but merely an acceptance of 'Western' values.[97] But he did argue that this culture would have to be defended resolutely against the cultural relativism of our times—other cultures would similarly defend themselves in their own territories (Huntington expects 'civilizations' to behave like states, and consequently to make war on other civilizations that presumably would also organize themselves like or as states). Structurally, Huntington's is a nearly classical postcolonial argument, in many senses; he has only to establish the victimhood, actual, or impending, of the 'West', to perfect it.

The bulk of the significant or formative debates in postcolonial history occurred in the period from the late 1980s to the early 1990s, which makes many of them over 30 years old. The terminology of the postcolonial

---

[96] Samuel P. Huntington, *The Clash of Civilizations and the Remaking of World Order* (New York: Simon & Schuster, 1996).
[97] Samuel P. Huntington, *Who Are We? The Challenges to America's National Identity* (New York: Simon & Schuster, 2004).

interventions has acquired a certain currency and legitimacy. The arguments have gradually lost their opponents, and some of them appear to be exercises in tilting at windmills. The term 'postcolonial' increasingly appears to be devoid of the polemical and political charge that it once carried.

2
Manifesto on Indirections
Histories, Collective Victimhood, and Postcolonialism

The impetus for this set of reflections comes from a sense that the political and academic directions of the last 25 or 30 years have led to the reification of subjectivities, the celebration of 'difference', the insistence on the importance of 'affect' and therefore on 'memory', collective, or otherwise. Such trends are epitomized by what is now known as 'postcolonialism'. Postcolonial theorists cannot be held responsible for them, but they often voice the trends in academically respectable language. And since 'postcolonialism' has in recent times been presented as a breakthrough in understanding Otherness and in achieving cultural understanding, this is a commentary on that claim. This is therefore an analysis of indirections not conducive to the (proclaimed) goal.

If one has, as I have, been in Germany for the last 10 or so years, one is struck by the return of the 'postcolonial'. The postcolonial moment has passed in the Anglo-American world (or has become the boring everydayness of academic life); however, this return in Germany has led to an Indian summer in the careers of the stars of postcolonial studies, who dutifully make their way to Berlin in the warm weather, flying first class to the evocatively titled 'Haus der Kulturen der Welt', in an academic version of the film *Sunset Boulevard*.

Postcolonial studies, though its origins are more diverse, and although many of its practitioners dispute its meaning and scope, disclaim many of these origins and even the name itself can be said to have come into its own in the context of 1980s and 1990s Anglo-American, and initially mainly American, anxieties about race, difference, and multicultural societies.[1] In Germany, these anxieties have now come to the fore,

[1] See for example Aijaz Ahmad, 'Orientalism and After: Ambivalence and Metropolitan Location in the Work of Edward Said', in *In Theory: Classes, Nations, Literatures* (London: Verso, 1992), 159–220; Ella Shohat, 'Notes on the "Post-Colonial"', *Social Text* no. 31/32 (1992): 99–113;

and the argument is whether the old debates from postcolonial studies are now relevant in Germany, and therefore that this 'rediscovery' is important, even though it seems to some academics that it is an unnecessary repetition.

The argument I am making is this: postcolonialism is attuned to an agenda of recognizing the subjectivities of subject peoples. It also requires the inheritance of that subjecthood by succeeding generations, a perpetuation of the role of victim and a perpetuation in collective memory of that understanding of victimhood, for its operation. This makes it unsuited to 'understanding the other' without stereotyping the 'other' either as perpetual victim or perpetual perpetrator, often with oneself in the role of the opposite in the binary. It often reifies and isolates 'cultures' in terms of a priori collectivities, gives voice to those who claim a continuity with 'communities' (and therefore 'cultures') that have been historically victims of persecution and delegitimizes those from 'perpetrator communities' (heterosexual, white, male, middle class, etc.) unless they choose to claim a voice by identifying with the victim communities (while at the same time acknowledging their own—inherited—historic complicity in the victimhood of the victim communities).

How does one identify 'victimhood' in this sense? The claim to victimhood has to be made collectively, and most often nationally, even when gestures of solidarity with other groups, oppressed by definition, are made.[2] This is connected with another question: who is to give voice to victimhood? Once it is, for instance, agreed that the voiceless need to have a voice, and that this voice has to be given to them by a representative, what qualifies one person as opposed to another to provide that voice?[3] Most often, it is the myth of common national origins that implicitly provides that voice, making non-nationals vicarious nationalists who choose to identify with the victims, or reducing them to illegitimacy, for the

Arif Dirlik, 'The Postcolonial Aura: Third World Criticism in the Age of Global Capitalism', *Critical Inquiry* 20, no. 2 (Winter, 1994): 328–356. For a broader analysis of postcolonial theory and history, see Chapter 1.

[2] Homi Bhabha, 'Introduction: Locations of Culture', in *The Location of Culture* (London: Routledge, 1995) [1994], 1–18.

[3] Gayatri Chakraborty Spivak, 'Can the Subaltern Speak?' in *Marxism and the Interpretation of Culture*, ed. Cary Nelson and Lawrence Grossberg (Basingstoke: Macmillan, 1988), 271–313.

legitimacy to speak comes not from any quality intrinsic to the argument but from the legitimacy of a vicarious victimhood of identification.

This leads to what I call the politics of comparative victimhood: a politics that is contested in terms of history, memory, and (compulsory?) belonging. This is particularly important in my own academic discipline; as historians are increasingly asked to serve the function of endorsing or at least respecting (and therefore being reticent about challenging) collective memory, the question as to what political and social roles they are to play, or indeed to seek to avoid playing, comes to the forefront. This is especially the case when historians are confronted with questions of victimhood and suffering, and are forced to negotiate a role or space between the subjectivities of various lived experiences of suffering, and the multiple appropriations, sometimes instrumental, of such suffering. Although much work has been done on the importance of collective memory and of memorialization in the construction of lives and of communities, it is apparently collective memory narrated *as history* that has a greater legitimating function than mere collective memory; the historian is therefore a 'site of memory' that is particularly legitimating.[4]

There is also an *asymmetry of recognition* that is shaped by this. Only victims and their inheritors, it would seem, have subjectivities that are relevant; perpetrators and their inheritors do not. Therefore, the way of gaining recognition of a subjectivity is to be able to claim, at least partially, a form of victimhood. Without this—although it is perfectly possible to imagine a perpetrator subjectivity that claims to be relevant because of its subjectivity—the subjectivity is illegitimate. Meanwhile, a world view composed of separate and reified subjectivities is not conducive to 'understanding the stranger'—at best, uneasy toleration can be achieved.

No small surprise, then, that the route to legitimation for other groups seeking recognition of their subjectivities is the claiming of victimhood. This does not work unproblematically in new political and 'national' contexts: for example, in the case of *die Vertriebenen*,[5] or the 'German'

---

[4] Pierre Nora, 'Between Memory and History: *Les Lieux de Memoire*', *Representations* 26 (Spring 1989): 7–24; Nora's comment about historians as custodians of, and consequently sites of, collective memory, appears on p. 7. For further discussions on this theme, see Chapter 3.

[5] The expellees from (mostly Eastern) Europe of German origin after the Second World War: see Pertti Ahonen, *After the Expulsion: West Germany and Eastern Europe, 1945–1990* (Oxford: Oxford University Press, 2003).

inheritors of the Dresden bombings, for whom the idea of Germans as a perpetrator *Volk* responsible for the atrocities of the Third Reich has to be tempered by the idea that Germans were also, at least sometimes, victims. Both a 'traditional' left, who sees these issues as ones for right-wing fringe movements and neo-Nazis and the new identitarian preconscious-postcolonial-left have no good rebuttal for these arguments. They seek instead to return these claims to sectional and partial ('German') victimhood to their larger ('German') framework of collective guilt for the ultimate horror of the Nazis' Holocaust: *'Oma, halt's Maul'*,[6] as the poster reads, also reminding us of the fact that this German guilt is now in the third and perhaps the fourth generation. The fact that this implicitly reifies a negative-nationalism-in-German-collective-guilt—imprisoning the argument in a framework of competing subjectivities that cannot be resolved—is ignored, and often deliberately so. This example problematizes one of the central assumptions of postcolonial argument in that it is about contestations within an already reified and unified subjectivity: 'German' (and this is not problematized as a category). That this picture is also one from the Federal Republic of Germany and not the German Democratic Republic is also notable.

It is usually taken for granted in all of this that the 'stranger' is the disempowered rather than the empowered, which of course is politically accurate but discursively inaccurate. As the spokespersons for the 'stranger' demand, and achieve, recognition for the strangers' subjectivities, their 'cultures' can be treated with respect even as it is a condition of this cultural recognition that the strangers remain politically disempowered. Otherwise, the legitimation-through-victimhood ceases to function. It is, however, important that the spokespersons for these subjectivities remain empowered—and they remain empowered only insofar as those they speak for remain disempowered.

But at the same time, attempts to break up the collectivity either of victimhood or perpetrator are met by a structure of argument that has incorporated individuals and sub-collectivities (defined from the perspective of an already reified collectivity) into the collectivity of either victims or perpetrators. Who has the right not to belong to 'their' culture? How does one identify 'one's own' culture? If I, as a 'Muslim woman',

---

[6] 'Grandma, shut your trap' is the best translation I could come up with.

swim naked, am I abandoning 'my' culture, and if you, as a person *von den neuen Bundesländern*,[7] also do so, are you asserting 'your' cultural rights, in the face of (for instance) West German cultural imperialism?

2.1. States and Values

It is of course easy to forget that these debates are staged by, and in, actually existing states that assume the right to adjudicate on these matters, at the same time as they pretend not to have cultural or values-based assumptions of their own. The state allegedly is forced to tolerate (others') intolerance in the name of a liberalism or pluralism phrased in universalist terms of cultural rights for all, and to surrender allegedly progressive principles in the name of diversity and (others') 'culture', rather than imposing a supposed *Leitkultur*[8]; states are reluctant to make explicit their implicit assumptions about belonging and non-belonging in a world of increasingly diverse populations. Cultural claims are also made upon the state and via the state; it is states' recognitions of claims to 'culture' that make cultures effectively exist. Without that recognition, and its concomitant reification, it is unclear what constitutes a 'culture' and its practitioners (in the example just quoted, without the pre-existing categories in which the two individuals are placed, we would just have two people swimming naked).

Groups with particularist and communitarian values might make (their own) culturalist claims to being more progressive and more inclusive than their competitors, thereby justifying (their own) intolerance in the name of liberalism, tolerance, secularism, etc., and seeking to have these adopted by the state. In some cases, then, the case for defending pluralism allegedly becomes a case for defending a community of faith or 'values', whether this faith is called 'tolerance' or 'culture' or 'liberalism', or the 'Hindu way of life', allegedly more tolerant and 'secular' than other

---

[7] 'From the new federal states': the 'new federal states' is the term for the former East German territories that were absorbed by West Germany after the reunification of 1990, a term that marks them out in a not-so-euphemistic euphemism as different.

[8] 'Leading culture' is a politically accurate translation, I think, for this phrase that has become a favourite of German conservatives and right-wingers, implying the importance of maintaining the 'culture' of the majority in the dominant position.

available ideologies[9] (it is worth noting that 'culture' and 'religious affiliation' become in many cases more or less operationally synonymous, especially for those designated as the outsiders, paradoxically mobilizing those religious affiliations as self-ascriptions even among those who might not normally identify with them).

Examples that come readily to mind include, for instance, the allegedly tolerant Dutch or Danish state's ability to justify stigmatizing 'Muslims' on the grounds of Islam's alleged intolerance of homosexuality or its mistreatment of women. The pattern is of course discernible in several public debates about the necessity of anti-terrorist legislation in 'democracies': 'our values' include respect for the due process of law, but anything from preventive detention to torture has been discussed in terms of the exceptional threat posed by those who threaten 'our values'. Opponents point out how these values are also under threat if they can be seen not to apply to potential 'terrorists' or outsiders, who in a circular argument are the one because they are the other. Such arguments have been so all-pervasive in recent times that it is useless to pretend that current discussions are untouched by them.

Inclusion, then, and the (often merely apparent) absence of markers of 'values'-based qualification to belonging within a state, can themselves be (presented as) 'values'. Such a state can define its exclusions in terms of excluding those who would otherwise do the excluding: even apparently unobjectionable principles such as 'freedom of speech' (most often defended in principle even as they are constrained or mutilated by states) are 'values'. It is also perfectly possible to imagine an exclusionary and secular democratic state: a 'confessional state', in an extended sense of the term, where the right to be a full member of that state requires conformity with a set of values that are often merely implicit.

The allegedly inclusive state (which is what most states try to claim they are), then, prefers to operate without claiming an explicit 'culture'; groups within it, almost by definition 'minorities', are allowed to have them, and

---

[9] The dilemma I have outlined here is also central to Anne Phillips, *Multiculturalism Without Culture* (Princeton: Princeton University Press, 2007): see especially 1–9. Her solutions are different from mine. She also distinguishes between 'culture' on the one hand, and 'religion', 'race', 'ethnicity', etc. on the other, categories which are often collapsed into the category 'culture'. This work also suffers from the assumption that it is states who should adjudicate amongst cultures by attempting to create a 'multiculturalism' without 'culture', in which model states do not themselves have, or ought not to have (dominant or implicit) cultures.

indeed, have 'culture' thrust upon them, in a paradoxical move of inclusion that marks them in that act of inclusion as exceptional.

2.2. The Potential Cultural Subjectivity of Occidental Civilization

There are several characteristics of the academic debates of postcolonial theory that have found their way into public debates on inclusion, representation, and 'culture' more generally. Central debates often hinge not so much upon the nature of the speaker's or writer's political engagements, but of the speaker's or writer's identitarian markers, with the result that positioning oneself in an identitarian manner sometimes becomes central to an argument: are you a Jew or a woman, or are you able to say 'shoah' and 'nakba' in the same breath? This of course can be seen as a logical and legitimate consequence of the death of 'objectivity': we are all interested parties, the personal is political, and our emotional cathexes are integral to our utterances;[10] however, there is a tendency for the structure of arguments to reduce speakers or writers to their origins, in a manner reminiscent of forms of stereotyping and essentialization that, it has been argued, are a feature of colonial thought.[11]

Academics' claiming of a privileged position as (post)colonized to (re)present the subjectivities of their fellow downtrodden subjects (and how downtrodden do you have to be to become a professor at a leading university?) requires an identification that is as uncertain as that of the inheritor of the perpetrator community identifying with the victim community and writing from that perspective.

This project of representation, and at times only this, is in danger of becoming the 'project' of postcolonial historiography or postcolonial theory, and some postcolonial theorists were able to recognize this: 'a certain postcolonial subject had ... been recoding the colonial subject and

---

[10] The phrase 'emotional cathexes' is the phrase used in the English translation of Sigmund Freud, *Introductory Lectures on Psychoanalysis* (trans. J. Strachey) (Harmondsworth: Pelican, 1974) [1915–1917].

[11] See in this context the distinction between 'identity' and 'youdentity' introduced in the Introduction.

appropriating the Native Informant's position.[12] However, a trend set in motion is difficult to arrest—the notoriously autonomous text, perhaps? And is it possible to draw back from the implications of the project without surrendering the cultural authority that has been won for oneself, and is sustained by, that project?

There is also the question of whom one is addressing. If the point of the non-universality of 'Western' thought and the disarming of its claim to being universal has to be made, the question of audience is central: such battles belong in newspaper offices, in schools, in first-year teaching, and in public fora rather than in scholarly journals and monographs, or recycled essays from scholarly monographs in scholarly books; accessibility and communicative skills are very important. It is also important not to have to rely centrally on the authority, say, as an 'Indian', a 'woman' or a 'Dalit' to speak for 'Indian', 'women's' or 'Dalit' pasts to the listener. And increasingly, it appears that some speakers claim that authority by virtue of their own alleged 'authenticity', ultimately derived from their privileged access to the 'indigenous'. This is myth-making and it is obscurantist.

Moreover, the acknowledgement of diversity, plurality, and a multiplicity of voices is now considered common sense; it is 'difference' rather than similarity that is assumed when two people are not of the same 'culture' (how can you tell?) come face to face. This is differently problematic; it is a semi-coercive assumption of alterity that produces conversations in which one assumes that the 'stranger' does not speak one's language.

And as to the dangers of universalistic claims that yield an oppressive cultural imperialism when left unquestioned: it is not by continuing to assert the universality of 'Western' thought and, therefore, the right of the 'West' to export its values by force to a reluctant world that must be administered the painful cure to an illness it is ignorant of that a new right wing operates; it is by acknowledging diversity and difference and by fighting that diversity in the name of the right of the 'West', which is self-proclaimed as particular rather than universal, to impose itself on its Others—as a matter of survival.

---

[12] Gayatri Chakravarty Spivak, *A Critique of Postcolonial Reason: Towards a History of the Vanishing Present* (Cambridge, MA: Harvard University Press, 1999), ix.

2.3. By Way of Conclusion

Those among the readers of this essay who have been watching the footnotes will have noticed that the bulk of the debates I have referred to as
significant or formative occurred in the late 1980s or early 1990s, which
makes them well past their twentieth anniversary. To my mind, the debates have not changed much over the years, although the terminology of
the postcolonial interventions has acquired a certain currency and legitimacy, becoming the common sense of our times.

And although there is now a tendency to think of them as conducive
to enabling an understanding of the (post)colonial Other by the (post)
colonizing Self, or by analogous victims by perpetrators—hence the
eager eavesdropping on these past debates in the (for instance German)
present—postcolonialism was in the first instance a model of conflict,
a challenge to the right of the (post)colonizer to continue to represent
the (post)colonial subject as if s/he did not have a voice (in fact, we may
note in parentheses that many of the challenges posed to postcolonial
theory and theorists came from a position that claimed a different axis
of confrontation—the argument was that internal conflicts among the
(post)colonized, for instance on 'class' lines, were being brushed under
the carpet, and a form of unproblematic and unified 'identity' of the postcolonial was being celebrated instead).

The way out of this conflict between (post)colonizer and (post)colon-
ized, in what we have already described as an asymmetrical model for
'understanding the stranger', was for the (post)colonizer to shed some
of the burdens of her inheritance of historic-guilt-as-perpetrator by accepting the subjectivities of the (post)colonized. This was a sort of vicarious redressal of grievances, an academic version of state apologies and
reparations for alleged or actual historic wrongs; however, it was not a
model for reciprocal understanding. At best, it could be a model of tolerance, in the Roman sense of 'sufferance'. Spheres of mutual incomprehen-
sion were, and are, not incompatible with this.

PART II

INSTRUMENTALIZATIONS

3

The Revolt of Memory

1857 in the Nationalist Imagination

3.1. Introduction: Nationalism, History, and Memory

This is about the awkward space in the intersection of history and collective memory that is the setting up of national *lieux de memoire*.[1] The phrase has been translated into English as 'realms of memory' by Pierre Nora,[2] or (the translation I prefer) 'sites of memory' and *Erinnerungsorte* in the German translation.[3] The customary form of such sites is concrete: *Denkmäler*, monuments, sites of memory, or mourning.[4] But they could also be more abstract: ways of interpreting historical events, the construction of an archive, the disciplined remembering of particular collective subjectivities recast as national history.[5]

According to Nora, 'There are *lieux de memoire*, sites of memory, because there are no longer *milieux de memoire*, real environments of memory'.[6] For Nora, of course, there is a distinction between 'real

---

[1] Pierre Nora, *Les lieux de Memoire* (3 vols, Paris: Gallimard, 1984–1986).

[2] Pierre Nora (trans. Arthur Goldhammer), *Realms of Memory: Rethinking the French Past* (3 vols, New York: Columbia University Press, 1996–1998).

[3] Etienne Francois and Hagen Schulze, eds., *Deutsche Erinnerungsorte* (Munich: Beck, 2005).

[4] Jay Winter, *Sites of Memory, Sites of Mourning: The Great War in European Cultural History* (Cambridge: Cambridge University Press, 1995); Jay Winter, *Remembering War: The Great War Between Memory and History in the Twentieth Century* (London: Yale University Press, 2006).

[5] For a critical survey of the literature on collective memory, see Wulf Kansteiner, 'Finding Meaning in Memory: A Methodological Critique of Collective Memory Studies', *History and Theory* 41, no. 2 (May 2002): 179–197; and, on Nora, 183–184. See also, for a warning against the overvalorization of memory and its potential oppositional status to history, Kerwin Lee Klein, 'On the Emergence of Memory in Historical Discourse', *Representations* 69, Special Issue: Grounds for Remembering (Winter 2000): 127–150; Kerwin Lee Klein, 'In Search of Narrative Mastery: Postmodernism and the People without History', *History and Theory* 34, no. 4 (December 1995): 275–298.

[6] Pierre Nora, 'Between Memory and History: Les Lieux de Memoire', *Representations* 26 (Spring 1989): 7–24; 7.

memory', which is 'social and unviolated' and exemplified by 'primi-tive and archaic', pre-'national' societies, and 'history', which is how our hopelessly forgetful modern societies, propelled by change, organise the past'.[7] He believes that 'archaic' societies have an 'unself-conscious' and uncritical, but therefore more authentic, 'memory without a past that ceaselessly reinvents traditions, linking the history of its ancestors to the undifferentiated time of heroes, origins, and myth'[8]—and he insists on this as pre-national and non-modern. This is a very strange distinc-tion, for he could equally be providing a commentary on modern na-tionalism. He maintains the old distinction between pre-historical and historical societies in a way that has long been associated with colonial knowledge-forms: 'Among the new nations, independence has swept into history societies newly awakened from their ethnological slumbers by colonial violation'[9] (it is, incidentally, something that seems to go without saying that 'sites of memory' will be national ones, which begs the ques-tion as to what social or institutional forms work towards the founding of these sites. What makes something successfully become a national site of memory? In what ways are these sites contested?).

Nora's claim of the 'fundamental opposition' in modern times of memory and history does not hold: 'memory is life', while 'his-tory ... is the reconstruction, always problematic and incomplete, of what is no longer'.[10] Invoking Maurice Halbwachs,[11] he goes on to say that memory serves the purpose of binding a group together, that 'there are as many memories as there are groups'; history is hostile to memory in this sense and seeks to destroy it. Nora's problematization, then, to rephrase it, is that of an anxiety about a loss of memory that has to be concretely embodied in some form of monumentalization, in a society now under the tyranny of history, 'for anchoring its memory'.[12] However, Nora's key distinction, that between history and memory in modern times,

---

[7] Nora, 'Between Memory and History', 8.

[8] Nora, 'Between Memory and History', 8.

[9] Nora, 'Between Memory and History', 7.

[10] Nora, 'Between Memory and History', 8.

[11] See Maurice Halbwachs, *On Collective Memory* (new edition, Chicago: Chicago University Press, 1992): his theorization dates from 1925.

[12] Nora, 'Between Memory and History', 9. Nora, situating himself in a (French) nationalist tradition, believes that once, during the Third Republic, history was expected to serve national memory—a time when many of the *lieux de memoire* he speaks of—the *Arc de Triomphe*, the *Dictionnaire Larousse*—were brought into being. Nora, 'Between Memory and History', 10–12.

between the authentic and subjective place of memory on the one hand, and history as the enemy of these subjectivities on the other, is one that Nora himself does not accept in practice, though he requires it analytically (for instance, he sees the role of historiographical critique as history discovering where and when it has become a 'victim of memories' that are 'alien impulses within itself', and he therefore implicitly situates history as a constant striving for objectivity, an ambition that he later acknowledges the discipline has now abandoned in favour of an explicit acceptance of positionality and the politics thereof).[13] Freed from the 'buttresses' of *lieux de memoire*, and left to survive in the hostile, wild outside world of history, memory would be swept away by history. So 'we must deliberately create archives', Nora says at one point, in order to preserve memory against the onslaught of history.[14] And this, he goes on to affirm, is an attempt of memory to become history: 'The quest for memory is a search for one's history'. Such memory is now a new kind of memory: 'Modern memory is, above all, archival'; it is not spontaneous, premodern, or archaic.[15] Or of course, since neither abstraction is an agent, is this not an example of the contestation over the category of history that Nora correctly sees as a legitimating one in modern times? The individual must take responsibility for remembering 'his' or 'her' history and becomes a 'memory-individual'—the (non-practicing) Jew whose Jewishness consists in remembering he is a Jew—and, as we now historicize memory itself, and the historian acknowledges his complicity with memory, the historian becomes, in himself, a *lieu de memoire*.[16]

To the questions 'Can there really be a collective history? Or is collective memory a better term?', we must therefore pose the further question: why must memory be presented as history? Because the legitimizing role of history is immense: it is, for that reason, modern. Both history and modernity are legitimizing categories that a national argument cannot do without. Or, in other words, what if a group—seeking to create solidarity—wishes to legitimize its memory as history? Which is of course the point many historians of nationalism have made: that nationalism writes its history backwards, narrates its nationness retrospectively.

[13] Nora, 'Between Memory and History', 10, 18.
[14] Nora, 'Between Memory and History', 12.
[15] Nora, 'Between Memory and History', 13.
[16] Nora, 'Between Memory and History', 16, 18.

3.2. 1857 and National Memory

1857 in various forms of collective imagination has come to overshadow the actual events of 1857; or, in other words, the questions of 'what happened' have been overwritten by those of representations of 1857, in particular in literary and popular cultural genres from that time on,[17] and not necessarily as Revolt or Mutiny, National War or feudal revenge, authentic subalternity or class revolt. It is now, simply as a date, a veritable cornucopia of polysemy.[18] It survives, in the imagination of professional historians, public intellectuals, amateur collectors of toy soldiers, and a lay public, in Britain and India. It is portrayed as a revolt of the Company's soldiers against a perceived threat to their religions, a general popular uprising of North Indian peasants and soldiers against British oppression, and a failed national war of independence; its stories are of martyrdom and sacrifice, of brutality and savagery, rape and massacre. This is a chapter, then, not on event-history, but on readings of a set of events that loomed large in the imagination of empire and colony alike. 'Popular cognisance of the modern history of the Indian subcontinent is limited', Eric Stokes wrote in the early 1980s, and speaking of Britain, of course, 'to three episodes dignified by the names of "Clive", "the Mutiny" and "Gandhi"'.[19] That 1857 is remembered separately and very differently in Indian and British national collective memory should be emphasized.[20]

---

[17] For studies of this, see for example Gautam Chakravarty, *The Indian Mutiny in the British Imagination* (Cambridge: Cambridge University Press, 2005); P. C. Joshi, *1857 in Folk Songs* (Delhi: People's Publishing House, 1994). There have been, of course, several novels, films, and plays on the subject of 1857 from various perspectives over the years, including the Bombay film, *The Rising: Ballad of Mangal Pandey* [2005]—criticized by academics for its historical inaccuracies, but nevertheless relatively successful—and Mahasweta Devi's first novel, *Jhansir Rani* (in Bengali) (1956), whose sometimes excessively nationalist tone might well have embarrassed her later in her life.

[18] It is, moreover, the single date that remains significant, although some of the events continued into 1858 and 1859.

[19] Eric Stokes, *The Peasant Armed: The Indian Revolt of 1857* (Oxford: Clarendon Press, 1985), edited by C. A. Bayly and published posthumously, 1.

[20] The argument that 1857 was a shared *lieu de memoire* connecting India and Britain has been put forward; it is difficult to sustain in the light of the non-overlap of the cultural products, discursive contexts, and audiences for the different strands of argument; the British and the Indian publics were largely separate in this regard, and, as I think this chapter at least implicitly argues, there was no unified 'national' space or audience for remembering 1857. See for example Astrid Erll, 'The "Indian Mutiny" as a shared Lieu de Memoire: Narratives, Media and Performances of Cultural Memory in Great Britain and India, 1857–2005', unpublished paper presented at the conference on 'Re-visiting Sites of Memory: New Perspectives on the British Empire' organized by the German Historical Institute, London, 29 June–2 July 2006. The methodological significance of digging up various texts, ballads, or other cultural products with a

This chapter deals with the 'Indian' side of these rememberings, awkward and contradictory as they were; and it uses the term 'Indian' with caution, given that it is all too easy to reify the assumed unity of the nation-state; indeed, it is one of the arguments of this chapter that the problem of dealing with 1857 is part of the problem of assigning an identity and unity to the Indian nation-state.

Despite its special status in the historical imagination of Britain and India, academic writing about the events of 1857 has been relatively sparse.[21] The exceptional moments in this regard have been anniversaries, and the 150th anniversary in 2007 provoked, inevitably, a scramble for that great date.[22] Previous to that, a spurt of writing appeared 50 years

Mutiny theme without knowing much about their circulation or impact needs to be questioned; this is a problem that also applies, for instance, to P. C. Joshi's (unfortunately unfinished) work, *1857 in Folk Songs*.

[21] Since the 1980s, writing on 1857 has been from the perspectives opened out by 'histories from below'. Following Eric Stokes, *The Peasant and the Raj: Studies in Agrarian Society and Peasant Rebellion in Colonial India* (Cambridge: Cambridge University Press, 1978); Stokes, *The Peasant Armed*, the question of the soldier as peasant and as rebel could not be ignored. The early practitioners of the craft of 'subaltern history' made something of this question, as they did of local power dynamics and everyday cultural practices. Ranajit Guha described their elementary aspects: Ranajit Guha, *Elementary Aspects of Peasant Insurgency in Colonial India* (Delhi: Oxford University Press, 1983). Gautam Bhadra wrote on four rebels of 1857: Gautam Bhadra, 'Four Rebels of 1857', in *Subaltern Studies IV*, ed. Ranajit Guha (Delhi: Oxford University Press, 1985), 229–275. Rudrangshu Mukherjee wrote on a local milieu: Rudrangshu Mukherjee, *Awadh in Revolt 1857–1858: A Study of Popular Resistance* (1984; new edition, New Delhi: Permanent Black, 2002); see his introduction to the new edition for a recontextualizing of his own contribution to the debates and those of others, in particular, his reading of Ranajit Guha's *Elementary Aspects*. Later he wrote on an incident of imperial outrage: Rudrangshu Mukherjee, *Spectre of Violence: The Kanpur Massacres in 1857* (New Delhi: Viking, 1998); Rudrangshu Mukherjee, '"Satan Let Loose Upon Earth": The Kanpur Massacres in India in the Revolt of 1857', *Past and Present* 128 (August 1990): 92–116. Tapti Roy wrote on another local context: Tapti Roy, *The Politics of a Popular Uprising: Bundelkhand in 1857* (Delhi: Oxford University Press, 1994). Military historians have used the Revolt as the implicit or explicit *telos* of their narratives of the development and structural tendencies of the East India Company's army: see Seema Alavi, *The Sepoys and the Company: Tradition and Transition in Northern India 1770–1830* (Delhi: Oxford University Press, 1995), which despite the chronological framework in the title, uses 1857 as its end-point. Chris Bayly famously used 1857 as the crucial juncture of the crisis of the imperial information order and the revolt of the Native Informant: C. A. Bayly, *Empire and Information: Information Gathering and Social Communication in India 1780–1870* (Cambridge: Cambridge University Press, 1996).

[22] There have been several anniversary-related projects and publications, not to mention a cluster of publications approaching the impending or actual anniversary, including Rudrangshu Mukherjee, *Mangal Pandey: Brave Martyr or Accidental Hero?* (New Delhi: Penguin, 2005); William Dalrymple, *The Last Mughal: the Fall of a Dynasty, Delhi 1857* (London: Bloomsbury, 2006); Tapti Roy, *The Raj of the Rani* (New Delhi: Penguin, 2006) on Laxmibai, and a special issue of *Biblio* (March–April 2007), to name a few—of the last, the contribution of Ronojoy Sen, 'Tilting at Windmills', 5–6, surveys a part of the academic historiography on the subject I address

before, on the occasion of the centenary in 1957.[23] Outside of academic arenas, of course, 1857 remains an evocative date that is to be remembered and memorialized for various purposes. In 1997, I was at the Red Fort in Delhi for an awkwardly concocted 140th anniversary of the events, which included a restaging of the sepoys' march to the Red Fort. The occasion for this invented anniversary, 10 years ahead of a conventional one, was the opportunity for underlining the allegedly non-sectarian and secular spirit of the rebels, among whom were both Hindus and Muslims, and who had appealed to the symbol of precolonial Indian sovereignty, the Mughal Emperor Bahadur Shah Zafar, to resume actual sovereignty and provide them with the legitimacy to mount a formal challenge to Company rule. The spectres that haunted the fort and hovered in the background that winter evening in 1997 were not those of the rebels or heroes of 1857, but those of the Sangh Parivar, that coalition of the self-proclaimed 'Hindu' nationalists and fascists who were on the verge of taking over the government of the independent state of India. Whether we, or others in their special edition t-shirts (the Rani of Jhansi or Bahadur Shah Zafar), succeeded in epitomizing communal harmony or revolutionary vigour I cannot tell.

It is difficult to interpret 1857 with any degree of comfort if one is committed to the values of a modernizing or a secular state. Events are embarrassing: was the British atrocity literature based on actual event-history (British brutality, of course, is well documented and even celebrated as the appropriately and truly manly response to the cowardly natives)? And then, there is the problem of placing 1857 in a narrative of national progress. Vinayak Damodar Savarkar (1883–1966) famously started the ball rolling in this debate (once again, the occasion was an anniversary, in his case, the 50th, in 1907). His association with later proto-fascist and fascist tendencies on behalf of a *völkisch* Hindu nationalism has made much of what he said distasteful, and therefore his 'history' of 1857 is not as canonical as it allegedly once was, or at least as canonical as its title was: it is

---

here, and David Lelyveld, 'Of Mixed Loyalties', 32–33, describes Sir Syed Ahmad Khan's experiences of 1857 in Bijnur.

[23] Surendra Nath Sen, *1857* (New Delhi: Publications Division, Ministry of Information and Broadcasting, Government of India, May 1957); Romesh Chunder Majumdar, *The Sepoy Mutiny and the Revolt of 1857* (1957; 2nd edn. Calcutta: Firma KL Mukhopadhyay, 1963); S. B. Chaudhuri, *Civil Rebellion in the Indian Mutinies 1857–59* (Calcutta: World Press, 1957).

doubtful that many have actually read this text overburdened with rhetorical excesses, and in its own time, it was impossible to find a legal and continuous copy of the banned text, which only circulated and existed in fragments.[24] Jawaharlal Nehru (1889–1964), on the other hand, representing the aspect of Indian nationalism that we have come to accept as the basis of a properly inclusive Indian state ideology, was in his most famous passages of historical writing rather dismissive of 1857;[25] in fact, he was more ambivalent about 1857 than the retrospective record allows for.[26]

The trouble with 1857 is that it inhabits inappropriable ground; a coalition of 'backward' elements drawn from the lower ranks of an army, elitist leaders, landowners, and world-historically obsolete kings and princes, speaking in a religiously inflected language of legitimation,[27] was difficult to celebrate among 'progressives'. And Indian nationalists of various types all wished to see themselves as progressives, even those nationalists we now see as somewhat backward. 1857, therefore, could be remembered as 'the dying groans of an obsolete aristocracy and centrifugal feudalism of the medieval age'.[28] And yet there were sentiments and moments that might well be used retrospectively to serve the needs of national mythology and mass mobilization.

A crucial distinction should be introduced here: that between anti-colonialism and nationalism. We need to maintain this distinction for ourselves, as retrospective analysts, even as we note that the difficulties of interpreting 1857 come from a desire to see the two as congruent. Anti-colonialism, whether clearly articulated or implicitly present, was not necessarily nationalism (the 1857 rebels allegedly lacked the 'modern' outlook that might have qualified them as Indian nationalists).[29] The corollary, that not all Indian nationalisms were anti-colonial, is seldom talked about—we are still told, however, that 'communalist' groups

---

[24] Vinayak Damodar Savarkar, *The Indian War of Independence 1857* (Bombay: Phoenix Publications, 1947).

[25] Jawaharlal Nehru, *The Discovery of India* (Calcutta: Signet, 1946). In his extremely long *Glimpses of World History* (London: Lindsay Drummond, 1949), written as history lessons for his daughter and as a means to keep himself occupied while in prison, he does not mention the Revolt at all.

[26] Jawaharlal Nehru, *An Autobiography* (London: Bodley Head, 1936), 2, 8.

[27] See Chapter 6.

[28] Majumdar, *The Sepoy Mutiny*, 58.

[29] See Guha, *Elementary Aspects*.

were not anti-colonial, or at any rate, not anti-colonial enough.[30] Anti-colonialism, then, might have been an easier fit with aspects of 1857; nationalism in the sense of its late nineteenth- or early twentieth-century use would have been an anachronism. We need to recognize that the idea of nationalism, in order to justify popular sovereignty in the face of the sovereignty of the monarch, was an innovation whose international acceptance was relatively late: it was not until the Bolshevik Revolution and Woodrow Wilson's Fourteen Points that 'national self-determination' became widely acknowledged as the language of legitimacy in which claims to collective political existence had to be made.[31] Anti-colonialism, a much more amorphous and non-ideological configuration or collection of sentiments, movements, and ideas, without typologies or predictable form, has by comparison been subject to the enormous condescension of posterity. But the clarity of this distinction is a retrospective and analytic one, rather than one that is contemporaneous and subjectively experienced. And it is a distinction that most historians do not make. There still seems to be a need to seek the 'precursors' of the Indian nation so that the 'Indian nation' has a longer genealogy than simply a colonial one, as if the acknowledgement that the 'nation' is a relatively recent concept is embarrassing. 1857 might thus serve a proto-national purpose even if it is, in the end, the wrong sort of nationalism, thereby giving the Indian nation a pre-colonial history and a non-colonial 'modernity' (since nationalism is a modern idea), and giving nationalism itself a non-'Western' genealogy.[32]

---

[30] We might recall, for instance, the debates on the *Towards Freedom* volumes compiled by the Indian Council for Historical Research: see Vinay Lal, *The History of History: Politics and Scholarship in Modern India* (Delhi: Oxford University Press, 2003), 2–3, for a brief account.

[31] For a study of this moment, see Arno Mayer, *Wilson vs Lenin: Political Origins of the New Diplomacy 1917–1918* (New Haven: Yale University Press, 1963) [1959]. For an inferior later text, see Erez Manela, *The Wilsonian Moment: Self-Determination and the International Origins of Anticolonial Nationalism* (Oxford: Oxford University Press, 2007).

[32] For the use of this argument by a historian of India who is not an Indian nationalist, see C. A. Bayly, *Origins of Nationality in India: Patriotism and Ethical Government in the Making of Modern India* (Delhi: Oxford University Press, 1998); C. A. Bayly, *The Birth of the Modern World 1780–1914: Global Connections and Comparisons* (Oxford: Blackwell, 2004). But for precolonial proto-nations more generally, see Rajat Kanta Ray, *The Felt Community: Commonality and Mentality Before the Emergence of Indian Nationalism* (Delhi: Oxford University Press, 2002); Irfan Habib, ed., *India: Studies in the History of an Idea* (New Delhi: Munshiram, 2005).

3.3. Framing 1857

In the case of 1857, monuments in a concrete sense do not serve this collective purpose; there are a few of these sparsely dotted around our urban
landscapes, but do monuments properly function without a prior or sim-
ultaneous metanarrative, however incoherent, of the significance of the
events that they attempt to embody? Perhaps there is a case for thinking
consistently in terms of more abstract sites of memory: collective memory
not directly experienced, but handed down so as to apparently be collectively, and intersubjectively, personal. But we must further note that such
memory is not archaic, and that it is often—though not always—in the
service of a national cause. Nationalism provides a rubric of disciplined
identities through which memories are themselves disciplined; non-
upper-caste or Dalit invocations of 1857[33] or folk ballads[34] can invoke
identities that are less or more than national, but must be incorporated
into the national to obtain their legitimacy.[35]

The question is whether a lack of what professionals might describe as
historical accuracy makes any difference when we are speaking about how
historical events become sites of memory—the success of Amir Khan's
film on Mangal Pandey being a case in point. '[I]n certain respects, the
past is up for grabs', as one writer put it. 'It is really the *meaning* of the past
that is of issue'.[36] This is of course especially important in terms of direct
personal involvement (by now inapplicable to 1857) or collective remembering that provides a collective belonging, which of course assumes an
identification with a past that is indeed remembered collectively, as belonging in some sense to 'us'.

Histories, for over a century now, since the paradigm of the 'national'
became (relatively) hegemonic in terms of its legitimating role for collective political and social existence, have been national histories even
when they have not. It is in this situation that 1857 proves defective in

---

[33] Badri Narayan, *Women Heroes and Dalit Assertion in North India: Culture, Identity and
Politics* (New Delhi: Sage, 2006).

[34] P. C. Joshi, *1857 in Folk Songs*.

[35] On the legitimacy of nationalism as a paradigm for collective identities, see my argument
in Benjamin Zachariah, *Playing the Nation Game: The Ambiguities of Nationalism in India*
(Delhi: Yoda Press, 2011).

[36] Michael G. Kenny, 'A Place for Memory: The Interface Between Individual and Collective
History', *Comparative Studies in Society and History* vol. 41, no. 3 (July 1999): 420–437, 437.

India. In terms of attempting to provide the Revolt with a successful place in a relatively coherent version of an official nationalist ideology, Indian nationalists were faced with a tricky problem: neither fully canonized nor properly disavowed, 1857 inhabits this peculiar space of non-belonging hovering on the brink of belonging. Such a situation was best illustrated in 1957, on the 100th anniversary of the Revolt. The foreword to the officially commissioned centenary history of the Revolt, Surendra Nath Sen's *Eighteen Fifty-Seven*, was written not by Jawaharlal Nehru, Prime Minister and habitual commentator on historical matters, but by Maulana Abul Kalam Azad (1888–1958).[37] Azad's piece, 16 pages long and divided into several sub-sections, was a careful analysis of the historiography of the Revolt, demonstrating both an impressive scholarship and an impressive engagement with the scholarship then extant. He claimed credit himself for having commissioned Sen's book; Azad pointedly said that prior to this, 'no objective history of the struggle had yet been written'[38]—a remark that provoked the wry remark from one of the book's reviewers, the Marxist historian Susobhan Chandra Sarkar, that 'Indian historical scholarship is still obsessed with the ghost of Ranke'[39] (this is incidentally an indication of how seriously Susobhan*babu* was willing to take the Maulana's claim to historical scholarship).[40] 'Dr. Sen', Azad wrote approvingly, 'has treated the subject objectively and dispassionately.'[41] Despite the book being an officially sponsored history, there had been 'no attempt to interfere with his work or influence his conclusions.'[42] Azad's stress on objectivity, which of course sounds strange to those of us trained in the post-1960s, or at least post-1980s, historical profession, was a matter of some importance. He conceded that 'an objective history of the uprising was more difficult to write before India became free', but believed that in 100 years, the passions raised by the events should have lost their hold.[43] Then he proceeded himself to write the emotive history of those passions,

---

[37] Sen, *1857*, foreword by Maulana Abul Kalam Azad, dated 9 February 1957, v–xxi.

[38] Azad, in Sen, *1857*, v.

[39] Susobhan Chandra Sarkar, 'Views on 1857', review article, *New Age* monthly, August 1957, reprinted in *On the Bengal Renaissance* (Calcutta: Papyrus, 1979, reprinted 1985), 115.

[40] A large amount of space in the review is spent discussing Maulana Azad's comments on objectivity, 'It is idle to pretend that one can shake off such points of view', and challenges Azad's claim that all of India had deep loyalty to the Mughal court. Sarkar, 'Views on 1857', 116.

[41] Azad, in Sen, *1857*, xxi.

[42] Azad, in Sen, *1857*, xx.

[43] Azad, in Sen, *1857*, vi.

in the rest of his own contribution to the book, while at the same time attempting to place it in a reading of national history.

Alongside the question of how to place 1857 in a national history, we might wish to consider the trajectories of the category 'national' as a legitimating category. 1857 was nine years after the 'springtime of the peoples' that was the 1848 revolutions in Europe, where the national principle resurfaced after a long underground existence under the Concert of Europe; it was, therefore, a radical idea whose incorporation into the language of resistance in India, such as it existed at the time, was gradual. By the turn of the century, Indians were engaging with the writings of Mazzini and celebrating the unification of Italy and the political economy of Germany. In the early twentieth century, all legitimate arguments about collective political existence and expression had to be made in terms of the national principle; however, even before its moment of universal acknowledgement, in the aftermath of the Russian Revolution of 1917 and Wilson's Fourteen Points, its obsolete nature—or at least its obsolescence—was already being proclaimed.[44]

In revisiting a number of readings of 1857, at different points of this chronology of the national principle as legitimating category, this chapter traces the history of attempts to map the Revolt onto the nation. Sir Saiyid Ahmad Khan (1817–1898), retrospectively anointed author of a 'two-nation theory' and therefore a 'forefather' of Pakistani 'nationalism', provided a contemporary account of the events, prior to the claiming of the axiomatic legitimacy of the principle of national self-determination for 'India'. Vinayak Damodar Savarkar (1883–1966) was from the 1920s a central spokesman for a Hindu nationalism that is by now generally considered fascist or at least proto-fascist by historians; however, his foundational, and in its time very influential, text on 1857 fits into that framework with difficulty. Jawaharlal Nehru (1889–1964), founder of a 'Nehruvian' nationalism that envisaged a tolerant, secular society of collective belonging in India, wrote of 1857 with difficulty. Sir Saiyid is only retrospectively a nationalist of any kind: he makes no use of the terms 'nation' or 'national', preferring 'native', by which he means both Hindu and Muslim inhabitants of India; his crucial distinction is between Hindus and Muslims, who for him are not 'nations', probably because

---

[44] See Mayer, *Wilson vs Lenin*.

the systematic use of the term had not yet arisen. Savarkar's reading uses the national category as central; however, even as he invokes Mazzini and the joint national belonging of Hindus and Muslims in India, he requires the nation to maintain its sacred (Hindu and Muslim, and sometimes Sikh) character. Nehru's nationalism, on the other hand, as I have argued elsewhere, is not properly a nationalism, for if nationalism is that which seeks to delineate proper belonging by demarcating those who belong from those who do not, Nehruvian nationalism refuses to do this.[45] These three narratives illustrate the difficulties of trying to find a coherent or inclusive 'nationalism' in 1857, and, indeed, to point out the impossibility of any nationalism to find a version that is truly inclusive. For nationalism, by definition, is a sectarian form of delineating identity. Two commentaries or (re)framing texts complete the set of readings selected for this chapter: Maulana Azad's foreword to the centenary history[46] and Susobhan Sarkar's review of the histories of 1857 written in the centenary year.[47] We need to understand how identities formed via actually experienced solidarities are encouraged or disciplined to make the imaginative jump to 'nationalism' or, alternatively, how they fail to do so.

3.4. Sir Saiyid Ahmad Khan's 1857

Sir Saiyid's narrative, as he presents it to us in the pamphlet *The Causes of the Indian Revolt* is, for us, perhaps of interest because he was an eye-witness; he lived through the events of 1857. He saw the British revenge in Delhi. He himself sheltered some British refugees from the events. Nonetheless, he lost his uncle and cousin, an aunt died of thirst and his mother died soon after despite having been rescued. Still, he insisted on a loyalist position, arguing only that an Indian representative in the Legislative Council could have provided the government with enough indigenous information to prevent the events from having happened.[48]

---

[45] Benjamin Zachariah, *Nehru* (London: Routledge, 2004), Interlude, 139–168; Zachariah, *Playing the Nation Game*, Chapter 5.

[46] Azad, in Sen, *1857*.

[47] Sarkar, 'Views on 1857'.

[48] Sayyid Ahmad Khan, *The Causes of the Indian Revolt* (Benares: Medical Hall Press, 1873; originally published in Urdu, 1859; new edition Oxford: Oxford University Press, 2000), 12. References are to the 2000 edition.

He maintained a resolutely *Sharif* point of view; in his treatment, Indian converts to Islam are foreign to his concerns because they are not of the ruling elite who came from without. He insists on the pride of Muslims as a former ruling elite. He criticizes land revenue policy largely on the grounds that the old landed elite has suffered, though he knows in the abstract that peasants have also suffered. The pamphlet was published immediately after the Revolt. Five hundred copies were printed, addressed to the government. Most copies were sent to England; it was written in Urdu, and only translated into English and published in 1873.[49] The original context for Sir Saiyid's intervention, it should thus be noted, was (if we phrase this in terms of a language of retrospective academic debate) his attempt to claim for himself the status of privileged native informant to the government, rather than to participate in any form of wider public debate.[50]

Sir Saiyid was of course arguing against the British view that it was mainly Muslims who were involved in the revolt. Through him, he believed, Muslims had to prove their loyalty. Among other things, he insisted that it was the British that had created solidarity between Hindus and Muslims by putting them in the same regiments, thereby creating unity between 'two antagonistic races'.[51] Even by the standards of the time, this is embarrassingly loyalist, although loyalism is of course a position that must be maintained to remain within a legitimate political language in any communication with the official hierarchies of the colonial state, and loyalism is itself subject to ambiguous feelings. As a result, of course, ambiguities in attitudes to, or support for, the Revolt must be read against other forms of communication to different audiences. The pamphlet starts by suggesting that much of the need to place the matter of the causes of the Revolt on record is now obsolete, since the takeover by

[49] Francis Robinson, introduction to Khan, *Causes*, xiv.

[50] On the colonial information order and the relative importance of the native informant and his (lack of) agency, see Bayly, *Empire and Information* versus Nicholas Dirks, *Castes of Mind* (Princeton: Princeton University Press, 2001); see also Michael Dodson, *Orientalism, Empire, and National Culture: India, 1770–1880* (New York: Palgrave Macmillan, 2007). The subtlest writings on this theme remain those of Bernard Cohn; see the collections *Colonialism and Its Forms of Knowledge: The British in India* (Princeton: Princeton University Press, 1996); *An Anthropologist among the Historians* (Delhi: Oxford University Press, 1987); also Bernard Cohn, 'The Command of Language and the Language of Command', *Subaltern Studies* 4: 276–329.

[51] Robinson, introduction to Khan, *Causes*, xii.

the Crown and the crowning glory of Queen Victoria as the monarch of India has actually already led to deliverance.[52]

Sir Saiyid was no supporter of popular protest:

> It must be remembered that the men who in those times raised so loud the cry of 'jehad' were vagabonds and ill-conditioned men. They were wine drinkers and men who spent their time in debauchery and dissipation. They were men floating without profession or occupation on the surface of society. Can such fellows as these be called leaders of a religious war? It was very little that they thought about religion. Their only object was to plunder Government Treasuries and to steal Government property. To be faithless to one's salt is to dis-regard [sic] the first principles of our religion. To slaughter innocents, especially women, children and old men would be accounted abo-minable [sic][53]

According to Sir Saiyid, the alleged *fatwa* of Delhi that had proclaimed *jehad* on behalf of the emperor was a forgery. Many Delhi *maulvi*s regarded the emperor as a heretic and did not even offer prayers in the Jama Masjid because they refused to pray in mosques under the emperor's patronage.[54]

He argued that a representative voice of Indians in the Legislative Council was important. Even this was a very limited argument:

> To form a Parliament from the natives of India is of course out of the question. It is not only impossible, but useless. There is no reason however why the natives of this country should be excluded from the Legislative Council.[55]

He doesn't say why it is useless. But it is a conduit of information to government to have Indians in the Council. Without it, there was the tendency of Indians to mistrust government-made laws, too. However good the intention of the laws—and Sir Saiyid is very quick to concede these good intentions—the people would fail to be convinced of this:

---

[52] Khan, *Causes*, 1.
[53] Khan, *Causes*, 8.
[54] Khan, *Causes*, 9–10.
[55] Khan, *Causes*, 13.

At length the Hindustanees fell into the habit of thinking that all the laws were passed with a view to degrade and ruin them, and to deprive them and their fellows of their religion. Such acts as were repugnant to native customs and character, whether in themselves good or bad, increased this suspicion.[56]

Here at least, Sir Saiyid is in consonance with Savarkar, who puts it more strongly: the English had no right to interfere with the customs of the country. Savarkar said that it was not a question of whether the Company's laws were good or bad; neither Muslim nor Hindu knew where the 'attack on their religions customs would stop'.[57] The abolition of Suttee, the Company's prisoners prevented from observing their religions, the Widow Remarriage Act passed by Canning, followed by a law for the abolition of polygamy brought before the Legislative Council—all these were examples for Savarkar of English 'insolence born of unbridled power'.[58] Sir Saiyid, as a loyalist, put it more gently. Interference in matters of religion made everyone believe that the government 'intended to force the Christian religion and foreign customs upon Hindu and Mussulman alike'.[59]

Sir Saiyid complains of missionary proselytizing and says that it appeared to people that the government was sponsoring and supporting missionary activities. Such appearances were given credence by details such as the decision to raise orphans in the Christian faith after the 1837 drought in the North-West Province.[60] On missionary proselytizing, he was quite firm:

They took to printing and circulating controversial tracts, in the shape of questions and answers. Men of a different faith were spoken of in those tracts in a most offensive and irritating way. In Hindustan these things have always been managed very differently. Everyman in this country, preaches and explains his views in his own mosque, or his own house. If anyone wishes to listen to him, he can go to the mosque, or

---

[56] Khan, *Causes*, 14.
[57] Savarkar, *The Indian War of Independence*, 57–58.
[58] Savarkar, *The Indian War of Independence*, 57.
[59] Khan, *Causes*, 16.
[60] Khan, *Causes*, 17–18.

house, and hear what he has to say. But … In violent and unmeasured language they [the Missionaries] attacked the followers and the holy places of other creeds; annoying, and insulting beyond expression the feelings of those who listened to them.[61]

He complains about all forms of missionary activity including schools, from which he slips easily into talking about education policy in general. Unveiled girls in schools are mentioned—there is a perception that girls were deliberately being unveiled or encouraged to unveil themselves at schools, which is 'obnoxious … to the feelings of the Hindustanees'.[62] The large colleges in the cities are also the cause of suspicion. At first, these were unfounded, and Islamic learning, Arabic and Persian were not neglected, so religious leaders supported the learning of English among other things. Then Arabic and Persian learning began to be replaced by Urdu and English—Urdu is clearly regarded by Sir Saiyid as inferior despite the fact that he wrote his pamphlet in Urdu.[63] Sir Saiyid was also sensitive to Hindu feelings. In jails, there was one cook in some cases. This was against the feelings of caste Hindus. This was not actually against the Muhammedan creed, but still, he says, it was annoying to them as well.[64]

It might be observed that this was not so much a pamphlet on the causes of the Revolt as a compendium of thoughts on what might annoy elite Indians, Hindus as well as Muslims. The Revolt is the excuse for writing about them. Sir Saiyid was acute on questions of interference with practices of property inheritance for converts, regulations on Hindu widow remarriage, on dispossession of traditional landlords for non-payment of arrears, etc. One suspects that he knew as little about the deeper causes of 1857 as Queen Victoria or Disraeli. The crux of his argument about the difference between Hindus and Muslims would not be out of place in a colonial ethnography of India. The government, he claims, does not know its subjects. He, Sir Saiyid, does, and can teach the government to know them too. Among Indian grievances, he mentions the drying up

[61] Khan, *Causes*, 18.
[62] Khan, *Causes*, 20.
[63] Khan, *Causes*, 21.
[64] Khan, *Causes*, 21.

of jobs under the British, and he says this affected Muslims more than Hindus:

> It must be borne in mind that the Hindoos, the original inhabitants of the country, were never in former days in the habit of taking service, but on the contrary they were each engaged in such work as their forefathers had been engaged in before them. The Brahmins never took service, the Vaishyas were always traders and bankers, the Kshatriyas, once lords of the land, never took service, but each kept his own small portion of land, dividing it amongst his kinsmen and preserving a semblance of authority. They had no standing army, but as occasion required they all united either to resist or to invade as the case might be ... There was one caste certainly that did take service and these were the 'Kayasths'.[65]

And then:

> The Muhammadans are not the aborigines of this country. They came in the train of former conquerors and gradually domesticated themselves in India. They were therefore all dependent on service, and on account of this increased difficulty in obtaining the same, they, far more than the Hindoos, were put to much inconvenience and misery. An honourable military service, distinct from that eagerly engaged in by the lower classes of the community, was with difficulty procurable under the British Government.[66]

In many ways, this is the lament of the old Mughal elite, disempowered in relative terms after the failure of the Revolt, and somewhat like the Nehru family's history, which Nehru recalls in his autobiography.[67] This was the Mughal service elite defending its ethos. The emperor himself is, however, not integral to this; Sir Saiyid dismisses him as a senile old man who did not know what he was doing.

Sir Saiyid's English text never uses the words 'nation' or 'nations'. 'Natives' is the preferred term. This is an indication that in the immediate

---

[65] Khan, *Causes*, 34–35.
[66] Khan, *Causes*, 35.
[67] Nehru, *Autobiography*, 2, 8.

aftermath of the Revolt, the argument about 'nations' is not yet a central legitimating argument. And the language of 'nations' is not yet ready for use in this manner. In passages from the writings of Marx and Engels, contemporary observers of the events, 'race', 'nation', and 'religion' are used as broadly synonymous:

> The outrages committed by the revolted sepoys in India are indeed appalling, hideous, ineffable—such as one is prepared to meet only in wars of insurrection, of nationalities, of races, and above all of religion ... However infamous the conduct of the sepoys, it is only the reflex, in a concentrated form, of England's own conduct in India ...[68]

Sir Saiyid foregrounds an argument about injury to elite pride. A petty British official thinks of himself as higher than the highest native gentleman. In the view of such an official, there is no such thing as a native gentleman. This is reprehensible, and since most Indians see government through these officials, it seems that all government has the same attitude. Sir Saiyid leaves open the possibility that the real government, that is, the higher-up government, recognizes that there are such things as native gentlemen.[69] This is an argument buttressed by arguments about Muslims in particular. Muhammedans seek honour, not money. And they were once exalted. Sir Saiyid teaches the British the virtues of Mughal practice: regular durbars so that the ruled could get a glimpse of the ruler, who had to befit the title of the shadow of God on earth.[70] The argument follows that there is now, finally, a rejoicing that Queen Victoria recognizes the principle. The people rejoiced that she accepted this principle. It is tempting to imagine Disraeli reading this pamphlet; it is a good lesson in inventing traditions. Sir Saiyid also knows how to address his audience: his text is laced with Biblical quotations, to make it easier for an assumed Christian audience to receive.

On military matters, the English made the mistake of having joint regiments of Hindus and Muslims: 'constant intercourse had done its work

---

[68] Karl Marx, '"The Indian Revolt"', *New York Daily Tribune*, 16 September 1857 (written 4 September); reprinted in Karl Marx and Friedrich Engels, *On Colonialism* (Moscow: Progress Publishers, 1959, repr. 1974), 152–155; 152.

[69] Khan, *Causes*, 41–42.

[70] Khan, *Causes*, 45–46.

and the two races had almost become one' (this would be a quasi-national argument, were he to regard the outcome as desirable; he does not).

> It is but natural and to be expected, that a feeling of friendship and brotherhood must spring up between the men of a regiment, constantly brought together as they are. They consider themselves as one body and thus it was that the difference which exists between Hindoos and Muhammadans had, in these regiments, been almost entirely smoothed away.[71]

This was clearly a mistake: he echoes Aristotle's famous argument about keeping the body of slaves diverse so that they cannot make common cause, but in reverse: that keeping diverse sepoys together creates a common cause. Nadir Shah, after conquering Khorasan, made sure that he kept the Persian and Afghan sides of his army separate and of equal strength:[72]

> If separate regiments of Hindoos and separate regiments of Muhammadans had been raised, this feeling of brotherhood could not have arisen and, in my opinion, the Muhammadan regiments would not have refused to receive the new cartridges.[73]

In this, and in the section on the grievances of the army, Sir Saiyid is most speculative, and there is no indication of how he would have had more information than the British government who sought to make enquiries in this regard.

3.5. Vinayak Damodar Savarkar's 1857

The history of the text of Savarkar's book is itself interesting. It was written in exile in Europe, in about 1908 when Savarkar was around 24 years old. Research was done at the India Office Library. Written in Marathi, it was

---

[71] Khan, *Causes*, 50.
[72] Khan, *Causes*, 50.
[73] Khan, *Causes*, 51.

smuggled into India and then, when police attempted to seize the manuscript, smuggled out again. Translated by various volunteers a chapter at
a time, separately, with no attempt to standardize style, it circulated in a
clandestine manner, while the manuscript itself passed into the keeping
of Madame Bhikhaji Cama in Paris; it was stored in a bank vault that only
she knew of and vanished after her death in 1936. All we have, therefore,
is the strange English translation, which appeared in various illicit and
promptly banned versions, the first legal version appearing in India in
January 1947.[74] The original publishers of the illegal 1909 version even
apologized for the style, not to Indian readers, for whom style allegedly
was not the important point, but 'to those sympathetic foreign readers
who might be inclined to read this book'.[75]

For those inclined to see Savarkar entirely in the light of his later fascist
or proto-fascist period, this is also a most interesting text. It was written
in a period of undifferentiated 'terrorist' politics: Indians in Europe,
America, or Bengal had not yet clearly differentiated into left and right,
and this was epitomized by the diversity of the circles that grew up around
Shamji Krishnavarma and his journal, the *Indian Sociologist*, in Europe,
or around Lala Lajpat Rai in his American years.[76] To pin Savarkar down
in this period as already a fascist would therefore give him the credit of
being one of the founders of that ideology. This may well be the case, if
we are to take a less Eurocentric and success-centric view of fascism, but
then Savarkar would hardly have been alone in this period.

Savarkar's opening remarks set the stage:

The nation that has no consciousness of its past has no future. Equally
true it is that a nation must develop its capacity not only of claiming a
past but also of knowing how to use it for the furtherance of its future.[77]

---

[74] Savarkar, *The Indian War of Independence*; see therein G. M. Joshi, 'The Story of This
History', ix–xx, to be read with caution, as it contains some errors.

[75] Savarkar, *The Indian War of Independence*, xxii.

[76] For a sense of this milieu, see Agnes Smedley's novel *Daughter of Earth* (New York: Coward-
McCann, 1929; new edition London: Virago, 1977); see also Nirode K. Barooah, *Chatto: The Life
and Times of an Indian Anti-Imperialist in Europe* (Delhi: Oxford University Press, 2004), 1–61;
Harald Fischer-Tiné, '"Indian Nationalism and the World Forces": Transnational and Diasporic
Dimensions of the Indian Freedom Movement on the Eve of the First World War', *Journal of
Global History* 2, no. 3 (2007): 325–344; Benjamin Zachariah, 'A Long, Strange Trip: The Lives in
Exile of Har Dayal', *South Asian History and Culture* 4, no. 4 (2013): 574–592.

[77] Savarkar, *The Indian War of Independence*, introduction, xxiii.

The author makes no apology for the instrumental nature of the history:

> The nation ought to be the master and not the slave of its own history. For, it is absolutely unwise to try to do certain things now irrespective of special considerations, simply because they had been once acted in the past. The feeling of hatred against the Mahomedans was just and necessary in the times of Shivaji—but, such a feeling would be unjust and foolish if nursed now, simply because it was the dominant feeling of the Hindus then.[78]

So the Savarkar problem is related to what to do about Muslims while using the rhetoric of the sacred and holy war by Hindus to purify themselves and their nation. For the purposes of this text, some Muslims at least can and must be admitted to the nation.

His narrative is that of the careful and well-planned uprising, scheduled for 31 May, being upset by the overeager Sepoys starting things up too early due to an understandably virile, manly patriotism that caused them to act prematurely:

> Mangal Pandey was a Brahmin by birth. He took up the duties of a Kshatriya and was a valiant young soldier. Into the heart of this young and brilliant Brahmin who loved religion more than his life, and who was pure in his private life and undaunted in battle, the idea of the freedom of his country had entered and electrified his blood. How could his sword be patient? The swords of martyrs never are.[79]

The association of virility and premature activity may be an unfortunate one; it is something that Savarkar seems keen on. The destiny of the high caste is also very important in this narrative. Rhetorically, the overuse of the phrase '*Maro feringheeko*' marks this text. Allegedly this was what crowds shouted at various stages of the Revolt.

The contention that the Revolt was to avenge the defeat at the Battle of Plassey is also central to Savarkar's narrative. He takes very seriously the rumour which was reportedly circulating, that British rule would last 100 years from the battle of Plassey, 23 June, 1757, and treats it as the

---

[78] Savarkar, *The Indian War of Independence*, introduction, xxiii.
[79] Savarkar, *The Indian War of Independence*, 104.

basis of the plot—which, however, was scheduled not for 23 June but for 31 May. But Savarkar has the prophets of modern nationalism to invoke. Mazzini appears as a legitimating character in the script: 'Mazzini, in a critical article on Carlyle's *French Revolution*, has said that every revolution must have had a fundamental principle. Revolution is a complete rearrangement in the life of historic man. A revolutionary movement cannot be based on a flimsy and momentary grievance. It is always due to some all-moving principle … As in private life, so also in history, the deeds of an individual or a nation are judged by the character of the motive'.[80] The sacred motives of 1857, allegedly, and thus the motifs of Savarkar's script, are the principles of Swadharma and Swaraj. Trivialities like greased cartridges were, he says, far too petty motives for figures like Nana Sahib, the Emperor of Delhi, the Queen of Jhansi, or Khan Bahadur Khan of Rohillkhand.[81] Indeed, these figures are the heroes of the plot, which lays him open to the charge of glorifying feudal heroes. He also has a rather patronizing view of the masses, and in many cases, the ordinary sepoy appears as brave and patriotic, but somewhat stupid, leaving the heroic roles to be played by those clearly of noble blood.

Reflections on causality require him to distinguish between 'real causes and motives' and 'temporary and accidental causes'.[82] 'The kidnapping of Sita was only the incidental cause of the fight between Rama and Ravana. The real causes were deeper and more inward'[83]; 'The seed of the Revolution of 1857 is in this holy inspiring idea, clear and explicit, propounded from the throne of Delhi, THE PROTECTION OF RELIGION AND COUNTRY'.[84] Savarkar, soon after, remarks: 'At least, orientals have never had the idea that Swadharma and Swaraj have no connection with each other. The Eastern mind has maintained a full and traditional belief, as is also said by Mazzini, that there is no vast barrier between Heaven and earth, but that the two are ends of one and the same thing'.[85]

Much of the point of the narrative is in its rhetoric, so I shall not attempt to paraphrase too much:

---

[80] Savarkar, *The Indian War of Independence*, 3.
[81] Savarkar, *The Indian War of Independence*, 5.
[82] Savarkar, *The Indian War of Independence*, 6–7.
[83] Savarkar, *The Indian War of Independence*, 7.
[84] Savarkar, *The Indian War of Independence*, 8.
[85] Savarkar, *The Indian War of Independence*, 10.

The war fought for Swadharma and Swaraj does not lose its lustre by defeat. The splendour of Guru Govind Singh's life is none the less, because his efforts did not immediately succeed at the time. Nor do we think the less of the rising of 1848 in Italy, because the Revolution failed completely at that time.

These are two bright pearls in the necklace of Mother India. Now, when dark night has overspread the horizon of the whole country, these two alone are shining as luminous stars. They are fiery *Akalis* ready to avenge their country's unjust wrongs with the last drop of their blood. They are two martyrs sacrificing their lives for Country, Religion and Freedom. They are two witnesses, sword in hand, to prove that the blood of Hindusthan that gave birth to Shivaji is not yet dead.[86]

And so on, speaking of Nana Sahib and Lakshmi Bai; of Azimullah Khan, of humble origin but his talent recognized by Nana Sahib; and of Azimullah's visit to Britain on behalf of Nana Sahib to advocate the latter's recognition despite his being adopted. Allegedly at the same time, Rango Bapuji, the Brahmin from Satara, was also in London; in Savarkar's account, he and Azimullah plotted the Revolt together in London.[87] And Azimullah's 'spirited mien and Oriental magnificence' caused many 'English women of respectable families' to become 'infatuated' with him.[88] Nana Sahib is his central figure, in his Marathaness: 'What did the portrait of Chhatrapati Shivaji say to him?'[89] His noble birth is referred to (although given that he was an adopted son, this presents a slight problem).[90]

It is Nana Sahib who has the foresight to see Muslims as assimilable to 'Hindusthan':

He [Nana Sahib], also, felt that the meaning of 'Hindusthan' was thereafter the united nation of the adherents of Islam as well as Hinduism. As long as the Mahomedans lived in India in the capacity of the alien rulers, so long, to be willing to live with them like brothers was to acknowledge

---

[86] Savarkar, *The Indian War of Independence*, 25.
[87] Savarkar, *The Indian War of Independence*, 33–34.
[88] Savarkar, *The Indian War of Independence*, 33.
[89] Savarkar, *The Indian War of Independence*, 35.
[90] Savarkar, *The Indian War of Independence*, 35.

national weakness. Hence, it was, up to then, necessary for the Hindus to consider the Mahomedans as foreigners. And moreover this ruler-ship of the Mahomedans, Guru Govind in the Panjab, Rana Pratap in Rajputana, Chhatrasal in Bundelkhand, and the Maharattas by even sitting upon the throne at Delhi, had destroyed; and, after a struggle of centuries, Hindu sovereignty had defeated the rulership of the Mahomedans and had come to its own all over India. It was no national shame to join hands with Mahomedans then, but it would, on the con-trary, be an act of generosity. So, now, the original antagonism between the Hindus and the Mahomedans might be consigned to the Past. Their present relation was one not of rulers and ruled, foreigner and native, but simply that of brothers with the one difference between them of reli-gion alone. For, they were both children of the soil of Hindusthan … all children of the same Mother.[91]

In Savarkar's stereotypical synecdochic histories, heroic figures personify virtue in historical shorthand:

And when the English had begun to take up the role of an Aurangzeb, there was no remedy other than that India must produce a Shivaji or a Guru Govind.[92]

The Marathas lived up to Shivaji in their participation in the Revolt; the Sikhs betrayed Guru Govind in their non-participation—that is another theme running through the book. Clearly, in his reading, 1857 was a war of religion, which is in India not separate from a war of national inde-pendence. He makes much of British insults to Indian religions: 'The Koran and the Vedas were openly defiled and images were desecrated!'[93]

Chapati rumours, lotus rumours, and other rumours were for Savarkar evidence of organization. Azimullah and Nana Sahib set off together to tour the country in March 1857, allegedly, so they said, on a pilgrimage. Which, says Savarkar, was obviously a pretext for the furthering of the plot: 'Indeed! A Brahmin and a Moslem are starting together, arm in arm,

---

[91] Savarkar, *The Indian War of Independence*, 75–76.
[92] Savarkar, *The Indian War of Independence*, 58.
[93] Savarkar, *The Indian War of Independence*, 60.

to visit the holy, religious places,—an event without a precedent!'[94] The Chapatis were the Angel of Revolution:

> Speed on, Angel of Revolution, speed on! Go thou forth to preach the Gospel to all the dear children of India, that the country is ready for a holy war to make everyone [sic] of them free ... Invite the spears of the Mahrattas, the swords of the Rajputs, the *Kirpan* of the Sikhs, the Crescent of the Islamites.[95]

The inflammatory nature of this book is in its keeping alive the memories of British atrocities in the Mutiny and thus justifying the violence of the rebels. Savarkar's resort to comparative history is not to be faulted. The argument is simple: some rebel leaders wished to have mercy on the whites at their disposal. But ordinary people were not willing to see this; if you do not kill a snake, it will strike you later. And this is what happened in the instances where the rebels spared the lives of English people. His account of the Kanpur massacre only barely manages to deplore the excesses of the sepoys; the tone is celebratory, for even though he says that Nana Sahib did not condone the massacre, he sees it as inadequate revenge for General Neill's sacking of Delhi: 'The whole Ganges became red'.[96] Violence is necessary to combat injustice; so in English history Charles I's beheading 'is a just deed',[97] but 'Hindustan' did not go to the extent of Cromwell's Irish massacres.[98] And so on.

The historical accuracy of the text is of course seriously flawed. Savarkar takes the conspiracy theories of British officials and writers and turns them into evidence for concerted national action; thus, this might be considered an early version of Ranajit Guha's method of reading against the grain, as advocated in 'the prose of counter-insurgency'.[99] Accuracy is not the issue here: how can the events be translated into a rallying cry for the 'nation'? There is a passage on ignorant Punjabi sepoys

[94] Savarkar, *The Indian War of Independence*, 95.
[95] Savarkar, *The Indian War of Independence*, 97–98.
[96] Savarkar, *The Indian War of Independence*, 235.
[97] Savarkar, *The Indian War of Independence*, 274.
[98] Savarkar, *The Indian War of Independence*, 277.
[99] Ranajit Guha, 'The Prose of Counter-Insurgency', in *Subaltern Studies II* (Delhi: Oxford University Press, 1984), ed. Ranajit Guha, 1–42.

not quite recognizing the nature of British rule, and therefore not joining the rebellion.[100]

Two uncomfortable questions are dealt with by Savarkar quite frankly. The first, on nationhood: admittedly, 1857 showed that India was not yet a united nation. But this is a lack that others have managed to overcome. The 'great and compact nations of the world' had all passed through their periods of disunity, such as Italy, Germany, or England under the Romans and the Saxons: 'But who can deny that the above countries have now united their several peoples into strong and powerful nations today, because they had been melted in the furnace of internal strife and the fire of foreign despotism?'[101] Second, the 'restoration' of the Mughal emperor at Delhi was not a restoration. The Mughal dynasty was an invading one. The appeal to the emperor was fundamentally new. The people had declared that 'the longstanding war between the Hindu and the Mahomedan had ended, that tyranny had ceased, and that the people of the soil were once more free to choose their own monarch'. Otherwise, 'the blood of hundreds of Hindu martyrs' who had fought the Muslim invaders would have been shed in vain.[102]

3.6. Jawaharlal Nehru's 1857

Nehru's 1857, unlike those of Sir Saiyid and Savarkar, is more ambiguous. He is clear that Indian history in contemporary times has been written from British sources and perspectives:

> The very circumstances of defeat and disruption prevented the Indian side of the story from being properly recorded, and many of the records that existed suffered destruction during the great Revolt of 1857. They remained dispersed, little known, and many perished in the manuscript stage from the incursion of termites and other insects which abound in the country.[103]

---

[100] Savarkar, *The Indian War of Independence*, 144.
[101] Savarkar, *The Indian War of Independence*, 144.
[102] Savarkar, *The Indian War of Independence*, 284–285.
[103] Nehru, *The Discovery of India*, 290.

Also foreshadowing Guha's 'the prose of counter-insurgency', Nehru wrote that 'the villain of the British in India is often a hero to Indians, and those whom the British have delighted to honour and reward are often traitors and quislings in the eyes of the great majority of the Indian People. That taint clings to their descendants'.[104] Nevertheless, Nehru's account is not clear whether it ought to rescue 1857 from the figurative termites of history; he is clear it is an important set of events, but is not sure, especially in a text that he wrote with the intention of narrating a serviceable national history for India, that 1857 belongs in the tradition. Nehru does, nonetheless, narrate a version of 1857, including its causes, course, and consequences. He was clear that the Revolt was not a national one, with his residual Marxism still in operation in the 1940s. Feudalism, princes, and loyalty are the motifs of his account, summed up in his dismissive summary that 'The Revolt of 1857–58 was essentially a feudal rising, though there were some nationalist elements in it',[105] as well as his comment elsewhere that:

Except for some minor defections the Indian princes not only remained aloof from the rising, but, in some instances, actually helped the British to crush it. This brought about a change in British policy towards them, and it was decided to keep them and even to strengthen them.[106]

The policy of direct annexation by the British was abandoned after the Revolt in favour of the earlier subsidiary alliance system. This was the essence of paramountcy:

Some of the princes are good, some are bad; even the good ones are thwarted and checked at every turn. As a class they are of necessity backward, feudal in outlook, and authoritarian in methods, except in their dealings with the British Government, when they show a becoming subservience.[107]

---

[104] Nehru, *The Discovery of India*, 290.
[105] Nehru, *The Discovery of India*, 327.
[106] Nehru, *The Discovery of India*, 312.
[107] Nehru, *The Discovery of India*, 312.

His narrative of the events themselves is swift and crisp. By 1857, much of India had come to terms with British rule, though not so in 'the upper provinces' where 'the spirit of revolt was growing, especially among the feudal chiefs and their followers'.[108] The masses were discontented and 'intensely anti-British'—for Nehru, this is not to be applauded, even when understandable, because he believed that racialism ought not to be a feature of anti-colonial struggle. In referring to the Quit India movement of 1942, he claimed (though not with great accuracy), that there was no such racial feeling. The masses suffered because officials were rapacious and ignorant; meanwhile, the upper classes were resentful of 'the insulting and overbearing manners of the foreigners'.[109]

The Revolt itself is brusquely characterized:

> Essentially it was a feudal outburst, headed by feudal chiefs and their followers and aided by the widespread anti-foreign sentiment. Inevitably it looked up to the relic of the Mughal dynasty, still sitting in the Delhi palace, but feeble and old and powerless.[110]

Is this in contradiction to what he says earlier in the same paragraph?

> In May, 1857, the Indian army at Meerut mutinied. The revolt had been secretly and well organised but a premature outburst rather upset the plans of the leaders. It was much more than a military mutiny and it spread rapidly and assumed the character of a popular rebellion and a war of Indian independence.[111]

It is a line that Maulana Azad, writing 11 years later, explicitly rejects: that it was organized and coordinated and went wrong. But Nehru is close in these passages to the Savarkar line on this (and indeed, it is clear that he draws upon Savarkar and cites his account in his own: views of 1857 are British ones, he maintains; Indian views are seldom printed. He mentions Savarkar's book, which is still banned over 30 years after it was written).[112]

---

[108] Nehru, *The Discovery of India*, 322.
[109] Nehru, *The Discovery of India*, 487.
[110] Nehru, *The Discovery of India*, 323.
[111] Nehru, *The Discovery of India*, 323.
[112] Nehru, *The Discovery of India*, 325.

Nehru has to be positive about signs of popular participation, though he recognized its limitations: 'As such a popular rebellion of the masses it was confined to Delhi, the United Provinces (as they are now called), and parts of central India and Bihar'.[113] 'Both Hindus and Moslems took full part in the Revolt'.[114] That is, both Hindus and Muslims were then feudal: 'The feudal chiefs had the sympathy of the masses over large areas, but they were incapable, unorganised, and with no constructive ideal or community of interest. They had already played their role in history and there was no place for them in the future'.[115] These chiefs had their final moment on a historical stage by craning their necks out of the dustbin of history, as it were, one more time. And many hedged their bets, waiting to see which side was winning, or helped the British and 'played the part of quislings': 'There was hardly any national and unifying sentiment among the leaders and a mere anti-foreign feeling, coupled with a desire to maintain their feudal privileges, was a poor substitute for this'.[116] Mere anti-foreign feeling; feudal privileges; inadequately national. Even the popular revolt was regional and limited:

> It is certainly to the credit of the British that they could win over the Sikhs ... whether it is to the credit or discredit of the Sikhs of those days depends on one's point of view. It is clear, however, that there was a lack of nationalist feeling which might have bound the people of India together. Nationalism of the modern type was yet to come ... Not by fighting for a lost cause, the feudal order, would freedom come.[117]

Still, it 'threw up some fine guerrilla leaders' like Tantia Topi and Lakshmi Bai.[118]

This is uncomfortable material for a nationalist movement; Nehru proceeds to talk about less problematic themes: British brutality, massacres, and revenge that shows itself from time to time in events like Jallianwalla Bagh: 'The rebel Indians sometimes indulged in cruel and barbarous

[113] Nehru, *The Discovery of India*, 323.
[114] Nehru, *The Discovery of India*, 323.
[115] Nehru, *The Discovery of India*, 323–324.
[116] Nehru, *The Discovery of India*, 324.
[117] Nehru, *The Discovery of India*, 324.
[118] Nehru, *The Discovery of India*, 324.

behaviour; they were unorganised, suppressed and often angered by reports of British excesses'. But British atrocities were worse: 'Some frank and honourable English historians have occasionally lifted the veil and allowed us a glimpse of the race mania and lynching mentality which prevailed on an enormous scale' (he mentions Kaye and Malleson, and Garrett [and Thompson's] *Rise and Fulfilment of British Rule In India*)— these accounts 'make one sick with horror'. He compares these brutalities with Nazism, remarking that 'One would like to forget all this, for it is a ghastly and horrible picture showing man at his worst, even according to the new standards of barbarity set up by Nazism and modern war'[119]:

> Biologists tell us that racialism is a myth and there is no such thing as a master race. But we in India have known racialism in all its forms ever since the commencement of British rule. The whole ideology of this rule was that of the herrenvolk [sic] and the master race, and the structure of government was based upon it; indeed the idea of a master race is inherent in imperialism. There was no subterfuge about it; it was proclaimed in unambiguous language by those in authority ... India as a nation and Indians as individuals were subjected to insult, humiliation and contemptuous treatment ... As an Indian, I am ashamed to write all this, for the memory of it hurts, and what hurts still more is the fact that we submitted for so long to this degradation. I would have preferred any kind of resistance to this, whatever the consequences, rather than that our people should endure this treatment. And yet it is better that both Indians and Englishmen should know it, for that is the psychological background of England's connection with India, and psychology counts and racial memories are long.[120]

1857 appears in Nehru's writing as comparator, with 'the most important ... since 1857' a recurrent phrase, notably of course in his description of 1942, the Quit India Movement: 'And so, for the first time since the great revolt of 1857, vast numbers of people again rose to challenge by force (but a force without arms!) the fabric of British rule in India. It was a foolish and inopportune challenge, for all the organised and armed force

[119] Nehru, *The Discovery of India*, 324–325.
[120] Nehru, *The Discovery of India*, 326.

was on the other side, and in greater measure indeed than at any previous time in history'.[121] His views on violence and non-violence are incidentally contained here: force is stupid if it is not likely to be effective—an instrumental and un-Gandhian view on the subject.

Nehru's account of 1857 in the *Discovery of India* is rather blurred until he can talk about the British brutality in its suppression. Otherwise, it is an uprising of feudal elements: 'The Revolt of 1857 was a joint affair, but in its suppression Moslems felt strongly, and to some extent rightly, that they were the greater sufferers. This Revolt also put an end finally to any dreams or fantasies of the revival of the Delhi empire. That empire had vanished long ago, even before the British arrived on the scene ...' So the point is that the Revolt 'tried to take advantage' of 'a symbol of a famous dynasty'.[122] The 'smashing of the symbol' after 1857 left a 'vacuum which sought for something to fill it'. He narrates how Sir Syed Ahmad Khan tried to fill this vacuum through Western education for Muslims and with the Mohammedan Anglo-Oriental College.

The ambiguity of Nehru's 1857 is more evident if one looks at other writings. In his autobiography, 1857 appears as the context of the fall from power and grace of two central families in the early part of the book: that of the Nehru family itself, who lost everything during the Revolt and had to build itself up from scratch, having sided with the mutineers and hence having had to flee Delhi, and that of the family retainer, Mubarak Ali, who was something of an early mentor for the young Jawaharlal, regaling him with the tales of and something of the feel for the events of 1857.[123] Something of the romance of the events seems to have stayed with Nehru, whose flair for the right phrase in the right place made his narrative of event-history surreptitiously attractive even to himself.

As a rationalist and a scientific socialist, Nehru was nevertheless to refrain from glorifying these backward elements who participated in the Revolt. In an address to an audience in independent India, on the occasion of the 100th anniversary, Nehru provided a quick history lesson for the people of the 'nation'.[124] He nonetheless began his speech by

[121] Nehru, *The Discovery of India*, 487–488.

[122] Nehru, *The Discovery of India*, 342.

[123] Nehru, *Autobiography*, 8.

[124] Jawaharlal Nehru, address at a public meeting, Ramlila Grounds, New Delhi, May 10, 1957, translation from All-India Radio tapes, in *Nehru and Azad on 1857* (New Delhi: National Book Trust, 2007), 1–23.

underplaying the date: it was May 10, coincidentally the 100th anniversary of the outbreak of the Revolt in Meerut, but also the day of the inauguration of the second Lok Sabha. Hundred years later, the anniversary 'adds significance' to the beginnings of the new Lok Sabha, but the date was not chosen 'deliberately'; it was a 'coincidence'.[125] Nehru explained that there was now a chance to provide a historical verdict on the events, 'objectively and without heat',[126] although it was understandable that Indians reacted emotionally to the events, which were still remembered by the people. That it was 'an Indian struggle for independence' and 'an expression of resentment against the yoke of foreign rule' he acknowledged, but noted immediately, '[w]hat might have followed if the movement succeeded is a different matter'.[127]

He placed this in the context of a quick reading of British rule: India had absorbed succeeding foreign invaders into itself without treating them as aliens; British rule was alien because the British chose to remain alien.[128] The British ruled India because of its superiority in terms of science and technology; Indians were divided into 'small compartments', in particular by caste.[129] After 1857, the unity of Hindus and Muslims was disrupted by the British (and Nehru leaves the question open as to whether he means 'again' or not, as he also does not weigh the 'small compartments' of caste against the different compartments of religion); 1857 was a historical moment lost at least in part because of the perfidy of Indians themselves (as in the case of 1757 and the defeat of the Nawab of Bengal by Clive).[130] He moved swiftly on from these backward glances to talk of the future: India, though 'one entity on the map', could only 'become a nation when there is full emotional integration'. Freedom was won with only 'a thin veneer of nationalism', beneath which was 'a strange hollowness and weakness'.[131] The language riots that had recently occurred were another indication of this weakness which would be overcome by not disrupting the Five-Year Plans, leading to industrialization and economic independence. The rest of the speech confirms the official narrative of Indian nation-building,

[125] Nehru, *Nehru and Azad on 1857*, 1–2.
[126] Nehru, *Nehru and Azad on 1857*, 3.
[127] Nehru, *Nehru and Azad on 1857*, 8–9.
[128] Nehru, *Nehru and Azad on 1857*, 4–7.
[129] Nehru, *Nehru and Azad on 1857*, 8.
[130] Nehru, *Nehru and Azad on 1857*, 9–12.
[131] Nehru, *Nehru and Azad on 1857*, 16.

the record of the Congress as party of independence and of the nation, of Gandhi as founding father and an uncomplicated account of official policy on non-alignment and non-violence, coupled nonetheless with an affirmation of the quality and strength of the armed forces and an admission that nuclear weapons made such armed forces redundant; but '[u]ltimately, if necessary, we will fight with sticks'.[132]

3.7. Anniversaries Again: Maulana Abul Kalam Azad's Version in 1957

Maulana Azad, commissioning the work of an officially sponsored history of 1857, two years before the anniversary, showed a keen scholarly interest in the details of the narrative, ruling out certain explanations as implausible, in particular, the argument that the events of 1857 had been planned.[133] He stressed that Dr. S. N. Sen's account would be 'a true history of the struggle of 1857', and not any 'partisan' account, despite the immense difficulties of such impartiality in the light of the passions raised.[134] Azad himself, however, sets up a teleology of nationalism when he asks the 'causes' question in terms of why it took 'Indians' almost 100 years (with 1757 as the baseline date) to revolt. His answer was 'slow penetration':[135] it took time for Indians to realize what was happening. The 'affair of the greased cartridge' then 'supplied the occasion when the underground discontent came into the open'.[136]

Writing his Preface to the officially commissioned history, Azad returns to these themes, and leaves little doubt that he is explicitly taking on Savarkar's view, but without mentioning him by name, with a whole section devoted to him: 'Some Indians ... have written ... not history but mere political propaganda. These authors wanted to represent the uprising as a planned war of independence organised by the nobility of India against the British Government'. But there was 'no evidence that the

---

[132] Nehru, *Nehru and Azad on 1857*, 20.

[133] Maulana Azad, from *Proceedings of the 31st Session of the Indian Historical Records Commission, Vol. XXXI*, reprinted in *Nehru and Azad on 1857*, 24–36.

[134] Azad, *Nehru and Azad on 1857*, 26–27.

[135] Azad, *Nehru and Azad on 1857*, 32.

[136] Azad, *Nehru and Azad on 1857*, 36.

uprising had been pre-planned', with the chapati rumour and the lotus rumour stories examined by the Government of India in colonial times and the planning theory discredited long ago: 'This has been my belief for a long time'. And newer research has not made him change his view.[137]

There then appears this problem: 'the revolt of the Indian people was delayed for almost a hundred years' after Plassey. Why was this? Azad's answer was that the people didn't understand what was happening: British rule was unprecedented, they came as traders and insidiously took over as rulers. To some extent, then, the delay of 100 years is understandable. But even after the first 100 years, the response was inadequate. Azad stressed the 'backwardness' of the rebels, although he conceded that some at least were 'moved by patriotic considerations'.[138] Then he made the necessary connections between national culture and 1857. In 1857, he wrote, 'Indian national culture had sunk very low. The leaders of the revolt could never agree. They were mutually jealous and continually intrigued against one another'.[139] The implications for the present were clear: a good national culture accepts the collective identity of the nation and maintains solidarity with it. The naturalness of that nation cannot be questioned, far less the definition of nations and nationalism.

3.8. Conclusions: The Marxist 1857?

'All discussion about the Revolt of 1857 must turn to the question of its characterisation' wrote the historian Susobhan Chandra Sarkar in 1957. This, he believed, involved three problems: 'Was there a popular revolt in 1857–58? Can the movement be regarded as a national struggle? Should the social content of the upheaval be labelled as a feudal reaction?'[140] His own answers are interesting: on the balance of evidence, he answers 'yes' to the first question.[141] The second is more ambiguous: it 'depends on what we understand by the term "national"'.[142] He believed that

---

[137] Azad in Sen, *1857*, viii.
[138] Azad in Sen, *1857*, xiv.
[139] Azad in Sen, *1857*, xv.
[140] Sarkar, 'Views on 1857', 117.
[141] Sarkar, 'Views on 1857', 118–119.
[142] Sarkar, 'Views on 1857', 119.

[t]he ideal of an unified all-India nation state or a democratic republic in India was certainly premature for most people in the 19th century, but that does not justify us in denying a national character to far-flung popular struggles for liberation from alien rule.[143]

Among his examples of nationalism were Joan of Arc driving out 'English intruders', Spanish guerrillas or Russian peasants fighting Napoleon, and the Italian Carbonari. He acknowledged the 'crude nature of the nationalism in the air in 1857', but found no reason to deny the 'national elements in the widespread upheaval'.[144] Susobhan*babu* finds it difficult to deny the 'strivings towards some kind of national outlook'[145] despite the lack of 'bourgeois democratic consciousness, the "conception of individual liberty"'.[146] Here is a predecessor to Dipesh Chakrabarty's argument about Indian history being written up as the history of a lack of something: as Dipesh criticized *inter alia* Susobhan Sarkar's son Sumit Sarkar for this,[147] Susobhan Sarkar criticized the conservative historian and Hindu Mahasabha supporter Romesh Chandra Majumdar for denying that India had a 'nationalism in the true sense' in 1857. But Susobhan Sarkar was interested in pointing out the lack of nationalism. He is, of course, if we maintain a distinction between anti-colonialism and nationalism, conflating the two, as is evident in his phrase 'a national struggle against foreign rule'.[148]

And finally, in answer to the third question, on the 'feudal character' of 1857:

Where feudal ideas are still very powerful, as in 1857, a general movement would be necessarily feudal to that extent. But in the usual characterisation of the 'mutiny', 'feudal' is quietly equated with 'reactionary'. The equation, however, is blandly forgotten when our scholars praise the traditional culture of the country also shaped by feudal times.[149]

---

[143] Sarkar, 'Views on 1857', 119.
[144] Sarkar, 'Views on 1857', 119–120.
[145] Sarkar, 'Views on 1857', 121.
[146] Sarkar, 'Views on 1857', 119.
[147] Dipesh Chakrabarty, 'Postcolonialism and the Artifice of History: Who Speaks for "Indian" Pasts?', *Representations* no. 37, Special Issue: Imperial Fantasies and Postcolonial Histories (Winter 1992): 1–26.
[148] Sarkar, 'Views on 1857', 119.
[149] Sarkar, 'Views on 1857', 121.

The great Marxist historian thus concluded that 1857 was indeed feudal, but not necessarily for that reason reactionary, because it was a war of liberation from foreign rule.[150] Marxist entanglement with nationalism in a stageist argument is a subject that requires further discussion; for now, it remains an open question as to why such entanglements, which are acknowledged as non-Marxist, remain so difficult to escape.

The problem here, as in the other attempts to instrumentalize the memory of 1857 as history in a national key described in this chapter, is one of translation into a new language of legitimacy. For characterizations of 1857 to work as national narratives, secular, Hindu, syncretic, or Marxist, the work done in 1857 by a contemporary language of legitimacy that appealed to religion, custom, and feudal deference had to be overwritten by a new language of the 'national' that provided a useable 'India' for the purposes of a struggle for independence, and thereafter as part of the national memory of the independent Indian state. The necessary resort to anachronism that this entailed made the translation an incomplete venture; because of the necessity of anachronism in the service of the 'national' cause, these translations would yield not 'history', in the (then?-) commonly understood sense of 'accurate tellings of the past', but parables for the present. Perhaps, then, 1857 could only provide local martyrs, memories of battles and deaths, histories of lost kingdoms and fiefdoms, that are less-than-national *lieux de memoire*.

---

[150] Sarkar, 'Views on 1857', 122.

4

Histories of Empire, Imperial Legitimation, and the Wartime Career of Penderel Moon

4.1. Introduction

By now, it is obvious that the service of history can always be called upon to provide legitimation for a wide variety of immediate political projects; history can also provide psychological solace to those suffering from a sense of being socially and morally out of joint with their political role. The historian's voice, we have been told often enough, must be listened to carefully for signs of where it is coming from. If the historian Ranajit Guha, following the Bengali litterateur Bankimchandra Chattopadhyay, accepted the importance of the project of 'we must write our own history' as an act of reclaiming control of 'our' pasts, and thereby 'our' futures,[1] the same could be said of other groups whose *esprit de corps* was to be historically justified. But the 'we' in question in each case was inflected with divergent and non-intersubjective ideas about the accuracy—in old-fashioned and pre-postmodern terms—of those historical narratives. What, then, if history was self-consciously intended as propaganda, and propaganda was written as history? This chapter is a study of such a set of circumstances, in which the instrumentalization of history was not subtle or hidden in the least.

If this chapter deals chiefly with the views of one British Civilian in India on the subject of imperialism towards the end of empire, it has nevertheless a wider significance than that of the trajectories of one individual's thought. The period of the Second World War was a crucial

[1] Ranajit Guha, *An Indian Historiography of India: A Nineteenth-Century Agenda and Its Implications* (Calcutta: K.P. Bagchi, 1988).

period in the catalysis of many of the ideas I discuss here: the war brought home to all concerned that the British departure from India, for long a part of the official rhetoric of Empire (though temporally placed in a near future that receded just out of reach as one approached it), was a matter of a quick few years. As this became evident, constructing a retrospective view of the achievements and significance of Empire became for many a way of coming to terms with it.

The critique of Empire which emerged from these discussions among British Indian civil servants and officials is significant in that it is a critique from within. These were no socialists, communists, or Hobsonian liberals: they had a strong sense of the role imperialism was supposed to play. Yet their critique also indicates that those committed to the idea were getting disillusioned, to the extent that the will to govern an empire through the level of coercion that such governance now called for was beginning to wane. The search for a retrospective view that ultimately justified and validated the British Indian experience was also a search for a way to close that experience honourably.

There has been a good deal of writing on British civil servants and the Empire in India. This has been seen to have a bearing on the way India was governed; the Indian Civil Service (ICS) was arguably the world's most powerful bureaucracy, and the Civilian wielded great power. As a vital cog in the wheel of Empire, his activities and the attitudes he brought to bear on them have been with good reason regarded as important in understanding the working of that Empire. There is, however, far less of this literature dealing with the late imperial period, and the years approaching the end of empire. This appears to stem from an understanding that the Civilian's absolute powers were in relative decline in twentieth-century India.[2] A sense of their own declining importance was shared by

---

[2] See H. M. L. Alexander, 'Discarding the "Steel Frame": Changing Images among India Civil Servants in the Early Twentieth Century', *South Asia*, new series, 2 (1982): 1–12; T. Beaglehole, 'From Rulers to Servants: The Indian Civil Service and the British Demission of Power in India', *Modern Asian Studies* [hereafter *MAS*] 11, no. 2 (1977): 237–255; H. A. Ewing, 'The Indian Civil Service, 1919–1942', unpublished PhD dissertation, University of Cambridge, 1980; H. A. Ewing, 'The Indian Civil Service 1919–1924: Service Discontent and the Response in London and in Delhi', *MAS* 18, no. 1 (1984): 33–53. An exception to this is David C. Potter, *India's Political Administrators 1919–1983* (New York: Oxford University Press, 1986). Potter is less interested in the ideas held by white Civilians at the end of the Empire than in the continuities between the ICS (in both its British and Indian constituent elements) and its successor organization, the Indian Administrative Service (IAS).

British Civilians at the time. This loss of importance, in the contemporary communications of white Civilians in India, was partly attributed to the increasing 'Indianization' of the services, which allegedly destroyed the high standards of work of the Service, and partly to the introduction of Indian ministerial government (albeit in miniaturized and caricatured forms) which interfered with the impartiality of the Civilian's governance. Certainly, the general complaint of British Civilians from about the 1920s onwards was that Indianization of the Services and ministerial government in the Provinces together had conspired to deprive them of their rightful powers and to bring about inefficient and corrupt government;[3] both could be connected to a perception of the passing of power from white to Indian hands. Things were clearly not the same for a British Civilian in India; a young Civilian fresh out of Oxford or Cambridge might just feel that he had come to India a little too late.

Even in reduced circumstances, though, and sometimes under Indian ministers or Indian fellow Civilians, the ICS man from Britain still had a lot to do, and a great deal of power to go with it. This seems to be reason enough for a continued interest in him, especially if, as has been argued, the experience of imperialism needs to be seen in its finer details and not merely in terms of the machinations of London and the Central Government in New Delhi. A closer attention to the activities and attitudes of the 'good white man' who sought to improve the country through painstaking work in his district might reveal a different face of imperialism, of doing good work unto the last, when the forces of nationalism finally displaced him.

Is there then a case for a good imperialism versus a bad imperialism? The question itself might appear quite illegitimate to those who do not acknowledge the possibility of a good imperialism. There are nonetheless ways of continuing to address this question, by shifting the focus away from the activities of the Civilians to the way they related to those activities. The question then becomes not the historian's own question, but that of the good white man himself. Did he see himself as fulfilling the imperial mission, or did he see himself as undermining it?

---

[3] See Philip Woodruff, *The Men Who Ruled India, Part II: The Guardians* (London: Jonathan Cape, 1954).

Clive Dewey's *Anglo-Indian Attitudes*, which seeks to make a contribution to the intellectual history of Empire, focuses on Frank Brayne and Malcolm Darling, two Civilians of the Punjab cadre, their intellectual and social backgrounds and their attitudes and approaches to the problems of village uplift, economic development, or the administration of social justice.[4] Implicit in many of these concerns were certain views of Empire and Imperialism, which, although gleaned from the early training of the ICS in the mythologies of Empire, as well as intellectual trends at Home, were tempered in many cases by experience and consequent cynicism. Dewey has argued, among other things, that 'each generation of Civilians took the intellectual fashions of their youth to the East, and spent the rest of their life putting them into practice'.[5] This statement needs, I think, to be qualified: however much a Civilian might have wanted to hold on to his ideas of Empire during his years in the Service, circumstances conspired to modify, and in some cases, change his attitudes. This is evident in the writings of a number of Civilians, who record how their initial attitudes about imperialism and its role, their own role in India, and their relationship to the natives changed over time. It would have been strange were this not so; it would attribute a rigidity and inflexibility to the British Civilian that was hardly compatible with operating in as swiftly changing conditions as those in which he was forced to operate in the last days of the British Empire in India.

Dewey's reading of Penderel Moon (1905–1987), the main protagonist of the present chapter—imperial civil servant, bureaucrat in post-independence India, and later historian of empire at Oxford University[6]—is particularly interesting in this context: 'Hard-core progressives, the Penderel Moon types, absorbed nationalist propaganda at one remove, from the *Manchester Guardian* or *A Passage to India*. By the time they sat the examination for the ICS, they were more than half-convinced that the Congress critique of British rule—all exploitation, repression and rudeness—was true'.[7] Moon's 'nationalist' credentials—as

---

[4] Clive Dewey, *Anglo-Indian Attitudes: The Mind of the Indian Civil Service* (London: Hambledon, 1993).

[5] Dewey, *Anglo-Indian Attitudes*, 14.

[6] See the biographical note in MSS.EUR.F.230/30, Moon Collection, British Library, London.

[7] Dewey, *Anglo-Indian Attitudes*, 223. This description of Moon's 'progressive' position sits uneasily with some of the material presented in this chapter, as indeed with Dewey's representation of some of Moon's views (see in particular Dewey, *Anglo-Indian Attitudes*, p. 207 and note 11, p. 251), and raises questions about Dewey's own position.

an *Indian* nationalist—have not been greatly discussed. However, his later career as a historian critical of British rule in India, and in particular of the British mishandling of Partition and the transfer of power,[8] not to mention his decision to stay on in India and serve under the Nehru government after 1947, notably as Secretary to the Planning Commission, seem to make it self-evident that he belongs outside the subset of committed paternalist imperialists of whom Dewey writes. But an Indian nationalist? Harsh words—or fulsome praise—indeed.

This chapter attempts to place Moon in his context, and thereby to re-read his particular rewriting of an imperial narrative for his particular time. The impending end of the Empire produced a good deal of questioning of imperial narratives, and there is a substantial literature on British attitudes to Empire, their origins, sustenance, or propagation. Most of this relates, however, to a period of confidence and strength within the British Empire, and deals with the higher ranks of Government officials in India and Britain or the training and manipulation of British public opinion regarding the Empire. The Second World War and the political developments which accompanied it further eroded the Service's already threatened sense of importance. By the end of the war, '[a]lmost everyone in the Service ... pictured an independent India and since few believed that it could rightly hold a place for themselves, their old whole-hearted confidence could hardly be maintained', and 'everyone ... was thinking of what was to come next'.[9] The sense of uncertainty which from the 1920s had bred both a reassessment and a hardening of attitudes— while some continued to cling to fragile certainties that they were too insecure to discard, others were more inclined to look the changes in the eye—now intensified to a point where to cling to certainties could only be seen as wilful blindness. The rhetoric of internal British debates about India and the Empire had changed accordingly; the distinction between 'die-hard' Tories and those who saw themselves as 'realists' from within

---

[8] See Penderel Moon, *Divide and Quit* (London: Chatto & Windus, 1961).

[9] Woodruff, *The Men Who Ruled India, Part II: The Guardians*, 338. Woodruff is here speaking of, and for, the British members of the service; although he goes on to point out that by the end of the war, the service was almost half Indian (339), it is doubtful that he meant to say the Indian members of the service doubted that there could be a place for them in the new scheme of things [Philip Woodruff was the pen-name used by Philip Mason, a Civilian who spent the last years of the Empire in India, serving the military administration during the Second World War. See his memoirs, Philip Mason, *A Shaft of Sunlight* (London: André Deutsch, 1978)].

the Conservative Party,[10] or 'social imperialists' in the Labour party,[11] had found echoes in the British Government of India as well as the ICS, though explicit and unambiguous anti-imperialist positions were difficult to come by in the Service (there were some, of course, notably the Bengal Civilian Michael Carritt, a member of the Communist Party).[12] After the war, 'ripeness for self-government'[13] was almost universally acknowledged, with only the 'communal question' and the attempt to transfer power to a united India delaying the British departure.

Penderel Moon's *Strangers in India* addressed the dilemmas faced by the Indian Civil Service towards the end of the Empire.[14] A lot of his correspondence following its publication indicates that the people he wrote about, and those who read the book, were indeed engaging with the questions he raised in it. It should be noted that this was an internal critique, a self-criticism session, addressed to British audiences, and in some cases, more specifically to his fellow Civilians. *Strangers in India* was a severe indictment, on several counts, of British rule in India, and a direct assault on a number of the most cherished and carefully nurtured views on the benefits bestowed on India by British imperialism.[15] Its central theme was an exploration of 'the alien character of our rule';[16] despite good intentions, Britain had brought no good upon India, as her 'foreign conceptions' had often led to results opposite to those desired. Even the much-vaunted impartial system of British justice was ill-adapted to the needs of the country.[17]

---

[10] See L. S. Amery's memoirs, *My Political Life, Volume III: The Unforgiving Years 1929–1940* (London: Hutchinson, 1955).

[11] See Stephen Howe, *Anticolonialism in British Politics: The Left and the End of Empire 1918–1964* (Oxford: Clarendon Press, 1993); Partha Sarathi Gupta, *Imperialism and the British Labour Movement 1914–1964* (London: Macmillan, 1975).

[12] See Michael Carritt, *A Mole in the Crown* (Calcutta: Rupa, 1986).

[13] For an exploration of this idea in the debates of the British Labour movement, and the contention that British tutelage in socialist practice and institutions was necessary before 'ripeness' for self-government could be achieved, see Gupta, *Imperialism and the British Labour Movement*.

[14] Penderel Moon, *Strangers in India* (London: Faber & Faber, 1944).

[15] A number of letters written to Moon after the publication of *Strangers in India* refer to this. See MSS.EUR.F.230/30.

[16] *Strangers in India*, 32.

[17] *Strangers in India*, 44–62. For a more tolerant acknowledgement that the British system of 'justice' as it operated in the districts had little to do with legal procedures, see Mason, *A Shaft of Sunlight*. For a much more searching and critical assessment of the farcical nature of the District Officer's role as judge, see Carritt, *A Mole in the Crown*.

4.2. Strangers?

Written just after he had resigned from the ICS as a consequence of severe disagreements with the Government of India, and with the Viceroy, Lord Linlithgow in particular, over the treatment of political prisoners during the Quit India Movement (the specific events leading up to Moon's resignation were not mentioned in polite company, but the resignation itself attracted much attention, and succeeded in causing a good deal of consternation in official circles at the time),[18] Penderel Moon's evocatively titled *Strangers in India* is a historical narrative within a novel whose barely fictional characters are allowed to speak their version of history through the medium of Moon's pen. The book reflects a period of helplessness in Moon's own life. He had spent a good deal of energy writing policy papers addressed to the Government of India pleading for a more reasonable and conciliatory policy towards India in the light of the need for Indian support during the War, but to no avail. It is possible to discern in this book a certain bitterness generated by a sense of betrayal: of the failure of the imperialism he had been taught to respect to live up to its noble ideals, and consequently the genesis in Moon himself of a sense of loss, as well as the guilt of complicity in a vicious system, a guilt he now sought to expiate.

The plot revolves around various incidents in the life of a young recruit to the ICS, Greenlane, who arrives in India in the 1930s full of idealism about the benefits of Empire, and his gradual disillusion with it. Greenlane's articulation of his doubts, and the cynical realism of his senior and mentor, Lightfoot, provide the space for the reassessment of

---

[18] See the biographical note introducing the Moon Collection, handlist to MSS.EUR.F.230. The story among those who knew Moon personally suggests that his closeness to the Congresswoman Rajkumari Amrit Kaur made him alert to the desire of a Congress left to co-operate with Britain against a worldwide fascist threat, but Linlithgow's mishandling of negotiations was a matter of some frustration. Moon's letters to his father in 1943 provide some clues as to the lines of disagreement. In a letter dated 31 January 1943, he writes regarding 'food difficulties out here. These are, in my opinion, to some extent due to the incompetence of the Govt. of India'. Certain remarks made regarding the treatment of political prisoners in this letter were deleted by the Censor. Two letters dated 16 May 1943 and 23 May 1943 talk about Moon having resigned, but provide no details as to why (presumably these would have been deleted if he had; all letters in this file are marked 'Opened by Examiner', and some have bits cut out, whose subject is difficult to ascertain). IOL: MSS.EUR.F.230/18. *Strangers in India*, when published, was examined as potentially subversive by the authorities before being cleared for import into India. See IOL: L/P&J/12/26, f. 55.

Empire undertaken by Moon. There is more than a touch of the auto-biographical in Moon's drawing of Greenlane, but Greenlane is also a prototype: the average idealistic raw recruit to the Service, fresh from training and having internalized the mythology of benevolent imperialism. Lightfoot, apparently based on an early mentor of Moon's, has a touch of Moon as he would like to be: the older Moon, Lightfoot, attempting to assist the younger Moon, Greenlane, to come to terms with the limitations of his situation. Malcolm Darling's review of the book put it succinctly: the 'strangers', the British, and what they have done or left undone, is discussed by three Civilians:

> one of them, young and eager, who finally retires, disillusioned; another called Lightfoot, older and wiser, and, as he says, 'too tangled up' in the country to leave it; and the third, the author himself—really a case of three in one, for all three represent different aspects of the same mind.[19]

Yet Moon is drawing on experiences and incidents which he regards as typical: dilemmas to be faced by every ICS man in the course of his service. In the ICS, as Michael Carritt wrote, 'there were some dedicated men who sincerely struggled against all the odds imposed by the system of Imperial Government to administer justice and to cope with the all-pervading rural poverty and ignorance. Not very many of these, I fear, as the twentieth century proceeded and even the best men in the service were frustrated by the contradiction between dedicated paternalism and their professional faith in the blessings of imperial rule'.[20]

'Facts and figures about India', Moon wrote in his preface, 'are easily obtainable. But these often tend to remain academic abstractions, unrelated to human life as it is actually led in that country ... it is time that Englishmen learnt to view their record in India more objectively than has been their habit in the past. Criticisms of the British Raj, though often ill-informed and ill-natured, are not on that account ill-founded. The critics may seem unreasonable; but psychologically if not logically, they usually have some justification, and this ought to be recognised and understood.

---

[19] *Asiatic Review* 1945, 108.
[20] Carritt, *A Mole in the Crown*, 4.

The customary idealisations of the British Raj are annoying to Indians, harmful to British interests, and quite unnecessary'.[21]

Why, in Moon's view, have Englishmen hitherto been unable to see the truth about India? A mixture of pecuniary interest and national pride, going hand in hand, have militated against it. English historians have ceased to be as objective, as 'brutally frank and critical about British rule in India since the end of Company rule, when the Company was not a national concern, and there were no politically-conscious Indians to worry about'. After India 'became unquestionably a national possession ... and incidentally the largest foreign market that any country has ever been able to control for its own advantage', India was 'too manifestly mixed up with England's national pride and prosperity for English writers to be able to give a full, judicious, and unbiased account of British-Indian history'.[22]

The central question which Moon asks, through Greenlane, a question dictated by the political scenario in which he was operating from the 1930s, is 'why it had been necessary to wait right up till their lifetime to take any substantial step towards Indian self-government, said to have been the goal of English policy for nearly 100 years'. The answer, provided by Lightfoot, is unequivocal: British national interests require the existence of the Indian empire. What follows is largely a representation of Indian nationalist arguments, whose substance Moon acknowledges, and his representation is rhetorically powerful. He accepts the 'Plassey plunder', 'deindustrialization', and 'drain of wealth' arguments, arguing that the system of exploitation through which India provided unprotected markets for British goods enabled Britain 'from about 1860 onwards to use the proceeds to set up as a vast moneylender'. Gradually, '[w]ith the profits from ... ever-increasing investments steadily rising, England could afford to see her share in Indian trade declining and to grant Indians greater freedom in the management of their tariffs'.[23] India as debtor simply had to pay:

After all, if you are so poor that you cannot develop your own resources without borrowing money, you must expect to pay for it. It matters not

---

[21] *Strangers in India*, 5.
[22] *Strangers in India*, 10.
[23] *Strangers in India*, 14.

whether your borrowings are wise or unwise, voluntary or involuntary. A bond is a bond. The creditor must take his pound of flesh.[24]

Here Moon uses an interesting reversal of arguments. The moneylender was a stock figure in the rhetoric of British India, representing unproductive parasitism: a creature who took advantage of poverty and weakness to extract his profits.[25] Although it was sometimes acknowledged that he provided an essential service in the absence of organized credit facilities, it was generally agreed that his usurious demands aggravated the problem of rural debt.[26] Representing the British Indian state, which represented itself as the protector of the peasant from the moneylender, as a 'vast moneylender', was calculated to provoke. Moon presses this analogy of parasitism, of the Britain-India relationship as the moneylender-peasant relationship, further: the period 1860–1900 saw the 'triumph of a parasitic class ... We fostered parasites; and, what is worse, we ourselves at the same time began to become parasitic'.[27] He wastes little space on the British claim that the use of British credit by the Government of India is essential for India's progress: 'a debtor can hardly feel that his interests are entirely safe when exclusively in his creditor's hands'.[28]

The analogy also drew on the negative connotations of the original use of the image against the cowardly *bania*: moneylending was un-Christian,

---

[24] *Strangers in India*, 14–15.

[25] This is an image Moon uses himself: see *Strangers in India*, 33.

[26] As is well known, a good deal of legislation had sought, at the end of the nineteenth century, to protect the peasant from the moneylender. In particular, protection was said to be necessary against the alleged danger of dispossession of 'cultivating classes' by non-cultivating classes. That this also reflected a concern for the continuity of commercial agricultural production, the essential element in the maintenance of India's export surplus, which subsidized Britain's trade deficit with the rest of the world, is also clear, but the point to be made here is that the official rationale for such acts was the need to defend the peasant against the rapacious moneylender. This image persisted strongly into the twentieth century and appeared strongly in the proceedings of the Provincial Banking Enquiry Committees and the Central Banking Enquiry Committee, summarized and amplified in the *Report of the Central Banking Enquiry Commission, 1931, Volume I Part I: Majority Report* (New Delhi: Government of India Press, 1931). On the rare occasions when a British officer was willing to defend the practice of moneylending, it was on the grounds that no alternative organized facilities as yet existed and hence that it was a lesser evil that nonetheless needed to be severely regulated. See Malcolm Darling, *The Punjab Peasant in Prosperity and Debt* (Oxford: Geoffrey Cumberlege, 1925), Chapter 10.

[27] *Strangers in India*, 35. On p. 33, he also argues that it is the 'foreign conceptions' of the British that have led to the ascendancy of the moneylender, with early rack renting by the British and British-created landlords weakening the peasants; later legislation could not solve the problem.

[28] *Strangers in India*, 35.

immoral, and foreign. In being a 'vast moneylender' and by implication un-Christian, immoral, and foreign, British rule was not only foreign to India, but foreign to itself. This is an implication made explicit elsewhere by Moon, which later links up with arguments that provide extenuating circumstances for English imperialism in India, for Moon has an interesting version of the 'canny Scot' argument up his sleeve.

In a speech beginning 'If I were an orthodox Englishman, I should have refused to give this talk', delivered sometime during the war, before an audience of predominantly if not exclusively Englishmen, Moon discussed Englishmen, the Empire and the social background they came from.[29] 'The mental sloth of the Englishman begins at school', he wrote: 'The English Public School is perhaps the only educational institution in the world where mental idleness is encouraged and even applauded ... In many of the best known of these world-famed establishments any noticeable mental exertion is reckoned as positively bad form. To work at all hard is simply not done. Even the masters are inclined to deprecate it'.[30] He recalled that shortly after arriving in India, he spent an evening 'dining with a number of middle-aged English officers, who throughout the evening vied with one another in explaining how singularly lazy and stupid they were at school. And, see what fine fellows we are now! This was the burden of their talk'.[31]

'This same tradition of idleness prevails at the older English universities', he added. A well-known don he recalls from his Oxford days, who used to take a keen interest in 'pushing young men into the Indian and African Civil Services, used to say that one came up to the University to drink, to row or to hunt. What an admirable training for an Empire civil servant! With a little "shooting" thrown in it would be quite perfect. It will produce considerable capacity for enduring and inflicting pain and hardship and very little else. And what else is required?'[32]

Why, despite all this, are the English people able to rule not only themselves but their Empire? Moon saw possible good in English 'mental

---

[29] MSS.EUR.F.230/40, 'If I were an orthodox Englishman ...'.
[30] MSS.EUR.F.230/40, 'If I were an orthodox Englishman ...', 1–2.
[31] MSS.EUR.F.230/40, 'If I were an orthodox Englishman ...', 2–3.
[32] MSS.EUR.F.230/40, 'If I were an orthodox Englishman ...', 3–4. Moon may have thought he was overdoing it a bit here: 'What an admirable training ...' onwards has been deleted from the draft, and was probably omitted when the speech was delivered.

lethargy', whose corollary, according to him, is 'easy-going tolerance'. The occasional genius is allowed to flourish as a 'crank'; when in a crisis he is required, he exists. Also, 'statesmanship is the art of the second best': logical consistency with stated principles never really bothered the English. But the principal reason for English imperial success, he felt, lies elsewhere:

> For the last 234 years they [the English] have enjoyed the inestimable advantage of having the assistance of the Scots. The inefficiency of the English throughout the world, and their (often) gross mental incapacity has been largely neutralised by the hordes of hungry, ambitious, uncouth but efficient Scotsmen, who ever since the Union in 1707 have poured forth from their gloomy towns and barren mountains into the English-speaking world and ended largely by dominating it. The Scotch can *think* as well as *act*. They have a rigorous sense of logic and a vast appetite for tedious mental drudgery if it holds out the slightest prospect of pecuniary profit. These useful and admirable qualities have been placed ungrudgingly at the disposal of the English.[33]

Here is a paradoxical position: having conducted a critique of the economics of imperialism which would not have been entirely unworthy of a Communist, and also a very nationalist prescription for economic development through planned industrialization,[34] Moon nonetheless seeks to escape from its implications in an argument based on race. But *Strangers* has its own search for extenuating circumstances; in it, Moon acknowledged the 'remarkable' British achievement in India—conquered by 'a tiny handful of Englishmen'—of planting 'in its somewhat uncongenial soil the great liberal ideals and institutions of England'.[35] The number of English officials in India was exceedingly small, at the time to which he is referring; some districts had only one, many none at all.[36] And (Lightfoot speaking):

---

[33] MSS.EUR.F.230/40, 'If I were an orthodox Englishman …', 5. 'If it holds out … pecuniary profit' has been deleted, as have further, and more offensive, anti-Scots remarks later on.
[34] *Strangers in India*, 38.
[35] *Strangers in India*, 5.
[36] *Strangers in India*, 5–6.

Indians are not unaware of what they owe to England. It is rather Englishmen who are apt to forget what they owe to India—not least how much of their own achievement in India has been dependent on Indian ability and co-operation. Neither the merits nor the defects of the British Raj are attributable solely to the British. Without Indian talent the great fabric of ordered government could never have been built; nor could it have been sustained with such impressive stability without certain qualities—which are also defects—of the Indian character—a respect for authority, a strong sense of personal loyalty, and a quick responsiveness to great ideas. The Indian Empire is the product of joint endeavours. Future generations will perhaps admire it.[37]

The consistency and rigour of Moon's arguments regarding imperial exploitation are not matched by a correspondingly exacting intellectual position with regard to his arguments on circumstances that reduced British (English?) culpability, as though he hesitantly searches for a way to rescue himself and his colleagues from being indicted in the logic of empire. This is much more of a struggle; however, as he argued himself, if one were to have told a young prospective Civil Servant that he was being sent out to defend British capital abroad, he would not have gone.[38]

What then, if any, were the good things about the Empire in India? *Strangers in India*, written as a critique of that empire, does not resolve this question clearly; nor could it be particularly easily done. Moon, writing in June 1947, seems to revert, possibly for a different audience, to the general contention that at least British rule maintained order— a position which he rejects in *Strangers*.[39] He never quite resolved this question for himself. Now, India is confronted with great violence and chaos: 'Already the hated British Raj, odious so long as it continued to exist, is being viewed with nostalgic regret. As it passes into history, there is a quickened appreciation of its merits and advantages'.[40] The younger generation of Indians seems prepared to suffer this chaos; the older generation, Moon felt, hoped that 'British influence and British administrative and technical personnel will ... still linger on and by their mere

---

[37] *Strangers in India*, 5–6.
[38] *Strangers in India*, Preface.
[39] *Strangers in India*, 44–62.
[40] MSS.EUR.F.230/47, f. 1.

presence contrive to preserve order and prevent a complete collapse of standards.[41] This is an adoption of the widely held line that British withdrawal led to the deterioration of standards of administration in India. As for 'the vast, voiceless, illiterate, inconscient masses, who inhabit the villages of India', Moon could comfort himself that '[t]o them, such terms as the "British Raj", "Independence", "Pakistan", if not entirely unknown, are at most meaningless abstractions'. Their lives could not be disrupted by colonialism, or by any other forces, continuing 'as they did before the Moguls came and before the British came and as they will continue to do for generations to come, preserving that age-old village life indestructible alike by calamity or progress'.[42]

This is a good resolution of the problem of imperialism and exploitation, with which Moon begins: colonialism is exploitative, yet it provides order in a society that would otherwise revert to chaos. The latter contention is of course part of an old argument. All this, however, recedes into the background if it can be argued that the vast majority of Indians, who clearly live in villages, are not significantly affected by colonial disruption. Yet of course this is not consistently argued, and there is an ambivalence written into it; it is both positive and negative, in the latter sense because the best efforts made by British rule to transform the country by benevolence will be destined to failure. It is these inconsistencies that provide a clue to the dilemma of the colonial official, uncertain of the moral propriety of colonialism, and consequently the moral propriety of his own position in its administration.

4.3. Resolving a Dilemma

Perhaps a perfect resolution to the dilemma was possible only in the realms of propaganda: propaganda not viewed as lies, but rather as a gentle smoothing-out of lines of conflictual interpretation, providing a softened picture that looks away from ugliness, and is as self-deluding as it is deluding. In January 1941, Moon gave a talk on All-India Radio entitled 'Totalitarian Facts and Fiction-2: Does Great Britain Exploit Her

---

[41] MSS.EUR.F.230/47, f. 2.
[42] MSS.EUR.F.230/47, f. 4.

Colonies?'. In it, he admitted that although it was impossible to answer this question truthfully with an unqualified negative, exploitation was 'not the avowed purpose for which Great Britain retains her colonies'. The purpose was the 'dual mandate' of 'adequate development of the resources of her colonies' and, as 'trustees for the native races', the promotion of their 'well-being and progress so that they may ultimately take their places as free and independent peoples'.[43] Moon claimed a divergence of interest between the British colonial Government and 'powerful financial interests seeking the development of mineral and other resources', the latter preventing British governments in the colonies from maintaining 'the paramountcy of native interests'.

With the above distinction in place, Moon was extremely critical of colonial 'exploitation': he quoted 'a British writer' as having said that 'We appropriate the natural resources of a country, develop them in our own way and for our own purpose, and of the wealth so produced we carry out of the country £11 for every £1 we leave behind'.[44] Here, however, appears a strange twist to the argument: since 'primitive African tribes' are not in a position to develop and use their mineral or other resources themselves, what moral claim might they have to resources 'of whose existence and significance they were wholly ignorant until the intrusion of Europeans'? There was, Moon felt, no moral ground to prevent British companies from developing these resources, but the appropriation of all the profits offended his sense of justice. And yet what would a fair division be? He could not, he said, resolve this problem, but he did not feel it could be solved 'by the British people becoming overnight a nation of philanthropists'.[45] Here it is unclear whether he was making a case for a benevolent imperialism or merely leaving his audience with an apparent dilemma; he ended by quoting an unnamed British communist quoting an unnamed West African Negro doctor on the 'highly progressive role' of British rule in Africa.[46]

In *Strangers in India*, almost three years down the road, Moon was making a surprisingly similar point: British rule was not itself responsible

[43] MSS.EUR.F.230/40: Text of All-India Radio Broadcast on 25 January 1941, Lahore Station, 8.15 p.m; 1–3.

[44] MSS.EUR.F.230/40: Text of All-India Radio Broadcast on 25 January 1941, 4–5.

[45] MSS.EUR.F.230/40: Text of All-India Radio Broadcast on 25 January 1941, 6–7.

[46] MSS.EUR.F.230/40: Text of All-India Radio Broadcast on 25 January 1941, 7–8.

for the poverty of the Indian masses, which was 'largely due to factors beyond our control, and even beyond our ken'. Any damage done to the already bad situation was the result of 'mistakes', 'shortcomings', 'unfortunate, though often not consciously intended, consequences of our association with India'.[47] Ultimately, though, Britain could be looked upon, in Marx's phrase, as just 'the unconscious tool of history':

> I am proud that our country should have been chosen by fate, nature, God or whatever you like to call it, to clear up the debris of the Mogul empire and to unlock for India the treasures of Western thought. I think on the whole we were worthy of it.[48]

This is Lightfoot speaking Moon's thoughts; at last, a worthy epitaph for the Empire has been found, worthy of the principle for which Moon always claimed to have taken up his calling as a Civilian in India, finally to hand over India to its own by now politically mature people.

4.4. Rewritten Mythology

Moon's All-India Radio speech was of course an official 'war effort' speech; what is interesting is that within its constraints, there was plenty of room for Moon's critique of imperialism. That critique fits into a narrative sought carefully to be put in place during the war to present an acceptable face of imperialism to allies, enemies, and subject peoples alike.[49] This narrative, far from being based on implicit and unarticulated assumptions, was explicitly provided to the controllers of public opinion involved in propaganda for the war effort. Briefing the staff of the British Embassy Publicity Committee in Washington on the line of argument which was to be the basis of their work, Mr. Jossleyn Hennessy suggested an analogy: what if India had conquered Europe? It is worth quoting from this analogy at some length, at the risk of appearing to digress:

---

[47] *Strangers in India*, 41–42.
[48] *Strangers in India*, 43.
[49] For the themes and audiences aimed at official wartime propaganda, see Sanjoy Bhattacharya, *Propaganda and Information in Eastern India, 1939–45: A Necessary Weapon of War* (Richmond: Curzon, 2001).

Let us imagine that Indian traders found it profitable to set up trading stations in Italy in the 17th and 18th centuries: Italy throughout that period was constantly in the throes of warfare between the unnumerable [sic] states into which it was divided; since Europe as a whole owed a vague suzerainty to the Holy Roman Emperor, the Indian traders duly sought his protection and secured licenses to trade from him. The Indian traders found the Emperor unable to protect them and their trade was frequently interrupted by local warfare, so that they were led to fortify their factories which they defended with Indian soldiers; the neighbouring Italian states soon learned the fighting value of these Indian soldiers and in some cases began to enlist their services as allies; in the event of victory greater trading facilities were granted or territorial acquisitions were made, in additionwhich the Indian traders learned that there were other benefits to be obtained by acquiring actual territorial possessions rather than mere trading rights.

To cut a long story short, the Indians who first came to trade soon became embroiled in European politics and in the course of time they became one of the European military powers—in the end the paramount power—this, let us say, by 1857.

Let us imagine the whole of the European continent ruled by a foreign Indian government since 1857: what would have been the effects on Europe?

In the first place, there would have been no war between Prussia and Austria in 1866; no Franco-Prussian War of 1870; no Balkan wars; no Great War of 1914–1918; and no Second World War of 1939.

The Indians (whom we imagine to have conquered Europe) formed a central administration which required a large Civil Service and although at first the higher positions were reserved exclusively for Indians, from the beginning thousands of secondary positions gave employment to Europeans. As the Indian administration was conducted in Hindusthani, all Europeans had to learn this language; Indian trading houses which came over in ever greater numbers and established businesses up and down the Continent from Cracow to Barcelona conducted their work in Hindusthani which thus became the common language for virtually all educated Europeans, so that for the first time, Finns in the north could converse freely with Spaniards in the south, and French in the West could converse freely with Bulgarians in the east.

The Indians established freedom of trade throughout this great area and they built roads and railways where none had been before.

A European Nationality

What would the consequences have been if this picture were real and not imaginary? Surely that as time went on the diverse race of Europe—the Rumanians, Turks, Greeks, Portuguese, Swedes, Estonians, Germans and French—would have begun to think of themselves less as Rumanians, Turks, Greeks, Portuguese, etc., and more and more as Europeans; they would for the first time have begun to consider their affairs from the viewpoint of Europe as a whole; once this idea had begun to establish itself, parallel with it would have come the consciousness of the difference of their civilisation from that of their foreign rulers, the Indians. A European Nationalist Movement would have been born. Agitations for a greater share by Europeans in the Indian Administration would have been followed by demands for an equal status for Europe in the Indian Empire. History suggests that nobody in possession of something readily gives it up. Consequently, the agitation would have lasted with growing impetus for many years; but we can imagine the Indians realising that the strength of the Indian Empire would be more likely to survive if it were converted into an Indian Commonwealth in which Europe would be a partner.

The Indian rulers granted various constitutional reforms, recruited up to fifty per cent of the higher Civil Servants from Europeans, and finally committed themselves to Dominion Status for Europe …[50]

This was an idealized picture of colonialism: if the Empire began as an accident, and progressed along lines determined by forces akin to natural laws, there could be no room for resentment or recriminations. It avoided using the old cliches of economic benefits, law and order, moral and material progress, as justifications of Empire, though these were built into the narrative as well. It was claimed that the Empire needed no justification, as in a similar situation, no one would have done any different. In any case, the argument went, the Empire was changing, British Imperialism becoming more humane, more representative, and accommodating the

---

[50] Secret: Minutes of Meeting of the British Embassy Publicity Committee, held at the British Embassy in Washington on 19 March 1942, British Library: MSS.EUR.D.725.

nationalisms it had itself created—despite the fact that '[h]istory suggests that nobody in possession of something readily gives it up'.

This was considered to be a particularly strong argument. As Hennessy put it, it was completely legitimate for Americans to demand an explanation of the British position on India, because (a) this was supposed to be a war for democracy, (b) because Britain had a good answer, and (c) because it offered a useful opportunity of explaining the British position. The argument was thus, as stressed in (b), expected to have persuasive powers beyond its target audience: like the character in the musical comedy who made believe he was brave,[51] it was meant to convince British speakers as much as American listeners of the justice behind the British presence in India.

By the time *Strangers in India*, written by December 1943, was published, Moon, in attacking British conceptions of colonial good government, was to an extent attacking a version of the imperial mythology that was no longer the projected official position. Civilians and imperial functionaries were clearly cynical of simplistic views of periods of tutelage and white man's burdens. It was still necessary to have some version of potted imperial history or moral philosophy which could at least attempt to maintain the Civilian's belief in his job, and to enable him to sound convincing when arguing the Imperial case before a critical audience. The explanations provided by apologists of empire during the war took these factors into account. In Moon's own account, although the origins of Empire in India are not foregrounded, the main thrust of his argument— the failure of British imperialism to live up to its promise—indicates the importance of the initial cause to his characterization of imperialism.

Strangers in India was enthusiastically received by many of Moon's colleagues and contemporaries who had been concerned with the Indian empire; others were sharply critical. Malcolm Darling, in a private letter to Moon, declared that it was 'worth resigning to write that'.[52] He nonetheless wrote elsewhere that Moon had perhaps overstated his case due to 'a certain animus against British rule in India'.[53] Reginald Coupland,

---

[51] *The King and I* (USA, 1956): 'Make believe you're brave/ And the trick will take you far/ You may be as brave/ As you make believe you are' ('I Whistle a Happy Tune', by Richard Rodgers and Oscar Hammerstein II).

[52] Malcolm Darling to Penderel Moon, 28 May 1944, MSS.EUR.F.230/30.

[53] Malcolm Darling's review of *Strangers in India* in the *Asiatic Review* (1945): 108.

Professor of Imperial History at Oxford, declared, 'As I expected, it is far the best book on India I have ever read', though he said that he differed on two or three points which he wanted to discuss later.[54] A retired police officer from the Punjab wrote, 'Never before have I seen it clearly stated in any book on India that what the uninitiated fondly conceive to be the one solid achievement of British rule, i.e. the gift of justice such as the East has never known before through great legal codes is nothing more than a myth', and added that he had been convinced of this throughout his service in the Indian Police.[55] A long dissenting letter, particularly critical of Moon's contention that parliamentary democracy was unsuited to India, made, among other things, a case for the exoneration of the Civil Service from indictment for the negative aspects of the Indian empire: 'You cannot as a District Officer be expected to take upon your own head the sins of H[is].M[ajesty's].G[overnment]., the Central Government, the Provincial Government, the Indian National Congress, the Muslim League, and the rest; you can only do your best with the instruments you have, and try to preserve your own professional standards'.[56] Another letter stated, 'You and I—and, indeed, all those who know anything of India—know that despite all our mistakes, on balance India is devinitely [sic] the better off for her contact with us. At least, I believe this to be the case. Possibly you don't?'[57] An old Army man, who had gone out to India in 1900, wrote to Moon, in a reprimanding tone:

Just as feminism is as old as history, and due, not to the real upsurge of womanhood but to the rotting of the manly virtues, so the complete-ness of our failure in India is due not to the real upsurge of the Indian peoples but to the decay and death of our own faith in ourselves, our mission and our destiny.[58]

For all the militant indignation of this last view, it can be seen as engaging with the same problem as Moon's own. This indeed can be said of the views of Moon's other correspondents, whether critics or supporters. The

---

[54] Reginald Coupland to Penderel Moon, 5 November 1944, MSS.EUR.F.230/30.
[55] F. W. Toms to Penderel Moon, 2 June 1944, MSS.EUR.F.230/30.
[56] Letter to Moon, 6 July 1944, signature illegible, MSS.EUR.F.230/30.
[57] Letter to Moon, 24 July 1944, signature illegible, MSS.EUR.F.230/30.
[58] Letter to Moon, 25 August 1944, signature illegible, MSS.EUR.F.230/30.

shared concern, at the impending close of Britain's imperial project in India, is with a good project gone wrong. This is an internal debate, a discussion not on the nature of India as much as on the nature and failures of the Imperial Briton.

Perhaps Moon himself did not altogether give up hope of contributing to the betterment of Indians. Consistent with the idea that the best intentions of imperialism can only be fulfilled by a fundamental transformation of India, Moon stayed on in India beyond the transfer of power, suppressing Communists in the North-East, serving in the Planning Commission, and generally providing a guiding hand to the new government.[59] The need for the friendly guiding hand was to him self-evident: in 1946, as Secretary to the Advisory Planning Board under the interim government, Moon wrote to his father:

> I am working directly under Nehru. He is very quick and intelligent, but exceedingly superficial. One has to steer him all the time through meetings at which he presides[60]

4.5. Conclusion

Most people read *Strangers in India* as a critique of British imperialism in India; it is not as apparent that it was equally a strong defence of the idea of Empire. Thus, in an exception is it possible to find the rule. Read alongside his other writing, and indeed alongside a good deal of the writing, public and private, of other Civilians at the time, it becomes clear that a belief that Britain should leave India at the earliest possible date was not incompatible with a belief in the imperial ideal, as against imperial practice, which was more difficult to defend.

It is clear that an erosion of the moral arguments that had hitherto justified the existence of empire, in the face of many good counter-arguments, had been taking place from the 1930s, and was accelerated by the war. In Moon's version, this change in attitude, the need to justify imperialism as

---

[59] For an idea of the work, he was involved with in these capacities, see MSS.EUR.F.230/36, MSS.EUR.F.230/37, MSS.EUR.F.230/43, MSS.EUR.F.230/44.
[60] Moon to his father, 19 October 1946, MSS.EUR.F.230/19.

a stage now past, and to close the chapter with a neat explanation, went hand in hand with the need to accept the fact of impending decolonization. Yet it was not pleasant altogether to abandon the idea that some good had come out of the empire; the futility of the exercise would then have been too patent. On the other hand, it had to be acknowledged that much that was bad had come of it as well; perhaps it was better to say that the empire had not meant anything significant at all.

I began this chapter with an assumption, that the Civil Service's work in India as agents of imperialism cannot merely be explained by cynicism and a willingness to remain tools of British capital; they felt a need to justify their position. Following from that, I argued, firstly, that towards the end of Empire, and especially by the Second World War, older versions of the imperial mythology, presenting the Civilian as a bulwark of civilization and a buffer that prevented the separate and hostile 'communities' in India from falling upon one another,[61] no longer worked among the ICS as adequate justification for their participation in the imperial project; and secondly, the 1940s' official version of the imperial philosophy, partly constructed from bits and pieces left over from the old versions, and partly from the needs of official wartime propaganda, were rather more subtle, and were slightly more suited to easing the Civilian's conscience. The 1940s version, however, was far less compatible with the British staying on for a long period. In this scheme of things, arguments based both on 'collaboration' and 'indigenous origins' were important strategies invented to cope with the moral dilemmas of Empire, particularly to alleviate the guilt associated with being involved in the exploitation, violence, and brutality of colonialism.

---

[61] See Thomas Metcalf, *Ideologies of the Raj* (Cambridge: Cambridge University Press, 1995).

5

History, Cinema, and the Politics
of Cultural Sensitivity in Interwar India

5.1. Introduction

British imperial rule in India was nothing if not culturally sensitive, looking after the potential sensibilities of Indian audiences in matters of the consumption of cultural products that they might find harmful or offensive, or that they might not recognize as harmful or offensive unless protected from their lack of such recognition by those better suited to judge. Long-standing practices of banning books and other printed material considered to contain subversive political ideas and/or subjects offensive to 'Indian sentiment' were supplemented by new regulations directed at new media as they emerged.[1] Cinema was one such medium. The India Office therefore took upon itself the task of liaising with the Government of India and the British Board of Film Censorship to ensure that anything which might offend the subjects of the Empire in India, British or Indian be kept from their sensitive spirits in their own interests. Of particular concern was the Hollywood motion picture industry, whose interest in spinning a good yarn, they knew, could not easily be curtailed by a sense of what the India Office considered suitable history and/or suitable entertainment which did not offend.

The principle of not offending sensibilities, however, ran into difficulties as newer interest groups, whose cultural sensibilities were not that easy to fathom or gauge, claimed inclusion within the protective umbrella of British Indian censorship. The fate of imperial cinema censorship became slightly more complicated when claims were made upon it by new

---

[1] N. G. Barrier, *Banned; Controversial Literature and Political Control in British India, 1907-1947* (Columbia: University of Missouri Press, 1974); Milton Israel, *Communications and Power: Propaganda and the Press in the Indian National Struggle, 1920-1947* (Cambridge: Cambridge University Press, 1994).

entrants in a very difficult encounter; for instance, the rise of Nazism, with supporters and opponents across the world, had to be negotiated in terms of (un)offended sentiments and the screening of films in India.

A suitable interpretation of the past was integral to many of the conflicts around cinema in this context, as new entrants began to claim or contest political positions in terms of their depiction in historical detail. What was available as history, mythology, tradition, or culture depended here very strongly on external factors, therefore, and not in any sense on 'organic' developments within the society that had to be defended. The question was usually not so much whether the history depicted was accurate or not, in terms of contemporaneous professional standards or regimes of truth, but rather whether an inconvenient depiction might create political difficulties in some way—or indeed whether a complaint or intervention by a foreign consulate could successfully change the nature of the public depictions of its country and its regime, to the better success of their image, ideology, and propaganda. One regime's culturally sensitive handling of public arenas was another regime's—or interest group's—triumph. And if it was not always possible to rely on the government's pre-emptive banning of potentially offensive material, it was usually possible to get the government to rethink its decisions by being very noisily and possibly violently offended afterwards.

5.2. Imperial Anxieties and Cultural Fixers

The question of what constituted acceptable material for audiences in India was of course centrally connected to an imperial government's concern about the governability of India. Anything likely to cause political unrest was to be discouraged greatly. We need not concern ourselves here with what exactly 'Indian cultural sensibilities' were, because there has been a great deal of writing on the invention of tradition, and in particular on how many so-called indigenous Indian traditions were invented under colonial rule. This does not mean that they were entirely invented *ex nihilo* by the coloniser's conspiratorial social engineering, but that the forms in which we know them—as 'tradition'—owed much to the colonial period.[2] Whatever the origins of a colonial official's definitions

---

[2] E. J. Hobsbawm and T. O. Ranger, eds., *The Invention of Tradition* (Cambridge: Cambridge University Press, 1983); Nicholas Dirks, *The Hollow Crown: Ethnohistory of a Little Kingdom*

or anxieties about Indian cultural sensitivities, these definitions and anxieties could be seen in action in various decisions made to defend them.

An example to bring us into this story that establishes the principles and informal mechanisms involved can be provided here. In January 1936, an early warning of impending disaster in the form of a film to be made by Warner Brothers, *The Charge of the Light Brigade*, was provided by F. A. Evans, of the British Consulate Los Angeles, California, to P. M. Broadmead, at the British Embassy in Washington[3] (Hollywood was obviously considered important enough by the British establishment to warrant diplomatic representation):

> It promises to be one of the worst films to have come out of Hollywood for some time, since it proposes to sacrifice history to the strange idea of dramatic values held by the writers of the script ... The script was lent to me by the man who will probably act as technical adviser in the film, and whose future would undoubtedly be jeopardised if it were learnt that he had shown me the story.[4]

This was in the nature of a kind of journalistic scoop that, unfortunately, could not be acknowledged or publicized, for as Evans noted, 'as I am not supposed to have seen the story, I cannot take the matter up directly with the Company'.[5] Evans was not certain whether correspondence with the Company would help: 'As no doubt you are aware', he wrote, 'Warner Brothers and the Hearst organization are closely identified, a fact which makes me the more hesitant to tackle them direct'.[6] William Randolph Hearst, the media baron on whose life Orson Welles based his film *Citizen Kane* (1941), is well known in his life for having, among other things, endorsed Adolf Hitler as a world leader, but he was far from alone in this. His legendary power as a political fixer was at the time at its height.

---

in South India (Cambridge: Cambridge University Press, 1987); Bernard Cohn, 'The Census, Social Structure and Objectification in South Asia', in *An Anthropologist Among the Historians* (Delhi: Oxford University Press, 1987), 224–254 [1984].

[3] F. A. Evans, of the British Consulate, Los Angeles, California, to P. M. Broadmead, British Embassy, Washington, 13 January 1936. India Office Records, British Library [IOR]: L/PJ/8/127, ff. 176–178.

[4] IOR: L/PJ/8/127, f. 176.

[5] IOR: L/PJ/8/127, f. 176.

[6] IOR: L/PJ/8/127, f. 177.

But Evans also had what he thought was a solution to the problem:

> It has occurred to me that the only way out of the difficulty is to allow the British Industry to know that this abomination is about to be perpetrated, in the hope that one of the British companies might be persuaded to produce a more faithful though perhaps no less romantic story in England, if possible in advance of the Warner production.[7]

In other words, what Evans proposed was to plagiarize the idea and produce a British film on the subject first—a proposal which, we might add here, shows good academic credentials.

Evans said he had already discussed this with two colleagues at the Los Angeles consulate, identified as Charlton and Cane. Cane had said that he had an old friend at the Federation of British Industries (or at the Department of Overseas Trade; it is not quite clear from context), one Neville Kearney; Cane said that if Sir Edward Crowe (who was then the Director of Marconi's Wireless Telegraphy Company) could be told of this situation, he could 'put the suggestion of a British production confidentially to Kearney, who in turn could discuss it equally confidentially with his contacts in the Industry'. However, since 'political considerations are involved', Evans said that he was talking to the Embassy first. There was not, however, a lot of time left: Warner Brothers was starting production in about two months.[8]

The correspondence also contains a plot summary, presumably provided by Evans' informant, a copy of which was sent to India on 20 February 1936.[9] This was the story which, the summarizer noted, would probably be in the film with minor modifications. Scenes depicted were in India and Crimea. The film opens in India in 1854, dealing with the life of a regiment of Indian native cavalry (lancers). There was a love interest involving the daughter of the Commanding Officer, one of the subalterns of the regiment, and his brother. The script also dealt with the family life of one native soldier, a Sikh, with his infant son, one of the

[7] IOR: L/PJ/8/127, f. 177.
[8] IOR: L/PJ/8/127, f. 178.
[9] IOR: L/PJ/8/127, ff. 179–181.

leading characters. The native regiment bears insignia similar to that of the British 17th Lancers (the Skull and Bones).

The Indian section of the story winds up with the headquarters of the regiment, 'with its women and children including the leading female character, defending a fort against a treacherous Indian Chieftain'. Defenders are persuaded to surrender by the besiegers' false promises, 'the surrender being followed by incidents based upon the massacre at Cawnpore'[10] (this was a sensitive point in British-Indian relations—the massacre of European civilians at Kanpur is one of the central atrocity stories of 1857 told to a British public across the generations).[11] Most of the characters die here, including Commanding Officer and Sikh child, although the hero and leading lady escape.

The perversion of history begins about this point, when Lord Raglan is found as Commander-in-Chief of the 'Army of India' with headquarters at Delhi, while the hero is an officer on his staff. Reference is made to the imminence of war with Russia, and quite surprisingly, it is decided that the Indian Lancer regiment shall form part of the British Expeditionary Force, which is being sent to Crimea. No consideration is given to the fact that there was such a thing in 1854–1855 as the East India Company and that the Company's troops were not normally employed in expeditions outside India, nor is any attention paid to the earlier portions of the Russian War. The transfer of the regiment is explained by the desirability of getting the troops away from the scene of the slaughter of their families, and a further and even more improbable reason is in the fact that the Indian Chieftain has quite inexplicably become attached to the staff of the Russian Commander-in-Chief in Crimea, and the regiment will have a chance for revenge in that theatre of war.[12]

The summary continues:

> Through deliberate disobedience and the forgery of orders, the hero arranges for the charge to be made upon the Russian batteries by the Light Brigade, in the first line of which ride the Indian Lancers. We are left with the impression that the charge is entirely successful and

[10] IOR: L/PJ/8/127, f. 179.
[11] See Barbara English, 'The Kanpur Massacres in India and the Revolt of 1857', *Past & Present* no. 142 (February 1994): 169–178.
[12] IOR: L/PJ/8/127, f. 180.

was instrumental, by diverting the attention of the Russian Forces, in enabling Lord Raglan to deliver a successful general attack against Sebastopol. The hero is killed; his brother, who has developed a fatal passion for the leading lady, is left to pursue his suit, and a posthumous V.C. [Victoria Cross] is awarded to the hero.[13]

And finally, the summary of reasoning as to why the film was considered so sensitive was provided:

it represents a painful incident in the Indian history which had better be left unrecalled, at the present time at least, and ... it takes extravagant and contemptible liberties with an incident which is probably one of the most sacred in the traditions of the British Army.[14]

Broadmead's reply was sceptical: 'From your account it seems to be a pretty rotten film and I agree that the depiction once more of scenes of bloodshed and political travail in Indian is objectionable, especially if episodes reminiscent of incidents in the Mutiny are included'. But he was not sure that a rival film from Britain would be worthwhile, especially as British film companies' commercial objects would not be served by a race with Warner Brothers 'merely to please some Department of His Majesty's Government or the Government of India'. And Warner would not necessarily halt production upon the news of a rival film, even if it were possible. Broadmead suggested instead that Evans should deal directly with the Company. Since he had been consulted on a technical point, he could even ask to see the script officially, rather than have it surreptitiously slipped to him, but of course Evans would be the one who had to decide. And he could suggest modifications, especially with a view to the sensitiveness of Indian opinion.[15]

The Foreign Office's America Department concurred: 'We agree with you that an approach to the British film industry with a view to the production of a rival film on the same subject would serve no useful purpose'. But they added: 'We have thought it worth while however to inform

[13] IOR: L/PJ/8/127, ff. 180–181.
[14] IOR: L/PJ/8/127, ff. 180–181.
[15] Broadmead to Evans, 17 January 1936, IOR: L/PJ/8/127, ff. 182–183.

the British Board of Film Censors very informally that Warner Brothers may be putting such a film into production. The Board, which as you doubtless know is now presided over by Lord Tyrrell, is, of course, a body entirely independent of government control and in fact represents a voluntary censorship created by the trade themselves. At the same time they are always very willing to listen to any views expressed by government departments and in the present instance have undertaken to scrutinise the film in question for any objectionable features'.[16]

Apart from these informal mechanisms of what might be called precensorship or self-censorship, there were of course measures in place to stop things getting out of hand closer to the point of contact with actual audiences. The Indian Cinematograph Act of 1918, as modified up to 1934, provided for licensing of places for 'exhibition by means of a cinematograph'—the licensing was to be provided by the District Magistrate, or in a Presidency town or in Rangoon, the Commissioner of Police. The Act required provisions for 'the safety of persons attending exhibitions therein'. Films had to be 'certified as suitable for public exhibition' by bodies appointed by Local Governments. And even after certification, films could have their certificates suspended and thereby count as uncertified films that could not be exhibited.[17]

The film was, of course, produced, starring Errol Flynn and Olivia de Havilland, and directed by the Hungarian *émigré* Michael Curtiz: his directorial instruction on that set, 'Bring on the empty horses', has become the stuff of Hollywood legend.[18] The film's fate in India was not without hiccups. *The Charge of the Light Brigade* was banned in the Central Provinces by the government in 1936, with the Mutiny-reminiscent incidents deemed 'derogatory to Indian self-respect'.[19] Mr. Peel at the India Office thought the Government of India was being 'a little unduly sensitive',[20] while an objection was raised that 'Suristan', the fictional

---

[16] Foreign Office, America Department, letter to Chancery, British Embassy, Washington, 20 March 1936 replying to letter of 17 January. IOR: L/PJ/8/127, ff. 160–161.

[17] Government of India, Legislative Department, *The Cinematograph Act, 1918 (II of 1918) (as modified up to the 15th March, 1934)*. Published by Manager of Publications, Delhi. Printed by the Manager, Government of India Press, New Delhi, 1934. Copy in file, IOR: L/PJ/8/127, f. 168 ff.

[18] David Niven, *Bring on the Empty Horses* (London: Hamish Hamilton, 1975).

[19] IOR: L/PJ/8/127, ff. 120–123; plot summary ff. 124–124v.

[20] IOR: L/PJ/8/127, f. 132.

country of the plot, was liable to be identified with 'the country of the swine' (if 'sur' was pronounced as 'suar') and therefore would be offensive to Muslim sentiment.[21] The phrase was consequently deleted and the massacre sequence was reduced by half. One reference to the North West Frontier was also replaced by the phrase 'Frontier'. Shots of horses falling were modified, and the British Board of Film Censors' letter exclaimed: 'and I cannot believe that anyone can take exception to the film as now edited'.[22]

The trouble with foreign films was that they could not be subjected to the jurisdiction and censorship of the Government of India or the India Office unless they were sought to be shown in India. Such was the fate of two German films of the time, *Der Tiger von Eschnapur* (1938) and *Das indische Grabmal* (1938) (*The Tiger of Eschnapur* and *The Indian Tomb*): since they had not applied to be shown in India, official concern with them was minimal, merely noting their existence. Occasional enquiries or complaints from private persons, officials, or unofficial organizations had to be turned away for those reasons. One complaint, that there had been a film crew clandestinely shooting footage of the Haj in Mecca in defiance of the laws of the Hedjaz, and that the Saudis had already complained against its showing in Egypt, was met with a profession of helplessness by the British Board of Film Censors: no such film had applied for classification, although it was possible that the footage might turn up in 'topical films'.[23]

Other films had their sensitive portions duly excised: *Sacred India*, showing various Indian themes that the missionaries found abhorrent, based on a book by one Father Lhand [sic], in 1938, dealing with the caste system, had several deletions made and was passed with a 'U' ('Unrestricted') certificate. Deletions included 'all scenes of mongoose and cobra'; 'all scenes described as "Poudjah" ["Puja"]'; 'All scenes of incineration, showing body being stripped of jewels, and monkeys and vultures feasting on the remains'; 'All shots of the mummified body of Saint Francis Xavier, in his coffin'; 'All shots of natives showing the ravages of

---

[21] IOR: L/PJ/8/127, f. 132.

[22] British Board of Film Censorship letter, 24 December 1936, IOR: L/PJ/8/127, f. 138.

[23] IOR: L/PJ/8/127: Pilgrimage to Mecca 1936: Foreign Office letter, 3 September 1936, ff. 106–108 to Peel, India Office. BBFC to Peel, 9 July 1936—no such film has been submitted for censorship. But footage might be used in topical films—signed J. Brookes Wilkinson. f. 109.

leprosy'.[24] Still, others were offensive less to Indian audiences 'out there' than to those who ruled them. One film, *Voice of India*, by Paul L. Hoefler, in 1935, was amended by its makers to be less objectionable. The summary by Evans, the British Empire's man in Hollywood, showed the film to be not really offensive.[25] But it included a fictional character, a disguised intelligence officer who travels with the entourage in India. The British Consulate in Los Angeles complained, rather disingenuously, that the film gave 'a false impression that espionage and unpleasant and obscure methods of censorship are practised in India'.[26] Which of course they were.

It was of course not only films made outside India with pseudo-Oriental colourings that made colonial officials uneasy. *Shiraz* (1928), produced by and starring Himansu Rai and directed by the Bavarian Franz Osten, director of *The Light of Asia* (1925), on the life of the Buddha, and the landmark *Achhut Kanya* (1936) addressing the question of untouchability, ran into trouble because of its treatment of a sensitive theme. A fictionalized account of the building of the Taj Mahal, *Shiraz* depicts the eponymous hero as a blind potter who designs the famous building because he was secretly in love with the Empress, Mumtaz Mahal; when the Emperor Shah Jahan wishes to blind the potter-architect who must not be allowed to surpass his wondrous creation in his next building, it is discovered, to the astonishment of all, that Shiraz is already blind.[27] This story was met with several complaints from 'Mahomedan' opinion before the film had been shown or presented to the Bombay Board of Film Censors. One indignant letter declared 'Shiraz the designer of the Taj Mahal and the alleged lover of Mumtaz Mahal only exists in the imagination of the author and one cannot trace any mention of him in history. That a lady of such dignity, purity, and piety, should be blackmailed by a modern writer to make the story attractive, is simply scandalous'.[28] The film had taken up considerable space in the discussions and report of the Indian Cinematograph Committee of 1928, in particular as a model

[24] IOR: L/PJ/8/127, f. 223.

[25] IOR: L/PJ/8/127, ff. 87–88.

[26] F. E. Evans, Consul, to Hoefler, 31 October 1935, IOR: L/PJ/8/127, ff. 79–80, 31 October 1935.

[27] See Gerhard Koch, *Franz Osten's Indian Silent Films* (Delhi: Goethe-Institut, 1983).

[28] Ghazanfar Ali Khan, M. L. A., Mehr Shah, to Home Member, Government of India, Delhi, n.d., Maharashtra State Archives [MSA]: Home (Political) file no. 236, 1928–29, f. 15.

example of Indian capital being used in the financing of Indian cinema.[29] But various other letters of this tone were received; in some cinemas, missiles were hurled at the screen when the film was shown.[30] The film had its certificate revoked in 1929.[31]

H. G. Rawlinson's handwritten note in the file, agreeing with the 'Mahomedans' and based on plot synopses rather than a viewing of the film, deplored the fact that Mr. Himanshu Rai, the Indian producer of the film, had made an Indian film every bit as full of 'depravity' as 'Western' films. He believed the film should have been banned by the censors in the first place, and was particularly horrified that a Muslim princess, of noble birth, and who by rights should not have been in the company of men at all, should be associated with a 'low-caste potter'. 'To pursue the parallel', he wrote indignantly, 'we might say that St Paul's Cathedral was designed, not by Sir Christopher Wren, but by a chimney-sweep'.[32] The film was, therefore, an 'uncertified film' in the whole of the Bombay Presidency, the United Provinces of Agra and Oudh, Assam, and several other Provinces besides.

5.3. Public Sentiment and Diplomatic Organization

The principles that protected Indian public sentiment—usually, of course, represented by an organized group—from being offended by films were also sought to be used by foreign governments desirous of maintaining control of public relations and propaganda in foreign countries.

In 1934, the Acting Consul General for Germany complained that the film 'Hitler's Reign of Terror', produced in the United States, was 'most objectionable from the German point of view' and requested the Board of Censors to 'prevent its exhibition'.[33] The solution was to leave it as an

---

[29] Indian Cinematograph Committee Report 1928.

[30] *Times of India* report, MSA: Home (Political) file no. 236, 1928–29, 23 May 1929, f. 19.

[31] S. G. Panandikar, Secretary, Bombay Board of Film Censors, to the Secretary, Government of Bombay, Home Department, 16 July 1929, MSA: Home (Political) file no. 236, 1928–29, ff. 29–31.

[32] Dated 3 August 1929, MSA: Home (Political) file no. 236, 1928–29, ff. 49–53.

[33] MSA Home Political File 141 of 1934. 'Cinema films: "Hitler's Reign" or "Hitler's Reign of Terror": Request by the German Consul General, Calcutta, that action be taken to stop the

uncertified film; under Sub-section (7) of Section 7 of the Cinematograph Act, 1918, as amended by the Cinematograph (Amendment) Act, 1919, the film 'shall be deemed to be an uncertified film in the whole of the Punjab'.[34] The Bombay Government followed the Punjab's lead as 'We have not got a synopsis of the film and so cannot satisfy ourselves of the Consul General's view that the film is objectionable from the German point of view'.[35] Under Sub-sections (6) or (7) of above, any action could only be taken for a certified film, and nothing could be done for an uncertified film.[36]

Other complaints of the same generic nature followed: the film 'Too Tough to Kill' elicited a complaint by the Consul General for Italy at Calcutta in 1936, and the film 'Everything is Thunder' by the Consul General for Germany at Calcutta in the same year.[37] On the latter, the German Consul wrote, 'The film is most offensive to German sentiment. All German soldiers, police and civilians are shown in this film as being of a most detestable type and open to all sorts of bribery. The only German person of an attractive appearance is the heroine, who however commits an act of high treason'.[38] On the former, the Italian Consul wrote, 'the said film is offensive to the dignity of the Italian Nation for the character of some Italians represented in it. My Government will appreciate it very much if, in case the distribution cannot be avoided, the Censor Boards of the different Provinces of British India be instructed to suppress those most humiliating scenes in which some characters figure and act in a manner absolutely contrary to the historical reality of the Italian Nation'.[39]

Here, technicalities came to the rescue of British Government officials. C. W. A. Turner, Chief Secretary to the Government of Bombay, wrote

exhibition of the ___ entitled ___'. Letter from Acting Consul General for Germany, E. von Selzam, 3 Lansdowne Road, Calcutta, dated 13 July 1934, f. 3.

[34] J. W. Hearn, Home Secy to Govt of Punjab, dated 18 August 1934. MSA Home Political File 141 of 1934, f. 11.

[35] MSA Home Political File 141 of 1934, f. 18.

[36] MSA Home Political File 141 of 1934, f. 19.

[37] MSA, Home Political File 83 of 1936–37.

[38] von Selzam, from 26, Lee Road, Calcutta, 10 October 1936, MSA, Home Political File 83 of 1936–37, f. 9.

[39] G. Sollazzo, Royal Consul General for Italy, 2 Camac Street, Calcutta, 12 August 1936, to Secy to Government of India in the Foreign and Political Department. MSA, Home Political File 83 of 1936–37, f. 3.

in response to the German Consul General's letter that 'the action of the Consul General in addressing the Government of a province other than the province in which he is stationed, is in contravention of the orders of the Government of India in the Foreign and Political Department'. Nevertheless, the Bombay Board of Film Censors would have a look at the film; it was clear that as far as possible, these complaints were not to be taken too seriously, though officials were careful in noting that in general a film offensive to the national sentiments of other nations should not be passed for viewing.[40]

Sensitivity towards film portrayals of Germany and Germans was not entirely a Nazi phenomenon. German consuls of the Weimar Republic had also had occasion to be offended by film portrayals of Germany and Germans, objecting mostly to the ridiculing of German militarism in the 1920s. In 1927, a German Consul even found Charlie Chaplin's *Shoulder Arms* (from 1918) objectionable on the grounds that it made fun of the former Kaiser and of Field Marshall (now Reichspräsident) Hindenberg. Officials commented that the film had been regularly shown since 1918, and was hardly to be taken seriously, implying a sense of humour failure on the part of the German Consul. It was however noted that the First World War was a sensitive issue; that in the interests of improving relations with former enemies, this should be taken into account; and that war films were falling in popularity in Britain, which might be the reason encouraging distributors to try their luck with such films in India.[41] *Shoulder Arms* was therefore reviewed and passed for viewing 'after excision of certain incidents which might be deemed likely to give offence to a patriotic German'.[42]

In 1937, the US film *The Road Back*, based on Erich Maria Remarque's novel of the same name, was the subject of the German Consul's attentions:[43]

[40] C. W. A. Turner, Chief Secy to Govt of Bombay, Political and Reforms Dept, to Chief Secy, Govt of Bengal, on the German Consul General's request, f. 10.

[41] MSA, Home Political File No. 206 of 1927, Consul's letter, 24 May 1927, f. 35.

[42] Chief Secretary to the Government of Bombay, Political Department, to Consul for Germany at Bombay, 16 September 1927, f. 85.

[43] MSA, Home Political File No. 239 of 1937.

The film, by several cleverly introduced scenes, is designed to represent the Germany front soldier and the German people in a despicable manner. Intentionally, individual fates and characters are shown which are meant to be typical and to give the impression to the spectator that the conditions and characters described in the film are generally applicable in Germany. The film is most objectionable from the German point of view as it signifies an insult to the German front soldier and deeply hurts German feeling. On behalf of my Government, I have the honour to ask you to prohibit a public exhibition of this film.[44]

By 1937, British Indian governments had begun to feel more confident about dealing with such consular objections: the Bombay Censor Board found 'nothing objectionable' about the film.[45] And about that time, there were also the first stirrings in the British Indian establishment that the Nazis were an international danger. About a year later, the state administration finally awoke to the danger of National Socialist organizations in India, and to their Indian representatives. They could rely in the first instance mainly on the very organizations they had regarded as enemies for so long, the communist and left press in India, and they began tapping into these information networks and reading these publications. There began, therefore, an arms-length collaboration between communist and socialist publications and the police and intelligence organizations that had persecuted them for so long.[46] The *Bombay Sentinel*, one such publication that pointed out the Nazi networks and their activities in India regularly, reported that *The Road Back* was of course the sequel to *All Quiet on the Western Front*, and the sub-heading read 'Famous Film that Nazis Threatened to Sabotage To Be Screened on Armistice Day'.[47] The article made it known that the German Consul had made what they

---

[44] Deutsches Konsulat, Bombay, 6 November 1937, Consul for Germany to Sir Charles Turner, Chief Secy to the Govt of Bombay, Political and Reforms Department, MSA, Home Political File No. 239 of 1937, f. 1.

[45] MSA, Home Political File No. 239 of 1937, f. 5.

[46] It was not clear to what extent the collaboration was acknowledged: surveillance methods aimed at controlling leftist networks were now employed in tapping into the leftist networks' own intelligence, while not a few of these leftist networks' publications dropped broad hints to government agencies as to who the Nazis in India were. See Benjamin Zachariah, 'Nazi-Hunting in India on the Eve of the Second World War', in *An Imperial World At War*, ed. Ashley Jackson, Yasmin Khan, and Gajendra Singh (Aldershot: Ashgate, 2016), 159–175.

[47] *Bombay Sentinel*, 10 November 1937, clipping in MSA, Home Political File No. 239 of 1937, f. 11.

regarded to be an ideological complaint from a Nazi perspective against the film's anti-militarism, and that the film was not anti-German per se.

And yet, the government's and the Bombay Censor Board's gentle cultural respect for Nazi sensibilities was maintained in several instances. The documentary 'Inside Nazi Germany', part of the *March of Time* series from the United States, was at first certified in 1938 despite an initial consular objection (which the Consul later withdrew despite continuing to claim the film was 'one-sided'), and then in 1940, it had its certificate withdrawn because it was not desirable to show the film 'at the present time', with more specific reasons not given.[48] The film *Confessions of a Nazi Spy* was dealt with very gingerly, being passed by the Bombay Board of Censors subject to the same cuts that the British Board had asked for—in particular, all direct references to the Führer that were likely to offend were considered necessary to cut; the Bombay Board, nevertheless, considered the film 'courageous'.[49] The Home Ministry of the Bombay Government was now under Provincial Autonomy (as a consequence of the Government of India Act of 1935) in the hands of an Indian elected government, and the Home Minister, K. M. Munshi, was a right-winger with proto-fascist sympathies; however, it is not known to what extent he handled these enquiries himself, though the Warner Brothers representative of *Confessions of a Nazi Spy* wrote to him on the question of the passing of the film for exhibition.

The Nazi Consul's objection to the film included the fact that it was 'produced by the notorious communist Korda' and was a

> typical example of the most unscrupulous and vile anti-German propaganda and, by a mass of outrageous lies and baseless accusations, is designed to degrade and insult the people and the Government whom I have the honour to represent, in the eyes of the world, and to incite ill-feeling and hatred against them.[50]

---

[48] MSA, Home Political file no. 267 of 1940; MSA, Home Political File No. 188 of 1938–40.

[49] MSA, Home Political file no. 247 of 1939–40. On anti-Nazi films made in the United States, see Thomas Doherty, *Hollywood and Hitler 1933–1939* (New York: Columbia University Press, 2013).

[50] Consul to Chief Secy, Govt of Bombay, Political and Services Department, 3 July 1939, MSA, Home Political file no. 247 of 1939–40, ff. 39–40.

He referred darkly to the world's political situation being 'none too good' and suggested that the British government ban the film to demonstrate its good intentions towards Germany.

Here, the officiating secretary to the Bombay Board of Film Censors replied directly to the Consul General that the Board had certified the film not on its own responsibility, but 'under orders of the Government of Bombay'. He further stated that the film had been passed in the version passed by the British Board of Film Censors, that all objectionable references to Hitler had been removed from the film, and that 'the director Alexander Korda has nothing to do with its production'.[51] The German Consul General replied that this was a mistake; he had meant 'the communist Kortner'.[52] He later wrote, somewhat cryptically:

> The german people, with their high standard of culture and education, will take offence at certain things which, by other standards, are looked upon as matter of course and quite proper—and vice versa.[53]

The *Bombay Chronicle*, another newspaper that watched Nazi activities in India closely, felt that *Confessions* was a very important film and that Nazi objections to it were natural given how close it was to the truth: ' "Confessions of a Nazi Spy" comes out at a time when the eyes of the democracies have been opened to the dangers of a regime in Europe which has surpassed everything in the form of ruthless oppression'.[54] The writer described Germany as a place where 'large portions of humanity, who have given up the right to think and act individually and who behave like dumb driven cattle, pushed on wherever the whims of their Fuehrer will lead them'.[55] The *Times of India*, conservative and pro-British, pointed

---

[51] V. N. Pai to Consul General for Germany, Bombay, 5 July 1939, MSA, Home Political file no. 247 of 1939–40, f. 47.

[52] Consul-General for Germany to V. N. Pai, 6 July 1939, MSA, Home Political file no. 247 of 1939–40, f. 53.

[53] Consul-General for Germany to Chief Secretary, Govt of Bombay, Political and Services Department, 12 July 1939, MSA, Home Political file no. 247 of 1939–40, f. 59.

[54] *Bombay Chronicle*, 13 July 1939, review by D. F. Karaka, clipping in MSA, Home Political file no. 247 of 1939–40, ff. 67–69.

[55] *Bombay Chronicle*, 13 July 1939, review by D. F. Karaka, clipping in MSA, Home Political file no. 247 of 1939–40, ff. 67–69.

out that the film was based on US Federal agent L.G. Turrou's book entitled *The Nazi Spy Conspiracy in America*, which in turn was based on his
investigations.[56] Comments on the cultural sensitivity argument also did
not resolve in favour of the German Consul-General's position:

> Incidentally, it is significant to note that while the Consul-General
> wants this film to be banned in India, his own countrymen have pro-
> duced and are showing to the world scandalously anti-Indian films like
> 'The Indian Tomb' and 'The Raja [sic] of Eschnapur'![57]

A letter to the editor concurred.

> I have not noticed the leaders of Nazi Germany being over solicitous
> for the sentiments of the many nations they vilify and castigate with
> their vitriolic rantings and brayings. There are many passages in 'Mein
> Kampf' that deeply wound the sentiments of the peoples of India and
> seldom a day passes without the German State-controlled press hurling
> abuse, in some form or another, at the British Empire.[58]

During the discussions on the *Confessions*, war broke out in Europe,
changing the ground rules;[59] it is possible that the ruling that withdrew
certification from the film *Inside Nazi Germany* was more concerned
with the anxieties of the war than with protecting the Nazi reputation in
wartime India. A revised version of the *Confessions*, with material dealing
with Nazi fifth columnists in Norway, Belgium, Holland, and France, was
certified in 1940.[60]

---

[56] *Times of India*, 17 August 1939. Clipping in MSA, Home Political file no. 247 of 1939–40, no
ff. nos.

[57] *Bombay Chronicle*, 19 August 1939. Clipping in MSA, Home Political file no. 247 of 1939–
40, no ff. nos. The title should have been *The Tiger of Eschnapur*.

[58] Letter to the editor, signed 'Naziphobe', *Bombay Chronicle*, 19 August 1939. Clipping in
MSA, Home Political file no. 247 of 1939–40, no ff. nos.

[59] Note, MSA, Home Political file no. 247 of 1939–40, f. 80.

[60] V. N. Pai to J. M. Sladen, Secy, Govt of Bombay, Home Department (Political), 29 November
1940, MSA, Home Political file no. 247 of 1939–40, f. 95; and J. M. Sladen's reply to Pai, 4
December 1940, MSA, Home Political file no. 247 of 1939–40, f. 101.

5.4. Conclusions

In these attempts to smooth the way for the public in the matter of not being offended, 'sentiment' was the operative category, which was considered self-evidently subjective. By 1939, the Home Department of the Government of India and the India Office had agreed on guidelines and definitions on what was to be considered offensive in a film that had to be shown in India:[61]

> Films to which objection is likely to be taken include:
> (1) those that are based on episodes in British Indian history or stories in the Kipling tradition;
> (2) those which show quarrelling or fighting between Europeans and Indians or between Hindus and Mohammedans;
> (3) those in which Indian religious or social customs are brought into ridicule or contempt: for example, films tending to over-emphasize the backwardness of certain classes in India or giving undue importance to social abuses or primitive customs which are not fairly representative of India as a whole;
> (4) those in which an Indian is portrayed as the villain and a European as the hero; and
> (5) in general, films which depict Indians as an inferior race with a 'slave mentality' cringing to and dominated by a superior white race.

> In this connection, I am to explain that the fact that a film will not be exhibited in India is not in Indian opinion the end of the matter. What Indian sentiment particularly objects to is the lowering of India in the eyes of the world, and the exhibition in other countries of films which would not be tolerated in India arouses for that reason no less sentiment.[62]

The issue was framed as relating specifically to whether Hollywood producers might be making films that for various reasons were offensive to

---

[61] IOR: L/PJ/8/126: 'Films Offensive to Indian Public Opinion: General Policy', file dated October 1935–May 1940. Home Dept, G/I letter to Secy, Public and Judicial Dept, India Office, London, dated Simla, 2 June 1939, ff. 21–24. Signed by the Deputy Secretary to the Government of India.

[62] IOR: L/PJ/8/126, ff. 23–24.

Indian audiences (and by this time, Kipling was quite apparently acknow-ledged to be offensive to Indian 'sentiments'), but there was also a concern expressed as to the maintenance of dignity in the depiction of the British rulers of India. It was clearly understood that while the India Office could not dictate what Hollywood produced, the Government of India recom-mended that it be made clear to Hollywood producers, *inter alia* through the British Consul in Los Angeles, that a Hollywood studio might clearly expect that an Indian ban on one of its films might affect the subsequent distribution of its later films; this was especially the case now that certifi-cation was in the hands of the Provincial Governments, elected under the Government of India Act of 1935, with ministerial responsibility in the Provinces in the hands of elected Indians.[63]

It might be possible, reading this, to forget that this protection of the 'sentiment' of Indians was in the hands of an imperial power in whose interest it lay to assuage the sentiments of a population it ruled—as a mechanism of control. No very firm or grounded idea of the 'sentiment' or 'customs' being protected was required for this exercise. This may be obvious, but it is worth reiterating for at least three reasons: one, the pres-ence of a fascist government in India that operates as I write this with a very reductive idea of 'Indian culture' drawn from that colonial period, and relies on its ability to present that culture as ancient and eternal; two, social scientists' apparent inability to function without some idea of cul-tural boundedness, even as they accept that they are themselves major contributors to framing those 'cultures'. Thirdly, of course, there is the question of the value of closely monitoring cinematic 'history', not for its accuracy or inaccuracy (which always appears as a secondary argument), but for its ability to offend 'sentiment'. This again is a worthy predecessor to present-day moral panics about books, films, or any other depiction of character or characters purporting to be historical and which similarly offend 'sentiments'.

---

[63] IOR: L/PJ/8/126, f. 22. This story was picked up by the film press in Britain, and a clipping from *To-Day's Cinema*, 80–82 Wardour Street, issue of 1 July 1939, was filed at f. 38 as evidence of the message being disseminated to the industry.

PART III
POSTDISCURSIVE
POSSIBILITIES

6

Moving Ideas and How to Catch Them

This is a set of reflections on the moving of ideas, and of the practical difficulties a historian has in tracking them across the usual national, linguistic, or 'cultural' boundaries. At one level, such an exercise must be a set of methodological reflections, but such reflections must be grounded in the specifics of particular historians' projects; I therefore attempt to ground these reflections in examples from my own work and concerns. In an academic context wherein we are now in a world of 'trans'-formations, as we abandon the comforts and mythologies of national and statist histories, and might still wish to resist the blandishments and glossy catalogues of 'transnational', 'global', and 'cosmopolitan' ones, we might wish to ask whether the aspirations contained in these projects are impossible to accomplish, or whether we might find the beginnings of a set of approaches via a struggle with the meagre methodological, textual, archival, or critical resources at our disposal.

The assumption of boundaries to moving ideas based on language, 'nation', 'culture', or 'community' are most often not the experiences of contemporaries but the retrospective assumptions of historians and the divisions of historiographical specializations. Ideas are notoriously bad at respecting boundaries, and to catch a moving idea, we need to unlearn many of our specializations. I have not attempted here to survey all the relevant literature that might be applicable to histories of moving ideas, in South Asia and elsewhere; nor have I analysed all attempts to import or instrumentalize the 'great theorists' of the current era in one or another field of study into South Asian, Indian, 'peripheral', or 'global' intellectual history. Such (mostly destructive) criticism sets up false oppositions and gives the work cited more importance than it deserves to have in its own right,[1] and I must add in this context my apologies to

---

[1] Two books that made their appearance shortly after the public debut of this chapter as a conference paper (in Heidelberg in 2012) are Samuel Moyn and Andrew Sartori, eds., *Global Intellectual History* (New York: Columbia University Press, 2013); and C. A. Bayly, *Recovering*

Herr Eugen Dühring, among others, whose name lives for evermore in Friedrich Engels' engagement with his work.[2] This is more of a set of excerpts from a historian's notebook on matters that he has found useful in his own work: mostly notes to himself and, then again, mostly notes on how not to do things. Two questions dominate the reflections contained in this chapter: how to read the material we have, and how to find material that might be relevant to read. These are not questions that are easy to separate.

6.1. In Search of an In-Between History of Ideas: Some Methodological Questions

'Man's articulate misery or articulate delight has never been a respecter of frontiers', Peter Gay, in his 1968 book, *Weimar Culture: The Outsider as Insider*, wrote:

> The German Expressionist theatre is unthinkable without the experiments of Strindberg, while German social realism drew on the realistic phase of Ibsen, whose plays were naturalised in Germany well before the First World War. A catalogue of Brecht's foreign sources—though Brecht's poetic diction is purely, superbly German—would have to be long to be at all meaningful, and range from Villon and Rimbaud to such improbable influences as Kipling, and from Chinese lyrics to Augustan satire. Spirits as diverse as Franz Werfel and Ernst Ludwig Kirchner acknowledged the inspiration of Walt Whitman. The philosophical irrationalism of Bergson and the brooding poetic irrationalism of Dostoyevsky appealed to sensitive spirits from the extreme

---

Liberties: Indian Thought in the Age of Liberalism and Empire (Cambridge: Cambridge University Press, 2012). The first suggests to its readers that 'global intellectual history' is 'about insisting on an implicit holism according to which cultural, social, linguistic, civilizational, or geographical boundaries are always occupied by mediators and go-betweens who establish connections and traces that defy any preordained closure'—thereby identifying it as a historian's category. Moyn and Sartori, 'Approaches to Global Intellectual History', *Global Intellectual History*, 9. The second compares 'classical British liberalism' with Indian variants: Bayly, *Recovering Liberties*, Introduction.

[2] Friedrich Engels, *Herrn Eugen Dührings Umwälzung der Wissenschaft* (Leipzig: Drück und Verlag der Genossenschafts Buckdrückerei, 1878), better known to us as 'Anti-Dühring'.

left to the extreme right, who could no longer bear the shape of modernity and were sickened by Wilhelminian culture. In architecture the American Frank Lloyd Wright, the Spaniard Antonio Gaudi, and the Belgian Henry van de Velde supplied the German rebels with most of their ammunition....[3]

We might well question what Gay means by 'purely, superbly German', except as the hyperbole of compliment, or else we might have to acknowledge that the great historian resurrects the boundaries of national belonging even as he denies their relevance; is he suggesting a model in which 'outsiders' contributing to 'Weimar culture' are—for that brief, shining moment—'insiders', but that they simultaneously, according to the teleological logic of nation-states, remain aware of this as an apparent transgression? Do we reify the boundaries we claim to abandon, by marking every border crossing as somehow exceptional? Or do we allow for the fact that what to us seems somehow strange or anomalous was to those who lived through those times perhaps neither strange nor anomalous, but self-evident (can we think back behind the Third Reich as if we suspend for ourselves the knowledge of all that we now know to have happened during that period, and can we therefore see the Weimar Republic as more than a doomed moment sandwiched between the real events of History)? And does Brecht belong so much to Weimar that his years in the United States of America or the German Democratic Republic are relatively insignificant in his life as artist, writer, or human being?

Let us try and relate this more closely to the problem of translational and international intellectual histories (there are views that suggest that intellectual history, a 'history of ideas' and histories of 'thought' or 'thinking' are different things; to that, we can add 'histories of knowledge', but let us leave these distinctions aside for now). For the purposes of this exercise, let us further situate ourselves in the first half of the twentieth century, from its early years to the interwar period. Let us deliberately use the term 'international', bypassing other candidates for the job, such as retrospective views on cosmopolitanism(s), which project particular attitudes and positions onto historical actors, and transnational history or

---

[3] Peter Gay, *Weimar Culture: The Outsider as Insider* (New York: WW Norton, 2001) [1968], 7.

global history, both of which are declarations of self-legitimation on the part of historians who are writing in retrospect.

This (necessarily partial) refusal to partake of the academic terminology of our own times is not merely a gesture towards (a modified) historicism[4] (in that 'international' would have made more sense to the times we refer to), but an attempt not to get entangled in a terminology which might actually distract from meaning. For after all, the same term could mean different things to different people, and different terms could mean the same thing, either to the same people or to different people. 'Internationalism' is not an unproblematic term either, and there were various varieties of internationalism to dispute and discuss: these must be addressed and disaggregated. However, although by now 'international' refers almost exclusively to relations between states, many contemporaries in the interwar period would have used the term to imply loyalties, connections, and solidarities that rejected the division of the world into states, nations, and nation-states: the Third (or Fourth) International was not an organization of a collection of states, though the League of Nations was, and the Third International was in danger of becoming the organization of a state by the time it was put to sleep (we note here the distinction between states—the monopoly of legitimate violence or organ of class rule—and nations: the sovereignty of the people, the claim to the congruence of nation and state).[5]

---

[4] I use 'historicism' here not in Karl Popper's sense of the term, as used in Karl Popper, *The Poverty of Historicism* (New York: Harper & Row, 1961) [1957; the argument appeared under that title in 1944–1945 in the journal *Economica*] or Karl Popper, *The Open Society and its Enemies* (2 vols, London: Routledge, 1945), in which there is an end in the beginning, but in the sense attributed often to Leopold von Ranke on the historian's judgement not being imposed in retrospect on the past (though Ranke was reliant on ideas of God, the German people, or Destiny, among other things: see for instance Leopold von Ranke, *Geschichten der romanischen und germanischen Völker von 1494 bis 1514* (Leipzig: Duncker und Humblot, 1874)), the latter view modified by the understanding that the questions one asks are based on one's own 'interests'; however, a distinction between a contemporary and a retrospective judgement as recognized by a historian is maintained. Problems of retrospectivism and the need for contemporaneous perspectives are stressed both by the Skinner/Pocock a.k.a. 'Cambridge' tradition of intellectual history and the *Begriffsgeschichte* approach, but neither approach seems to reflect much on the role of the historians themselves in their systems of analysis.

[5] Max Weber, 'Politik als Beruf', lecture, Munich University, 1918, reprinted in translation as 'Politics as a Vocation', in *From Max Weber: Essays in Sociology*, ed. and transl. H. H. Gerth and C. Wright Mills (new edn., London: Routledge, 1991), 77–128; the definition appears on p. 78: 'a state is a human community that (successfully) claims the monopoly of the legitimate use of physical force within a given territory'; see also Mikhail Bakunin, *Statism and Anarchy* (1874), VI Lenin, *The State and Revolution* (1918); online at http://www.marxists.org/reference/archive/bakunin/works/1873/statism-anarchy.htm, accessed 29 December 2018 and http://www.marxi

If we are interested here in what we might call intermediate intellectual histories, or an in-between history of ideas, not completely coherent, nor always formulated as philosophically defensible arguments, but as traces or assumptions that show themselves in different forms of communication, we might have to ask a number of supplementary questions to add to that about not respecting frontiers.[6] Is the tracing of the movement of ideas something that is only an elite possibility, tracking down references in footnotes and citations, looking at academic texts and manifestos? Or can the influence of ideas, at a less rarefied level, also be traced and tracked by a historian? If intellectual history is written as the history of successive publications, and the methodology is merely chasing down the footnotes to trace influences and sources, it can of course be resolutely elitist. Can there be a social history of ideas, and through that, a social history of the 'carriers' of ideas? Of the networks that sustain and amplify them?

Another large question has always been to what extent ideas can or should be traced directly or indirectly to actual events, practices, movements, or institutions. Many historical narratives on ideas or ideologically driven movements often focus on activities rather than ideas, activities being easier to trace and ideas always possible to attribute to the historical figures concerned as motive for their activities (although motive and intention remain notoriously opaque to retrospective readings). Zeev Sternhell has written, for instance, on fascism as a set of ideas already in place before the First World War. That it became important in practice only after the Great War is not to suggest that it was entirely a post-war phenomenon, even if its manifestation in movements and its experience of state power was in the post-First World War years. If we are not to take ideas as a part of social movements, Sternhell says, we ignore more than a generation of writings by leading European intellectuals (he says 'European' intellectuals, because Europe is his field of study, but that need not reduce his argument to Eurocentric applicability alone). And he insists that intellectual history is also social history, or in his words,

sts.org/archive/lenin/works/1917/staterev/, accessed 29 December 2018, respectively; on 'nations' see Ernest Gellner, *Nations and Nationalism* (Oxford: Blackwell, 1983).

[6] See Benjamin Zachariah, 'Internationalisms in the Interwar Years: The Travelling of Ideas', in *The Internationalist Moment: South Asia, Worlds and World Views*, ed. Ali Raza, Franziska Roy, and Benjamin Zachariah (Delhi: Sage, 2014), 1–21, for an earlier version of the arguments that follow in this section.

'the relationship between the history of ideas, politics and culture is a direct one'.[7]

The dangers of a teleological reading are clear here.[8] We also need to take into account that some of these ideas did not 'lead to' fascism, were a part, but not always a necessary part, of several fascisms, and in some cases survived their encounter with and incorporation into fascism with their legitimacy only partially compromised, to rise again in different forms—and expressed in different terms.[9] Then again, there is the question of whether ideas only need to be taken seriously when they manifest themselves in practices—in other words, we need only take 'successful' ideas seriously. To my mind, this is a rather instrumental reading of ideas. How coherent has a set of ideas to be before it is considered worthy of study? According to the criteria of coherence and internal consistency, fascism is, for many commentators, not an ideology. According to the criteria of success, only Italian Fascism and German Nazism need to be studied in any depth; and if there are only two examples, the generic category 'fascism' makes no sense—either as a name, for only one group ever called itself 'fascist', or as an idea, because poor imitations and distant engagements are not to be taken seriously. This is especially true with a 'European-ideas-exported-elsewhere' framework: why Romanian fascism has been taken more seriously than Indian fascism cannot be fully explained without acknowledging this implicit framework, which often operates alongside the framework of an 'incomplete-or-improper-reception' of ideas as they leave their European 'natural habitat'.[10]

To this Eurocentric prejudice can be added a (post)colonial-indigenist one, which reinforces the tendency to see 'Europe' or 'the West' on the one hand, and 'Asia', 'Africa', or the 'periphery' more generally on the other as a priori separate spaces. Much of the writing of the 'reception' of 'European' or 'foreign' ideas in India has been overdetermined by retrospectivist or

---

[7] Zeev Sternhell, 'How to Think About Fascism and its Ideology', *Constellations* 15, no. 3 (2008): 280–290; quote from p. 284.

[8] Kevin Passmore, 'The Ideological Origins of Fascism Before 1914', in *The Oxford Handbook of Fascism*, ed. R. J. B. Bosworth (Oxford: Oxford University Press, 2009), 11–31.

[9] See Benjamin Zachariah, 'Rethinking (the Absence of) Fascism in India, c.1922–1945', in *Cosmopolitan Thought Zones: South Asia and the Global Circulation of Ideas*, ed. Sugata Bose and Kris Manjapra (New York: Palgrave Macmillan, 2010), 178–209.

[10] See Federico Finchelstein, *Transatlantic Fascism: Ideology, Violence, and the Sacred in Argentina and Italy, 1919–1945* (Durham & London: Duke University Press, 2010) for a notable avoidance of this problem.

nativist readings about the separation of the 'indigenous' and the 'foreign', a trope that was ironically also common during the colonial period. The formula 'indigenous'-and-'foreign' was also all too often mapped onto the 'spiritual'-and-'material' spheres (Gandhi and the Gandhians); this distinction was more or less continued in a different form in a 'dominance without hegemony' argument in which the 'subalterns' inhabited a separate mental world from elites, colonial, and 'national' (Ranajit Guha),[11] or in another version in which the Indian 'elites' were and are colonized and inauthentic, cut off from the 'true' people and 'their' true 'culture' by virtue of their 'foreign' education and ideas (Ashis Nandy).[12]

Clearly, from this perspective, histories of ideas in use in a space such as India cannot be about the interaction of various strands, taking place in a public domain in which spheres of communication are not separate—the tendency is to assume the relative stability and completeness of a set of ideas coming in from 'outside', and the relative stability and coherence of the 'outside' and 'inside'. When an idea is adapted in usage to something that is not immediately recognizable as the 'original', it is perceived as a 'misreading'.[13]

There is often a sense that an idea has a supposedly recognized form, and so it is easy to assume that it moves in that shape. But ideas develop as they move (in the 1920s, 'communism' was hardly the Stalinized beast that is invoked with the term nowadays, so what was a 'proper' set of communist ideas supposed to look like, especially in conditions of illegality and censorship?). Perhaps they were not 'fully developed' in metropole

---

[11] Ranajit Guha, 'Dominance without Hegemony and its Historiography', in Ranajit Guha, *Dominance without Hegemony: History and Power in Colonial India* (Cambridge, MA: Harvard University Press, 1997), 60–80; Ranajit Guha, 'On Some Aspects of the Historiography of Colonial India', in *Subaltern Studies I*, ed. Ranajit Guha (Delhi: Oxford University Press, 1982), 1–8.

[12] For instance, Ashis Nandy, 'The Political Culture of the Indian State', *Daedalus* 118, no. 4 (1989): 1–26; Ashis Nandy, *The Intimate Enemy. Loss and Recovery of Self Under Colonialism* (Delhi: Oxford University Press, 1983).

[13] One thing to avoid is an 'impact-response theory', as Paul Cohen put it in the 1980s. Cohen had then called for a more 'Sino-centric' approach with an attention to mutual moving together of ideas, and without assuming that the 'West' has an 'impact' on 'China' in any unidirectional sense: there are no stable sets of ideas, and a creative reworking of ideas is not a 'distortion'; he now says that 'Sino-centrism' has led in large measure to forms of indigenism, and that this was not the point he had sought to make earlier. Paul Cohen, *Discovering History in China* (New York: Columbia University Press, 1984); Paul Cohen, 'Revisiting *Discovering History in China*', in *China Unbound: Evolving Perspectives on the Chinese Past*, ed. Paul Cohen (London: Routledge Curzon, 2003), 185–199.

or periphery—unless we wish to claim that we know when an idea is 'fully matured', after which, in the Stalinist sense, those who don't accept that version can only be deviationists or revisionists (at various points in Windmiller and Overstreet's monumental 1950s history of communism in India, the authors express surprise that the Indian party was sometimes out of joint with Moscow; Uncle Joe's version of what world communism and the socialist fatherland should do together was by now triumphant, and accepted even by ardent enemies).[14]

Much of the literature that exists on the movement of ideas between a 'centre' and a 'periphery', then, struggles with an 'original' and 'copy' problem: the original is in a 'centre', such as 'Europe', and the outside world copies it, either properly and correctly, or imperfectly and incorrectly. We have here a more or less ideal-typical model of an 'ideology', which no one actually holds, against which the 'copies' must inevitably be imperfect and ideas always 'flow', if somewhat 'asymmetrically', from the centre to the periphery, both of which are pre-defined and reified. Instead of this, we might want to consider a model of ideas gravitating towards each other—for example, the recognition by Indians of concepts they already considered desirable in European fascisms, which were already to some extent concepts in existence in India, and already sought to be realized in India, though expressed in different terms. Once a successful version of a set of ideas provides a language to legitimate what other versions attempt, the versions gravitate towards the successful variant, not through a top-down *Gleichschaltung* imposed by a state, as in the case of Nazi Germany internally or occupied Europe under Nazi rule, but in a relatively consensual process, where the individual variants retain the ability—and indeed demand the right—to insist on variations.[15] But in the process, nevertheless, something of a change happens to the sets of ideas that come into contact: they recognize one another, borrow from one another, and coordinate their ideological propaganda and publicity, even as the degree of coordination and explicit cooperated must be disavowed in the interests of the unique genius of each particular people, nation, or race.

---

[14] Marshal Windmiller and Gene D. Overstreet, *Communism in India* (Berkeley: University of California Press, 1959).

[15] Benjamin Zachariah, 'A Voluntary *Gleichschaltung*? Perspectives from India Towards a Non-Eurocentric Understanding of Fascism', *Transcultural Studies* (December 2014): 63–100.

Many of the existing narratives on travelling ideas focus on those who led movements, on those who were articulate and active. These are often seen as 'elite' histories; but elite and non-elite are relational categories, statuses can change as people travel through different contexts and one can often lose elite status in cases where one moves context. It is nevertheless expected of persons that they are relatively coherent and consistent in their positions, and it is not always the case that they were: social status is thus not completely transferable, although some abilities (language skills or literacy, for instance) might equip persons better to adapt to and make their way in new contexts. But not all testimony or surviving narrative is necessarily 'elite' either; if it is, relationally speaking, elite, then perhaps there is more to be said on the distance between a leadership and a set of people whose casual and partial engagement with that leadership, or with the environment of ideas in which both operate, is worth studying. These are often the carriers of ideas at a more informal level: whereas an argument made at a consistently philosophical level in a forum dominated by textual exchanges is easier to trace in retrospect, it may well be the least effective way in which an idea can travel.

6.2. Clusters, Framing, Legitimation

In tracing ideas that move across (presumed) boundaries, linguistic, ideological, or territorial, the framing of the (re)presentation of ideas must be taken seriously: these framing statements are made, often in didactic mode, when a text seeks to present an idea, often regarded a priori as 'foreign', to a new audience. The texts themselves are often opaque without the framing statement to explain them. These framing statements are often contained in 'paratexts'[16] that help us situate the author(s), something of their proclaimed communicative intent and the desired outcomes of their communication, which again is illuminative of much more than the content of the text. The political projects sought to be enabled by the text itself are enabled and legitimated by the framing that is suggested by the

---

[16] See Gerard Genette and Marie Maclean, 'Introduction to the Paratext', *New Literary History* 22, no. 2 (Spring 1991): 261–272. Paratexts can include prefaces, introductions, guest forewords, communications among publishers, authors, translators, and distributors, advertisements and their placing, and reviews quoted either in advertisements or in the books themselves.

paratext. This becomes central to the use of the texts by readers as well as by various intermediaries for whom their own roles in the furthering of the didactic project are set out and clarified by the paratext.

In this respect, the by-now proverbial 'autonomy of the text' is matched by an 'autonomy of the paratext', whose programmatic nature makes it important in its own right, apart from the text to which it is attached. In another respect, the paratext seeks to constrain the autonomy of the text by laying out the ways in which the text ought to be read and, therefore, to direct, or often to curtail, the range of readings that might otherwise be available: the author of the paratext, whether or not s/he is the author of the text itself, seeks to maintain authorial control over the dissemination of meanings in the furtherance of particular didactic projects. Here is a case for not passing over the paratext quickly in our haste to get to the text, though of course this should not be a call to ignore the text. There are, however, also instances of the paratexts acquiring a life apart from the texts for which they were intended as paratexts, in these cases becoming texts themselves and even acquiring paratexts in their own right.

These (para)texts, in the Indian context, are to be found in English (the language in which many of these first appear) and in a number of Indian languages (languages into which they are often translated). In paying attention to them, the processes of mediation through which the attempt to domesticate and operationalize 'foreign' ideas,[17] and the processes of legitimation or indices of legitimacy of politics in India, as also the relevant engagements of that politics, can be better understood. Another set of paratexts (acknowledgements, advertisements, and institutional affiliations, for instance) point to the networks that disseminated similar sets of ideas and created the crossovers that enabled the movements and translations of ideas of which we are speaking here. The paratextual material also leads us back to a distinction we have already made between terms and concepts. It is often taken for granted that the same terms in the same language, or in self-evident translation, even when in use in different contexts, are more or less assimilable to one another: or, in other words, that they refer to similar concepts. What is often therefore overlooked is that the same terms might actually refer to different concepts,

---

[17] On 'domestication', see Dhruv Raina and S. Irfan Habib, *Domesticating Modern Science: A Social History of Science and Culture in Colonial India* (Delhi: Tulika, 2004).

and similar concepts might be rendered by different terms. This could happen within a relatively stable linguistic context or time frame if variations such as class or caste context or specialized usage are taken into account. But the question is pertinent in bilingual or multilingual contexts in a significant way.

Let us take the case of an attempt to build a modern political vocabulary during colonial rule. There is, firstly, the question of how particular concepts are received by a group of people adept at using the new language: let us say English, for the sake of our example. These adepts often self-consciously look for parallels or similarities in their language in order to translate the new set of terms and become the mediators of a process of attempted domestication of the new language. In this process, two sets of concepts, in two linguistic milieux, are assimilated to one another and, in the process, gravitate towards one another.

This is of course a simplified model, but it begins to illustrate the problem of equating terms with concepts unproblematically, assuming relatively stable meanings. What we can in fact observe is an attempt to create, in a 'native language', a set of terms that express new ideas from a newly acquired but desirable language. But the semantic range of the neologisms thus found might retain, to users of both languages or to those without access to the new language, something of the old usages, or in the case where the neologism is completely new or appears too artificial, not catch on at all. Equally, concepts are not transferred in some pristine form because they do not exist anywhere in a pristine form, constantly being negotiated and remade. The shift to a new context might result in the same term, in the same language, among one set of users (let us say one particular public domain) being used with reference to a concept that is subtly or significantly different from the concept among another set of users of the same term.

More to the point, terms tend not to be used individually and in isolation, and a historian's search for individual terms or their cognate translations will provide more indirections than directions, given the different uses to which a term can be put. A far better method is to observe how terms cluster together: those clusters of terms might be useful in providing a set of clues to associated ideas and to potential institutionalizations that might not otherwise be visible. Instead of looking at single terms, then, we can observe ways in which clusters of terms operate together, following, leading, or informing practices and meanings in proliferating, interconnected contexts. To take the example of an important 'keyword' from the twentieth century:[18] there is generally a penumbra of ideas that inform conceptions of 'development'. In the Indian case (but not exclusively the Indian case), this would include 'progress', the need to overcome 'backwardness', or the moral nature of 'nationhood'. 'Development' in the 1930s incorporated themes that had earlier been autonomous—'social reform', 'village uplift', 'rural reconstruction', 'rural development', 'constructive work'—many of which had strong moral and extra-economic connotations. Wider moral concerns were equally linked up with the 'village uplift' initiatives of the poet Rabindranath Tagore, Mohandas Gandhi, the Punjab cadre of the Indian Civil Service (ICS),[19] or the Young Men's Christian Association (YMCA), though in different ways. The significance of these debates, even when framed in predominantly economic terms or containing strong claims to economically rational argument, extended well beyond the merely economic. The terms of reference for these debates—'development', 'modernization', 'industrialization', 'backwardness'—contained in them connotations not too far removed from other categories of 'backwardness', which remained scarcely veiled under colonialism. This was not, however, conceived merely in terms of a political problem of 'constructing the nation' (or state), but situated in the context of wider philosophical, social, and moral questions: what 'improvement' consisted in, the conditions of human well-being, the laws of history, the social responsibility of science.[20]

Clusters of ideas can achieve enough weight and significance in the public domain to produce languages of legitimation (or languages of legitimacy), which form the basis of the accepted political rhetoric of public arenas. They define the boundaries of publicly acceptable political behaviour and, therefore, define public standards to which people are expected to conform: a language of politics that becomes inescapable inasmuch as claims to political legitimacy must be made in that language. This creates the basis for public debate and the standards for acceptable action.

---

[18] See Raymond Williams, *Keywords: A Vocabulary of Culture and Society* (rev. edn., 1983) [1976].

[19] See Chapter 4.

[20] See Benjamin Zachariah, 'British and Indian Ideas of "Development": Decoding Political Conventions in the Late Colonial State', *Itinerario* 3–4 (1999): 162–209.

Deviations from such norms need to be hidden, or justified as exceptions, or as only apparent deviations, ultimately assimilable within the bounds of the norms.

Any statement or argument takes place within the framework of a language of legitimacy. In such a context, that language is a resource for making legitimate arguments; to avoid it is to reduce one's effectiveness. But the same individual can be seen to argue within more than a single language of legitimacy. Caution should therefore be used before a historian attempts to attribute ideological persuasions—as 'belief'—to individuals: what we could say is that they identify with a particular set of ideas in public.

6.3. Ideas and the Terms That (Do Not) Bear Them

Let us linger a little longer on the problem of the comparability and compatibility of terminology used to describe ideas. This can, as we have said a few times by now, be confusing, as the same terms might be used by some protagonists in different contexts, for instance, both metropole and periphery, but used for different ideas or different purposes, in different immediate contexts, or vice versa: different terms for the same thing. This is made more complicated in language switches (both literally and figuratively); as terms in different languages or idioms find themselves gravitating towards each other, one needs to develop a vocabulary to express new ideas in the language that is going to be used as the central language of communication, perhaps as a central agitational language, even if the vocabulary originates in or is borrowed from another language, and its resonances in the new language into which it is translated might be different from its resonances in the language from which it is borrowed.

We need to keep in mind not so much the world as a language game, in which we are imprisoned in language alone, but that new experiences and new ideas require innovations of linguistic expression for someone to order and make sense of them. The problem of language thus has several dimensions: in a bi- or multilingual context, there is the question of translations of terms, and the gravitation of similar ideas towards one another, with the resultant transformation of both or all. There is the question of whether the term retains a semantic range that belongs to one group of users, from an earlier usage, whether for a bi- or multilingual set of users, the term retains all of the semantic ranges in all the languages into which s/he now habitually (and unconsciously?) translates the term, whether writer or reader or both can switch between ranges and whether a historian can read the wider semantic range that is relevant for a particular communicative context. Then there is the question of language as legitimation, in the sense of rhetorical register and political vocabulary: of what can be said in public, and to different publics, as opposed to what might be said outside those spaces, among people convinced of one's point of view.

We could summarize the sets of problems we encounter with reference to a number of schools of thought that have been influential in studying ideas. The Skinner/Pocock school of thought stresses close attention to context, intention, and communication in addition to content of a text. Political language, they stress, is always both normative and descriptive, and it is impossible to treat it as transparent across contexts. What is important is to read, from the context in which a statement appeared, what its author intended to say to an audience in his or her own times and spaces.[21] It is to be wondered how helpful these hints are in spaces where there is more than one audience to consider, and where a statement must operate across a number of contexts, linguistic, class, 'culture', etc. Here, different audiences would have their own conventions of reading statements; a stability of meaning cannot be predicted (we need not reduce this to a 'nothing-outside-the-text' argument of infinite possible meanings: not every meaning is plausible, and/but a historian is not going to be able to reproduce an entire set of plausible meanings). In addition, there is the problem of the opacity of intention, as read by the historian in retrospect: what we have is proclaimed intention, according to the normative rules of a given space, and it is a case, as Skinner himself might have put it, of tailoring your argument to fit an available language.[22] Given that intention may even be opaque to the subject himself or herself (if we take on

---

[21] See James Tully, ed., *Meaning and Context: Quentin Skinner and his Critics* (Cambridge: Cambridge University Press, 1988). Political language is both normative and descriptive; 'liberalism', 'pluralism', 'democracy', 'nationalism', etc. are normative claims that seek legitimate political activity (i.e. political claims are made in these terms) but are often in danger of lacking any agreed-upon descriptive content.

[22] Quentin Skinner, 'Language and Social Change', in *Meaning and Context*, ed. Tully, 132.

board anything at all of the psychoanalytic tradition), we are in difficult territory.

Scaling down from entire texts read in context(s), we can agree that words, too, are important, but are they useful as units of analysis?[23] According to the *Begriffsgeschichte* approach pioneered by the editors of the *Geschichtliche Grundbegriffe*, and associated now mainly with the name of Reinhart Koselleck, one cannot understand the politics of a given society without understanding the relevant political concepts or categories through which that politics is rendered intelligible and practised: one must understand the key *Begriffe* with which a society speaks about itself.[24] This, if applied in the way suggested, is elite history, because no 'society' speaks about 'itself' in an intelligible voice with a shared vocabulary; to suggest that it does so is to attempt to create a 'community' beyond fractures of class, gender, social standing—in a word, beyond specific contexts. One might of course suggest that the possible blindness to this elitism is based on the reificatory assumption that a 'society' is a coherent, organic whole—inviting an interrogation of the roots of *Begriffsgeschichte* in National Socialist ideology.[25] The sense that its users can be unproblematically inferred from the *Begriffe* in an assumption about 'society' that is tinged with a sense of the organic unity of the community of users never quite leaves a reader of a number of these texts. Observers of the 'language of the Third Reich' noted that an ideology of fascism could be carried by language; however, we do not always know whether a language of legitimation obligatorily imposed from above is more than the initial shibboleth without which trouble ensues for the

---

[23] See for instance Hans Erich Bödeker, ed., *Begriffsgeschichte, Diskursgeschichte, Metapherngeschichte* (Göttingen: Wallstein, 2002).

[24] On the issues involved, see for instance Reinhart Koselleck's programmatic introduction in volume 1 of Otto Brunner, Werner Conze, and Reinhart Koselleck, eds., *Geschichtliche Grundbegriffe: Historisches Lexikon zur politisch-sozialen Sprache in Deutschland* (8 vols, Stuttgart: Klett, 1972–1993), which many reviewers have pointed out is not entirely in consonance with the approaches of all contributors to the *Geschichtliche Grundbegriffe*. See also Reinhart Koselleck, 'Richtlinien für das Lexikon politisch-sozialer Begriffe der Neuzeit', *Archiv für Begriffsgeschichte* XI (1967): 81–99; and Reinhart Koselleck, 'Begriffsgeschichte and Social History' in *Futures Past*, ed. Reinhart Koselleck, (Cambridge, MA: MIT Press, 1985, transl. Keith Tribe), 73–91 [in the original: Koselleck, 'Begriffsgeschichte und Sozialgeschichte' in Koselleck, *Vergangene Zukunft* (Frankfurt a. M.: Suhrkamp, 1979), 107–129].

[25] See for example James Van Horn Melton, 'Otto Brunner and the Ideological Origins of Begriffgeschichte', in *The Meaning of Historical Terms and Concepts: New Studies on Begriffsgeschichte*, ed. Hartmut Lehmann and Melvin Richter, Occasional Paper No. 15 (Washington, DC: German Historical Institute, 1996), 21–33.

non-user of that language, or whether it makes sense to treat that language of legitimation as if it is somehow 'transparent'.[26]

The inflections of different groups of users of the same *Begriff* need to be grappled with, and of course, a term that has specific specialist uses might be the same term that is in common circulation with a less rigid or wholly different set of meanings (this is something that Raymond Williams, for instance, stressed, in his own understanding of the uses of 'keywords').[27] The problem seems to be one of wanting to map terms too closely onto concepts—perhaps a problem of translation of '*Begriff*', which is both term and concept: the same term could refer to different concepts, and the same concept could be rendered by different terms. The difficulties with the arbitrary sign have not been fully grappled with in this tradition, although *Begriffsgeschichte* makes something of the Saussurean distinction between the synchronic and the diachronic. This is also not a school of thought that can grapple with the problems of translation; there is a certain arbitrariness in its identifying a set of users, and an elitism in assuming that terms have a set of agreed-upon meanings even within the same linguistic context—and language is sometimes too easily confused or conflated with (national) space.[28]

Things begin to look even more tricky if we begin to consider Michel Foucault's idea of a 'discourse' as not what is explicitly said, but the implicit assumptions that confine what we can plausibly think, let alone say, within certain boundaries.[29] How does a historian read the silences without imposing his or her assumptions on the readings? And if we look at Roland Barthes' studies of surrounding sets of semiological significances, of surplus meanings in what he formulated as the hamburger and caviar question (which are not just two kinds of food, but connote a

---

[26] Victor Klemperer, *LTI* (Leipzig: Reklam, 1966) [1946]; Eugen Seidel and Ingeborg Seidel-Slotty, *Sprachwandel im dritten Reich: eine kritische Untersuchung faschistische Einflüsse* (Halle: VEB Verlag Sprache und Literatur, 1961).

[27] Williams, *Keywords*. The difficulty here is the impressionistic nature of Williams' reading; he does not share with the reader the set of texts or utterances from which he draws his conclusions.

[28] An assessment of the possibilities of *Begriffsgeschichte* from the early 1990s stressed 'the extraordinary difficulty of translating the meaning of terms and concepts from one language into another, from one cultural tradition into another, and from one intellectual climate into another': Detlef Junker, 'Preface', in *The Meaning of Historical Terms and Concepts: New Studies on Begriffsgeschichte*, ed. Hartmut Lehmann and Melvin Richter, Occasional Paper No. 15 (Washington, DC: German Historical Institute, 1996), 6.

[29] Michel Foucault, *The Archaeology of Knowledge* (London: Routledge, 1995) [1969].

whole range of things beyond eating), we are indicating our problem of different, coexisting, and overlapping semantic ranges.[30]

We might fruitfully attempt here to make an inventory of the variables we have encountered so far. Language: bi- or multilingual situations and contexts; translations of terms; the connotations and semantic significances of terms in each language; the gravitation of similar ideas towards one another, with the resultant transformation of both. Language: the question of legitimation: what can be said in public, and to different publics. Context, intention, and communication; normative and descriptive content (the Skinner-Pocock debates). The arbitrariness of identifying a set of users, and the elitism of assuming that terms have a set of agreed-upon meanings across social divisions; terms versus ideas (the *Begriffsgeschichte* approach). Roland Barthes and surplus meanings. Michel Foucault and what is taken for granted by contemporaries and what is therefore unvoiced and often unintelligible in retrospect to historians.

6.4. Communicative Contexts and the Pre-Education of the Collective

What, then, do contemporaries know that we cannot know in retrospect? Is there a way we can try to read or hear the unvoiced or the unwritten? And why is it important to try? There is itself a social history to this reading: an unexpected (to us) reading renders a social and intellectual history of a different dimension to the assumptions of cultural intelligibility and elite reception of texts that we have discussed so far. And as a quick counterexample of historians' interpretations of unexpected readings, we might wish to return to Carlo Ginzburg's attempted reconstruction of the 'cosmos' of a sixteenth-century miller from his testimony at his trials before the Inquisition, which could only with difficulty and via the imaginative jumps of the historian be read by the historian from the books the miller is known to have possessed and read: what did the miller

---

[30] Roland Barthes, *Mythologies* (transl. Annette Lavers) (New York: Hill and Wang, 1972) [1957].

know, in what contexts did he process what he read and how can we attempt to know this?[31]

Consider the following scenario: an artistic project in a public building in a small town in Poland, which had once been a synagogue and during the Nazi occupation had been turned into a swimming pool for the German Wehrmacht. The building has survived to the present day as a public swimming pool. No explicit evocation of the building's past as synagogue was required for an artistic project's photograph of a showerhead in the building to invoke Auschwitz quite effortlessly. But it was a showerhead from a cubicle at a public swimming pool.[32] Should it have evoked this? Does it, indeed, invoke this, outside of specific audiences? The connection is obvious to professional historians, even if they are not historians of the Third Reich. But it is also relatively transparent to a far wider audience, who have grown up with images and narratives of the Holocaust. Historical memory is important for the art to work, in order for the context to be present in order to ensure the 'correct' reading. 'History' present(ed) as collective memory—in other words, the importance of historical and conceptual pre-education: Picasso's *Guernica* might be an impressive painting even without the knowledge of the bombing of the market town on 26 April 1937,[33] and is probably read differently when viewed without that knowledge.

These are cases where our pre-education is adequate to the purposes of reading, and is sufficiently congruent with the pre-education of contemporaries whose readings we choose to study (there are also cases where we think it is, but we're missing the fact that it isn't because the worlds of our presents and their pasts appear similar enough for us to make the assumption that it is adequate). And there are cases where the congruence of pre-educations doesn't work quite so smoothly. The satire in Jonathan Swift's *Modest Proposal* relies on a general awareness of utopian and simplistic schemes for 'improvement' and on conditions in Ireland,[34] without

---

[31] Carlo Ginzburg, *The Cheese and the Worms: The Cosmos of a Sixteenth-Century Miller* (London: Routledge & Kegan Paul, 1980) [1976].

[32] Dorota Glowacka, 'Art and Community: Aesthetic Practice as Exposure to the Other', in *Cultural Politics and Identity: The Public Space of Recognition*, ed. Barbara Weber et al. (Berlin: Lit, 2011), 229–243.

[33] Pablo Picasso, 'Guernica', completed June 1937, now at the *MOMA* in New York.

[34] Jonathan Swift, *A Modest Proposal for Preventing the Children of Poor People in Ireland From Being a Burden to Their Parents or Country, and for Making Them Beneficial to the Public* [1729], accessed 27 June 2011, http://www.clintbridges.com/ebooks/swift-amodestproposal.pdf.

which awareness (which we no longer have), satire fails to reach its audience. Satire is of course a genre particularly suitable for enabling a retrospective reader to gauge the contexts in which it needed to be read: the allusions and the wit function only against these contexts.[35] Consider the frustrations of the satirist who fails to reach his audience with the subtlety of his wit and is therefore forced to rail at his audience in passages where the subtlety of the originally deft formulation is re-enacted with the equivalent of a literary sledgehammer, the author forced to explain every joke, lay out the context, and write his piece a second time for an audience that simply doesn't get the picture. That second writing, which we seldom encounter in our sources, is what we must reconstruct.[36] And most often, we have not much with which to construct it.

An implicit language of legitimacy, and therefore a register of ways of framing, is 'collective memory'. 'Collective memory' is a disciplined form of 'remembering'; if the 'collective memory' debate has told us much, it is that the collective creates the memory as well as the memory that creates the collective.[37] For many historians of 'collective memory', the collectivity invoked in memory is the 'nation' or the 'community', often defined through collective victimhood. The custodian of 'collective memory' is therefore the institutionalized collective (the French 'nation', European Jewry, *die Vertriebenen*), retrospectively operationalized, with the historian playing the enabling role of the 'site of memory'.[38] The ways in which these self-proclaimed collectives read their own histories are also prescriptive: there is a relatively small level of variation permissible. This is best illustrated through the failure of some types of disciplining of a collective imagination to come into being even when sought to be institutionalized: the 'working class' as the universal class, shorn of particularisms and acting self-consciously as an agent of historical change, for instance. Some forms of collective memory are in conflict with others, and since the same individuals are claimed by (and must

---

[35] See Hans Harder, 'Prologue: Late Nineteenth- and Twentieth Century Punch Versions and Related Satirical Journals', in *Asian Punches: A Transcultural Affair*, ed. Hans Harder and Barbara Mittler (Berlin: Springer, 2013), 1–11.

[36] Such a case is recounted by Alok Rai, 'The Possibility of Satire: Reading Pratap Narain Misra's *Brāhmaṇ*, 1883–1890', in *Asian Punches*, ed. Harder and Mittler, 65–74.

[37] See Chapter 3.

[38] Pierre Nora, 'Between Memory and History: *Les Lieux de Memoire*', *Representations* 26 (Spring 1989): 7–24.

legitimize themselves through) participation in different and sometimes conflicting communities of collective memory, there are always moments of differently successful collective memories. For the historian of ideas, these differences need to be readable; the work of recognizing and assimilating an idea is done with reference to the needs of a relevant and legitimate collective memory.

The question of legitimate political expression is an important one, especially if your research project deals with banned political movements: since much of the activity of political subversives working against a state or an empire is either illegal or takes place underground or both, it is sometimes hard to find traces of opinions actually recorded, or actually recorded when they go against the grain of the legitimate political language of the time and context. Much of the material that makes its way to us is filtered through a version of what Ranajit Guha called the 'prose of counter-insurgency';[39] only the police and intelligence agencies that gathered the material had an interest in letting the subject speak for himself, not least in pursuit of the legal basis for prosecution. As a result, the 'colonial state' perpetuates different voices: its own, at various levels, which turn out often to be different voices; those of the insurgent, whom the colonial state requires to speak for himself, but who must speak in the formulaic language of the state (or at least in what he understands to be this language) in order to protect himself. This can be seen as 'approver's testimony',[40] or more usefully, a way of gesturing to the requirements of the formulae of communication that protect an individual from the powers of the state that he seeks to resist—a phenomenon that has been examined, for instance, in the conventions of the petition letter.[41] There is thus is a delicate act of sifting to be done by a historian who reads an alleged 'prose of counter-insurgency' in the voice of the state reproduced, or to some extent subverted, by the subject, who himself has to learn to use and reproduce the language that will to some extent formularize the encounter—in order not to speak.

[39] Ranajit Guha, 'The Prose of Counter-Insurgency', in *Subaltern Studies II*, ed. Ranajit Guha (Delhi: Oxford University Press, 1983), 45–88.

[40] Shahid Amin, 'Approver's Testimony, Judicial Discourse: The Case of Chauri Chaura', in *Subaltern Studies V*, ed. Ranajit Guha (Delhi: Oxford University Press, 1987), 166–202.

[41] Majid Hayat Siddiqi, *The British Historical Context and Petitioning in Colonial India* (Dr. M. A. Ansari Memorial Lecture) (New Delhi: Jamia Millia Islamia, 2005).

In a number of situations, the potentially insurgent subject is being examined for what he thinks, not what he has done, because what he thinks is perhaps a clue to what he might in the future do. And since the subject is aware of what he is being examined for, he is able to avoid saying what he doesn't want to—which is of course easier in an interview with a policeman than in a conversation with an informer he doesn't know is one. Either way, the question of what a legitimate language of political expression is, and how to stay on the right side of that line, plays an important role. But given corroborating evidence of what a person said or did, or the circles in which he (or occasionally she) moved, one can read an avoidance as an awareness of what must not be said—which is good information on the context in which any statement had to be placed.[42]

6.5. Some Conclusions

For much of the time, the professional historian's work can consist in disrupting existing understandings of the world, thereby generating the typological cliché of the historian's generic statement: 'it's more complicated than that'. The work of the historian of ideas consists often in resimplifying the more complicated. We might know, retrospectively and ethically, that things are more complicated, but we also know that contemporaneously and emically, things were often deliberately kept simple—and often simplistic. But we also draw together into relative coherence strands that might have been dissociated among contemporaries, its 'logic' only completely visible to us when we have cleaned up the 'noise' around them to give it coherence. Both are important and complementary moves; one is never only, or completely, a fascist or a communist, and one's ideas are never completely coherent or ideal–typical.

We are trained, perhaps, to hear resonances or dissonances with the 'real thing'—and it might well be said that both the resonances and dissonances are the result of seeing the whole to which the part is connected

---

[42] Quentin Skinner, 'Language and Social Change', in *Meaning and Context*, ed. Tully, 119–132. This is not a world of stable political terms in which one has an accepted set of *Begriffe* whose usage one can unproblematically trace: see on this question, though not in the South Asian context, Melvin Richter, 'Reconstructing the History of Political Language: Pocock, Skinner and the *Geschichtliche Grundbegriffe*', *History and Theory* 29, no. 1 (February 1990): 38–70.

in the 'complete' idea. Why are we allowed to assume, however, that these resonances and dissonances are not available to those who do not observe the boundaries that their perception of the resonances and dissonances should lead them to? Had they been academics or intellectuals, they might have taken the time to tell us. But is this a process of selection, appropriation, disassembly, or reassembly, or is it necessarily a failure to 'get the ideas right'? We don't always know whether the protagonists in these in-between spaces, neither academic nor entirely popular, had read the 'real thing' and had decided to use apparently contradictory ideas in a self-conscious or at least deliberate way, or had collected elements in a more accidental way. But if we are interested in a social milieu (which includes, surely, ideas that are commonly held), we need to try and find these ideas in unrewarding sources, and accept their contradictoriness and their inconsistencies, rather than look for the ideas cleaned up and presented in academically compatible forms.

So much of the writing one can read on histories of ideas, or intellectual histories, concentrates on the production of the ideas, and can tell us little or nothing about their reception. Since historians deal with traces, this is often a matter of the serendipitous find: correspondence with an author upon reading his book, for instance.[43] But it does oblige us to help serendipity to find its way, which in practical terms means trying to find archival evidence to back textual reading. The assumption of the self-determined nature of an authored text seems at least to have implicitly survived in historians' readings, despite the trends of the last thirty-odd years; for who, among intellectual historians, would be seen digging in an archive, when texts are so easily available for close reading? This of course is a longer story about the changing nature of historical scholarship itself.

---

[43] See Chapter 4.

7

Travellers in Archives, or the Possibilities of a Post-Post-Archival Historiography

7.1. Introduction

Over the years, the idea of an archive has undergone a number of changes, and we seem to be coming out of a tunnel towards the light of a sudden blinding insight, or at least we ought to be: we need not think of an archive merely as a grand building storing a static state-created collection of self-serving and self-legitimating documents that reiterates and reifies elite and statist perspectives. Perhaps this should be obvious; however, the peaceful co-existence of different kinds of history, with widely divergent views of what a source is, archival or otherwise, and the relationship of that source to what we write, is indication enough that a few clarifications might be in order. My perspective is that of a historian who started off, in area studies terms, as a 'South Asianist', a label imposed rather than earned or claimed, and is now apparently a practitioner of 'global history' or 'transnational history', new labels that I have likewise not been born to or achieved, but have instead had thrust upon me. The advantage of the disciplinary, area studies, and specialization perspectives pulling in different directions, however, have made it possible to map certain trends and disadvantages better.

At least a generation of historians trained in 'postcolonial' forms of history writing had more or less abandoned archives to the more 'traditional' historians, with archives being viewed more or less as a conspiracy of (especially colonial) state power with which the historian must not collude. 'The colonial archive' was the repository of prejudice against the 'native', who was only visible when he (usually he) was a problem, as insurgent, criminal, or savage, and a malaise was diagnosed among historians (especially of South Asia) where they were deemed to be reproducing the assumptions of the archive and/or the authors of its documents. A suggestion that the historian 'read against the grain' of the archive required, of course, an attention to that grain, and therefore some acquaintance with that archive,[1] but very soon the archive, along with 'Eurocentric models' were seen as causes of the oppressive nature of history itself,[2] and by then there was nothing outside the text,[3] and certainly nothing much of value deemed to be in the archive.

If this seems like a caricatured view of the developments in historiography told here in a condensed narrative, I would argue that it is this condensed and caricatured view that was absorbed as received wisdom by much of the historical profession working in postcolonial mode, serving to remind us of the literary origins of postcolonial studies which in turn also gives us license for such a condensed narrative as we now seek to provide for what we now affectionately call PoCo (this sentence should be three or four sentences, but it would then lose its gravitas).[4]

Given that, at least in fields such as South Asian history, the narrow interpretations of transparency that has led to the flouting of the limited rules of archiving that the state has deemed fit to provide (in India, for instance, there is in theory a 50-year rule for the depositing of official records in the National Archives of India), there is no such thing as a 'postcolonial archive' to speak of, there has therefore been less material to 'read against the grain' for the period after formal independence. And the discussions on the nature of historical narrativization suggesting that historians simply made up their stories like every other writer, backing them up with 'truth-claims' made from the 'archive', then directed attention to our strategies of representation rather than at our archives.[5] 'Archive fever'

---

[1] The classic statement of this position can be found in Ranajit Guha, 'The Prose of Counter-Insurgency', in *Subaltern Studies II*, ed. Ranajit Guha (Delhi: Oxford University Press, 1983), 45–88.

[2] Dipesh Chakravarty, *Provincializing Europe: Postcolonial Thought and Historical Difference* (Princeton: Princeton University Press, 2000).

[3] Jacques Derrida, *Of Grammatology* (London: Johns Hopkins University Press, 1976) (transl. Gayatri Spivak).

[4] See Chapter 1 for a less condensed view.

[5] Paul Ricoeur, 'Narrative Time', *Critical Inquiry* 7, no. 1 (Autumn 1980): 169–190; Paul Ricoeur, *Time and Narrative* (3 vols, Chicago: University of Chicago Press, 1984–1987); Hayden White, 'The Question of Narrative in Contemporary Historical Theory', *History and Theory* 23,

was described;[6] 'dust' celebrated;[7] still there was a touch of derision attached to those who actually believed that trying to find archival evidence for a claim was a worthwhile activity. 'The archive' became a monolith and a straw man, even as some historians refused to abandon archives and still others returned to them in self-effacing embarrassment.

It is possible now to discern a slow process of recovery from this post- or anti-archival condition. Perhaps this is an over-optimistic reading (and this is the place to confess that I think archives are a good thing); however, I think that as historians learn to operate with a more active conception of an archive, 'the' archive is revealed to be a rhetorical move rather than a place where documents are deposited, and 'archives' become the body of material we draw upon, or can plausibly draw upon, to answer our research questions—which makes the unusualness of an archive proportionate to the unusualness of our research questions. This modest proposal can serve therefore as a hope and a conclusion. What, then, can you get out of a specific set of sources from particular archives? Before you read your sources, we might paraphrase E. H. Carr as potentially having said read your archive[8]—or rather, we might add, describe it, and in describing it, invent it. I shall explore this question by providing an assessment of the readings I have made as a historian of the archives I have used over the years to answer specific research questions; but here, I shall talk about the archives concerned rather than the research projects that led me to them. Two archives stand out as peculiar archives whose own histories need to be written into the historiography that draws upon them, or specifically two collections, put together by individuals: P. C. Joshi's collection at the core of the Archives for Contemporary History, Jawaharlal Nehru University (JNU), Delhi and the Horst Krüger Nachlass from the remains of the East German Academy of Sciences, at the Zentrum Moderner Orient in Berlin.

---

no. 1 (February 1984), 1–33; Hayden White, *The Content of the Form: Narrative Discourse and Historical Representation* (Baltimore: Johns Hopkins University Press, 1987).

[6] Jacques Derrida, 'Archive Fever: A Freudian Impression', *diacritics* 25, no. 2 (Summer 1995): 9–63.
[7] Carolyn Steedman, *Dust: The Archive and Cultural History* (New Brunswick: Rutgers University Press, 2002).
[8] E. H. Carr, *What Is History?* (Harmondsworth: Penguin, 1990) [1961].

What follows is a brief set of notes in part based on observations in the archives, by which I mean an ethnographic account of academic and non-academic practices involved in the imagining and creating of an archive in addition to archival research, with the added caveat that the methodology of an anthropologist is mostly 'someone told me' added to 'I was there'—one day the archival evidence for some of this might be available, but then we ourselves will be citing our own writing from this period as *Zeitzeuge* and memoirists.

7.2. Archives: Accessible and Private

Given that 'archive' refers both to the space where records are stored and to the records themselves, a certain ambiguity can arise as to which is meant when 'the archive' appears as an entity in a set of writings. In much of this writing, the metaphoric, metonymic, or polemical value of the term 'the archive' relies on the awkward palimpsest of a large official-looking building that embodies the authority, power, and (discursive) violence of the state and the documents it contains being inscribed upon and sharing the power of the building itself. The document or the building, or the document and building together, becomes a metonymy of the state and a metaphor of violence at the same time. While we can, and should, separate the uses and definitions that archivists habitually make about archives from this metonymic-discursive complex that 'the archive' has become in the usage of historians who don't use them, we should recognize that the power attributed to 'the archive' relies on the failure to make these distinctions.

Making such abstract distinctions, however, are seen by many re-searchers who never abandoned their archives as self-indulgent luxuries. In a world that South Asianists in particular (though not exclusively South Asianists) will be familiar with, where so many archives are treated by archivists as their private domain where the researcher is an intruder into their uninterrupted contemplative hours, and where anything sensitive or liable to generate uncomfortable narratives for states or other vested interests disappear into archives' most inaccessible corners, it becomes important to identify ways to make an archive speak to you, and through you, to your (often imagined) readership. By now, historians are acutely aware that all archives are actually engaged in hiding things: sometimes very cleverly, in plain sight, sometimes by making certain things overly accessible to divert your attention from what they do not wish you to see. Many historians, like magpies, can be persuaded to gravitate towards the shiny objects put before them.

All states have had a long history of the 'secret state', whose existence and records were for the longest time not fully acknowledged to exist, but also whose records in their own times were hidden from the non-secret state's operatives, and not just from a larger public. The necessary illusions of democratic transparency by which many of us choose to live give us a sense of archiving practices that are illusory (one needs only to wait for the requisite number of years to elapse and the state will 'come clean' by placing its documents recording its dastardly deeds as well as its benevolent ones on the table before us). Recent times have provided plenty of such examples, where colonial atrocities' records have mysteriously been relocated to spaces whence they do not emerge at the appointed time of 30 years.[9] But democratic states, and still more so democratic archival practices, should not be assumed by historians to exist; different 'democracies' have varied and divergent archiving practices; the 'secret state' is an integral feature of stateness, which makes the 'democratic' part more of a vocabulary of legitimation than a substantive set of transparent or enforceable rights and duties; and there are substantial parts of what might 'normally' conceive as material that belongs in a state archive that, if acknowledged to exist at all, will be withheld from view for reasons of 'state security', or in order to protect the servants of the (secret) state from public scrutiny or opprobrium. Translated into historiographical and methodological terms, what this means is the old axiom that what gets to be archived is far from 'complete', whatever one's view of completeness might be, is still relevant; there are dangers of assuming that the 'logic' of archival practices, proclaimed or implicit, are consistently observed, observable, or readable.

To provide a quick example: the Indian Political Intelligence (IPI) files were not known to exist until their release in 1995; IPI was considered a

---

[9] See for instance https://www.theguardian.com/uk/2012/apr/18/britain-destroyed-records-colonial-crimes?CMP accessed 07.09.2022.

predecessor of MI5 and MI6,[10] and its information on Indian political activities at home and in the wider world, based on testimony gathered by blackmail, the use of secret informants, interceptions of mail, and occasionally by torture, was seldom admissible in a court of law. Magistrates were known to refuse to convict on the basis of secret evidence, and a plea was often made by the government prosecutor that to make the evidence public would be to compromise the source, whereupon the magistrate could simply dismiss the case. Meanwhile, colonial policemen had occasionally to make the trip to London to consult the IPI records, from which they made notes—and even though the IPI records were in part drawn from the police records themselves, it was the collation of police records with various kinds of information the police did not have that made the IPI files worth consulting.[11] The conspiracy of the state archives thus cannot be a conspiracy, and if you are reading 'against the grain' or 'with the grain', part of the excitement of the archive is to learn how to read an archive's grain.

These files have now become central to those who are interested in South Asians abroad in the first half of the twentieth century—and can be delved in by non-South Asianists, in particular those without knowledge of a South Asian language who want some 'transnational' window-dressing. But there were archival resources for this set of themes before. When Mushirul Hasan was the Director of the National Archives of India, he found a cache of files on the travails and movements of Indians abroad in the early part of the twentieth century in his office—and he asked S. Irfan Habib whether he was interested in working on them (the latter suggested that since this was not his current work, the files ought simply to be replaced on the shelves).[12] But this cache explains why ever since Tilak Raj Sareen, still active and travelling among his old contacts from the days of the German Democratic Republic, had been Director of the NAI and had written several slight books on Indians abroad,[13] these

---

[10] See for instance Richard Thurlow, *The Secret State: British Internal Security in the Twentieth Century* (Oxford: Blackwell, 1994).

[11] 'Notes made by Mr. Kidd in London regarding Bolshevism and Indian agitation abroad', West Bengal State Archives (WBSA), Calcutta, IB Sl No 124/1921, File No. 83/21.

[12] Conversation with S. Irfan Habib, Berlin, Summer 2010, reconfirmed in subsequent conversation January 2017.

[13] The least unsound of these is Tilak Raj Sareen, *Indian Revolutionary Movement Abroad (1905–1920)* (New Delhi: Sterling, 1979).

files had vanished from the collection at the NAI, and why so many of us had the experience of ordering files that he and others had once cited and the requisition slip came back with 'NT' on them—the joke was that 'NT' stood for 'not transferred' (the official explanation, meaning that it had allegedly never been transferred from the original government department to the archive), 'not traced', or 'no time'. Coincidentally, a small group of people working on aspects of this phenomenon of political exile had been active in the few years prior to this discovery, and we have collected our slips; should Mushirul Hasan's cache have been listed or catalogued in some way, we'd like to do a comparison of our 'NT' slips with those 'discovered' by Mushirul Hasan. But the route to some, if not all those files, was not altogether closed: they would often surface either at P. C. Joshi's collection at JNU, or at the Horst Krüger collection at the Zentrum Moderner Orient (ZMO), Berlin.

7.3. Joshi, Krüger, and the Communist History Plot That Failed

Puran Chand Joshi (1907–1980) was General Secretary of the Communist Party of India from 1935, when the CPI was still illegal, to 1947. He was therefore, General Secretary for the difficult years of the Second World War, and before that during the Popular Front years—the Indian interpretation of the Dimitrov Line is usually attributed to him. It would seem that Joshi was eased onto the back-burners of the by then slow-burning communist movement after Indian independence and the partition of India—expelled in 1949, and reinstated two years later, Joshi began to take refuge in history. He set himself the task of collecting and collating documents relating to the foundational years of the communist movement and the part played by the Communist Party of India and its fellow travellers and exiles across the world. In doing so, he gathered extensive material from archives mainly in India and Germany on the great movements of the first half of the twentieth century: socialism, of course, with all its contradictory strands; fascism, in its occasional meanderings in and out of socialist thematics and rhetoric; and many entangled strands in-between, caught in the cross-currents of the century's opening decades. This is a collection that is self-consciously pioneering

of a more international history of Indian movements abroad[14]—Joshi collected a large amount of information on Indian activities in Germany, the United States, Japan, and elsewhere—activities of both left and right-wing political engagements, plus an engaging social history of varieties of anti-imperial networks. The histories that he might have written from these strands were never written, although from December 1970, the documents found a home at the newly founded (in 1969) JNU, becoming the core of its Archives for Contemporary History. Joshi himself lived in semi-retirement from political life in JNU for the last 10 years of his life.[15] Had he written his histories of the early years of the CPI under his own name from the documents he gathered, he almost certainly would not have been able to keep his party membership.

Horst Krüger (1920–1989) can be said to have been the senior historian of South Asia in the German Democratic Republic; trained in history and *Germanistik*, among his first published works was a monograph on Prussian manufacturing in the eighteenth century.[16] After a period from 1957 to 1959 as 'Kulturberater an der Handelsvertretung der DDR in Indien' (Cultural Advisor to the GDR Trade Representation in India), he was assigned, from 1960, to be a historian of contemporary India, at the AdW (Akademie der Wissenschaften) and at the Institut für Orientforschung (Institute for Oriental Research)[17] (his West German colleague and younger contemporary Dietmar Rothermund (1933–2020) completed a PhD on the American colonial period in 1959, and only later, in 1968, a *Habilitation* on India: careers in South Asian history in both Germanies were made by Cold War imperatives).[18] When Krüger died in March 1989, his collection of books and papers became

[14] See Ali Raza, Franziska Roy, and Benjamin Zachariah, eds., *The Internationalist Moment: South Asia, Worlds and World Views, 1917–1939* (New Delhi: Sage, 2015)for a sense of these engagements.

[15] Jawaharlal Nehru University (JNU), Archives for Contemporary History (ACH), http://www.jnu.ac.in/SSS/Archive accessed 07.09.2022; Bipan Chandra, 'P C. Joshi: A Political Journey', *Mainstream* XLVI, no. 1 (2007), http://www.mainstreamweekly.net/article503.html, accessed 29 August 2016. Bipan Chandra's history of the CPI in this article is deeply flawed, and no endorsement of those details should be implied by my citing the article here.

[16] Horst Krüger, *Zur Geschichte der Manufakturen und der Manufakturarbeiter in Preußen* (Potsdam: Rütten & Loening, 1958).

[17] https://www.zmo.de/biblio/sammlung_krueger.html, accessed 29 August 2016.

[18] Dietmar Rothermund, *The Layman's Progress: Religious and Political Experience in Colonial Pennsylvania, 1740–1770* (Philadelphia: University of Pennsylvania Press, 1961); Dietmar Rothermund, *Die politische Willensbildung im Indien 1900–1960* (Wiesbaden: Harrassowitz, 1965).

a part of the collection of AdW, and thereafter of the Zentrum Moderner Orient, an institution created from the debris of the East German Academy of Sciences. At a time when the GDR's academic landscape was being remodelled in Cold War revenge format, bits were cut out of the East German Academy of Sciences that were deemed usable in the new dispensation. The ZMO was the site where those deemed useful for the project of 'Modern Oriental Studies', whatever that might have meant in a post-Saidian-critique world (Said's book appeared in 1978; the 'Forschungsschwerpunkt Moderner Orient' was founded in 1992, becoming the 'Zentrum Moderner Orient' in 1996).[19] Krüger's career as a historian of India was not a *Beruf*, a 'vocation', in the sense that it was connected with historical privilege among the *Bildungsbürgertum*; in addition to his days as cultural attaché to a trading delegation, he had earlier been a motorcycle courier for the Nazis during the Second World War (as his interlocutor in India Majid Siddiqui, who shared his joy of motorcycles, remembers).[20]

If Joshi did not to a large extent write what he set out to write, neither, for that matter, did Horst Krüger, though in comparison, he was by far the more productive of the two on the subject of contemporary India and the world. The ideological imperatives of writing in East Germany were often no more than an obligatory set of formulae in the introductory remarks, but writing on India had often to be more clearly delineating of the onward march of India towards a progressive and potentially socialist political order that justified the GDR's special relationship with a non-socialist state—the politics of Cold War friendships were often pre-emptive government-to-government contacts to prevent the other side from cashing in on the need for alliances. As historian of India, Krüger's contribution to the telos of socialist emancipation was a planned four-volume history of modern India, *Die internationale Arbeiterbewegung und die indische nationale Befreiungsbewegung*, of which two volumes saw the light of day: *Indische Nationalisten und Weltproletariat* (1984) and *Anfänge sozialistischen Denkens in Indien* (1985).[21] Krüger was, however,

---

[19] Edward W. Said, *Orientalism* (New York: Pantheon, 1978).
[20] Conversation with Majid Siddiqui, New Delhi, December 2009.
[21] Horst Krüger, *Indische Nationalisten und Weltproletariat: der nationale Befreiungskampf in Indien und die internationale Arbeiterbewegung vor 1914* (Berlin: Akademie-Verlag, 1984); Horst Krüger, *Anfänge sozialistischen Denkens in Indien: der Beginn der Rezeption sozialistischer Ideen in Indien vor 1914* (Berlin: Akademie-Verlag, 1985).

as a practicing historian and quasi-diplomat, a prolific presenter of papers, some of which were published and some of which appear in P. C. Joshi's archive, in some cases at second remove, having been presented first at the Nehru Memorial Museum and Library; there is a good deal of material that he published in various fora that bears the heavy burden of his official hat. For his 'beginnings of socialist thought in India', there were many questionable figures he claimed for the socialist cause—he even argued that the Bengali writer and anti-Muslim ideologue Bankim Chandra Chattopadhyay (1838–1894) had been a socialist in his early thinking, before moving to less progressive themes.[22] For this latter claim, he had the support of no less a person than the philosopher and Marxist Debiprosad Chattopadhyay, with whom he shared a correspondence; it seems that Debi*da* allowed Krüger to make this claim by providing him with the requisite hints as to a selective reading of sources.[23]

The two collections are to a large extent a set of archiving from other archives, with an added insight available in the collections themselves into the politics of access to such other archives, the politics of (non-) writing of the expected research papers or monographs that could have been written from the new collections, as well as a hint of the nature and demands of self-censorship. There are also some interesting overlaps and intersections between the two archives, which indicate the continued co-operation of communists beyond the government-to-government layer that settled into the convenient Cold War lies of the Congress Party in India as a progressive government and therefore a partner-state of the GDR. Some of Joshi's material comes from the Potsdam archives of the GDR, especially on the activities of Indians in Germany; his research assistant Helga Meier was provided by the East German Academy of Sciences.[24] Meanwhile, Krüger, with semi-diplomatic status in India, had access to materials that ordinary mortals like us still do not: the Bombay Police records, which were sent to him as photocopies by order of the

---

[22] Krüger, *Anfänge*.

[23] Debiprosad Chattopadhyay, letter to Horst Krüger, including typed extracts of the book by Bankim Chandra Chattopadhyaya, 'Samya', dated Calcutta, 24 June 1974, in Krüger Nachlass Box 48 No. 352, 1, ZMO, Berlin.

[24] Conversation with Helga Maier-Singh, Zentrum Moderner Orient, Berlin, May 2012; file references from P. C. Joshi's papers: see for example P. C. Joshi's Papers on the League Against Imperialism: File 76: LAI, IML, ZPA, Berlin, 'Support the Indian revolution. Appeal to LAI', *Rote Fahne* no. 104 (6 May 1930). Notes by P. C. Joshi, dictated by Dr. Helga Meier, Berlin, 1967.

Maharashtra Government, for instance.²⁵ A complicated politics of the interaction of movements can be seen here: Krüger represented a state that was seeking to appropriate the histories of an anti-statist internationalism from the interwar years, but Joshi represented a movement that in India was not anywhere near state power. As the interwar anti-statist internationalism became the statist internationalism of the Cold War years, the movement-that-became-the-state, Krüger's GDR, dealt with the state-that-excluded-the-movement, India-without-Joshi. Joshi's archiving-the-movement project could be assisted by Krüger's statist patronage.²⁶

Both archival projects sought to cover the period of the formative years of the twentieth century's greatest movement, the communist movement. The emplotment sought, to borrow from the textualists' dictionary, to narrate the history of the attempted creation of a more progressive world. But both archival projects ran into the difficulty that in creating their archives, they were undermining their own narrative, and opening up other narratives that they had perhaps not expected to find: Indian collaboration with and enthusiasm for Fascism and Nazism, Soviet Union-returned pan-Islamists-turned-Nazis, communists-turned-police-informers, and the like.²⁷

7.4. How to Do Things with Archives

Could you and I with fate conspire to grasp the sorry scheme of things entire, we might return to the discovery that there is an infinity of possible narratives in any archive, even those that someone self-consciously invents in the concrete or abstract sense; to which the correct response would be that yet there are less than infinite numbers

²⁵ See for instance Bombay Police Commissioner's Office File No. 3120/H in Krüger Nachlass, Box 85 No. 624.
²⁶ See Raza, Roy, and Zachariah, 'Introduction: The Internationalism of the Moment', *The Internationalist Moment,* for the difference between statist and non-statist internationalism.
²⁷ Benjamin Zachariah, 'Indian Political Activities in Germany, 1914–1945', in *Transcultural Encounters Between Germany and India: Kindred Spirits in the 19th and 20th Centuries,* ed. Joanne Miyang Cho, Eric Kurlander, and Douglas T McGetchin (New York: Routledge, 2013), 141–154, summarizes some of these trends.

of plausible narratives—and we are no further than before. However, before a longing like despair sends us yearning for the unity of knowledge or any other larger-than-life framework, let us linger on the notion of the frame, and use it as a visual metaphor. Presuming that we use pre-existing archives but frame our questions and reframe those archives as we frame our questions, the two being mutually dependent, we might suggest that the frame (and the lens that frames) are active parts of a visual field. Pushing any analogy too far or attempting too detailed an explication of a metaphor destroys its efficacy, of course, but nevertheless, it is these reframings that are the everyday, even subconscious, acts of historians, with the predilections of historians the lenses. The archive is approached with these framing devices, and the more peculiar the framing (the more peculiar the photographer or painter and the lenses or points of view s/he chooses), the more peculiar the outcome. For 'peculiar' read 'unsettling', and for 'settled' read 'historiographical consensus', and I think a reader will get the picture, or at least the metaphor.

In the two instances selected here, various 'official' archives were trawled by two pioneers of research who did not do much of the writing they planned to do, but in not doing so, nevertheless created (or invented) an archive. We have here a sense of how political activists or party functionaries (applied variously in ungenerous or generous manner to the two central characters behind the collections) turned historians turned accidental archivists; their archives then became the basis for archival collections that formed the core of future archives, the Archives for Contemporary History at JNU, or the ZMO, Berlin. It is of course bad practice simply to use someone else's primary sources to write histories she left unwritten: we don't quite know their framing practices or the focal lengths of their lenses in order to do this safely. But we are also able to reframe our research into these collections in terms of other questions: the relations between the GDR and India, the politics of the Cold War and its operation in the creation of historiographical frameworks, the victims of Stalinist terror and their posthumous reinstatement (albeit only in the realms of historiography), the rehabilitation of Indian collaborators with the Nazis and their elevation to diplomatic power, or the status of the Indian Communist Party in its undivided and post-split forms (the CPI split in 1964 largely as a consequence of the Sino-Indian border dispute and the war of 1962),[28] to name a few possibilities (and it is beyond the scope of this chapter to do more than name them).

7.5. 'The' Archive? In Lieu of a Conclusion

Even an archive created for a particular purpose, then, is not the equivalent of a tuna-friendly net, and even a tuna-friendly net is intended not to catch tuna, while its user doesn't quite know what else it might accidentally catch, and even less what else it has failed to catch. While publishing archivists have indeed spent some time understanding the anxieties of archive-users or archive-refuseniks, they have also continued to focus on seemingly banal considerations such as the usability of an archive, the expectations of archive users, and the purposes of archives other than for historical research.[29] Discernible nevertheless, in the move from a passive to a power-knowledge view of archives, was the acknowledgement of the possibility that archives, and therefore the archival profession itself, had an intellectual history.[30] That an archive was expected to assist the process of collective memory was acknowledged: and it was possible to raise questions as to the deliberate effacement of memory by non-archiving or by strategic destruction of the built environment, itself an archive.[31] We have known, of course, since the 1920s, that collective memory is taught, rather than being anyone's actually lived memory;[32] and it was acknowledged that archives produced memory and identity, with archivists complicit in the process.[33] It made sense, therefore, that in order to cement memories or identities that were not part of a dominant narrative, other archives could be self-consciously created to serve that purpose, to be

[28] Neville Maxwell, *India's China War* (London: Cape, 1970).

[29] See for example Louise Craven, ed., *What Are Archives? Cultural and Theoretical Perspectives: A Reader* (Aldershot: Ashgate, 2008), which attempts a survey.

[30] Tom Nesmith, 'Reopening Archives: Bringing New Contextualities into Archival Theory and Practice', *Archivaria* 60 (Fall 2005): 259–274.

[31] Kenneth E. Foote, 'To Remember and Forget: Archives, Memory, and Culture', *American Archivist* 53 (Summer 1990): 378–392.

[32] Maurice Halbwachs, *On Collective Memory* (new edition, Chicago: Chicago University Press, 1992): his theorization dates from 1925. See also Chapter 3.

[33] Joan M. Schwartz and Terry Cook, 'Archives, Records, and Power: The Making of Modern Memory', *Archival Science* 2 (2002): 1–19: Joan M. Schwartz and Terry Cook, 'Archives, Records, and Power: From (Postmodern) Theory to (Archival) Performance', *Archival Science* 2 (2002): 171–185.

part of such a differentiated diversification of archivally available voices.[34] But as we still had to read 'the colonial archive', we needed to pay attention not just to the content of colonial archives but also to their form, because 'the archive was the supreme technology of the late nineteenth century colonial state'.[35] And of course, before we could read against the grain, we had to know how to read with the grain.[36] In some ways, we can consider all of this in the vein of Bernard Cohn's article on the census and the production of hard categories of social stratification:[37] it is both obvious and necessary to place on record that archives produce the realities that they claim merely to collect descriptions of. But they cannot do that without the historians, and the historiography, that draw upon them. And if we work, as all of this implies, with an active as opposed to a passive conception of archives, then historians definitely produce, or invent, the archives that produce the realities they choose to call into being.

Let us, for the sake of argument, call this process of production 'playing the archival game'—there isn't an obvious archive for the study of 'x' or 'y', so let's create it and start collecting, creatively looking for material wherever we may find it—and whether we house it in a particular physical space or it remains in our imagination, collated and ordered, though its component bits come from different archives (in both senses, repository and content), is not important. But you cannot control the meanings of the archives you create: your own emplotment is undermined by what you have invented as an archive, in your own ordering and of course in others' reordering (or partial reconjuring, following footnotes and bibliographies to reconfigure that which remained in your imagination), where you cannot control what meanings or narratives it generates. Why, though, is this not true of 'the' archive, state-run celebrations of the state's stateness? Given the scale and nature of the operations, does the dream-catcher not catch other people's dreams?

---

[34] Catherine Hobbs, 'The Character of Personal Archives: Reflections on the Value of Records of Individuals', *Archivaria* 52 (Fall 2001): 126–135; Shaunna Moore and Susan Pell, 'Autonomous Archives', *International Journal of Heritage Studies* 16, no. 4–5 (2010): 255–268; Andrew Flinn, Mary Stevens, and Elizabeth Shepherd, 'Whose Memories, Whose Archives? Independent Community Archives, Autonomy and the Mainstream', *Archival Science* 9 (June 2009): 71–86.

[35] Ann Laura Stoler, 'Colonial Archives and the Art of Governance', *Archival Science* 2 (2002): 87–109: 87.

[36] Stoler, 'Colonial Archives and the Art of Governance', 100.

[37] Bernard Cohn, 'The Census, Social Structure and Objectification in South Asia', in *An Anthropologist Among the Historians*, (Delhi: Oxford University Press, 1987), 224–254.

Jacques Derrida reminds us of what he thinks are the origins and meanings of the Archive:

> the Greek arkheion: initially a house, a domicile, an address, the residence of the superior magistrates, the archons, those who commanded. The citizens who thus held and signified political power were considered to possess the right to make or to represent the law. On account of their publicly recognized authority, it is at their home, in that place which is their house (private house, family house, or employee's house), that official documents are filed. The archons are first of all the documents' guardians. They do not only ensure the physical security of what is deposited and of the substrate. They are also accorded the hermeneutic right and competence. They have the power to interpret the archives.[38]

Obviously the European impulse to return, etymologically or historically (the distinction is often forgotten), to a Greek or Latin origin (mirrored today by counter-indigenisms from South Asia) does not make for a reliable history of that origin, far less of the continuation and continuities of the entities themselves. Does this power exist in the collections described in this article? What power to interpret, with any authority, resides in these collections that have become archives? Is the act of archiving them an attempt to challenge the Archon? Or is a 'real' archive, in the Derridean sense, only that which embodies the power of the state? And to complete the journey round the circle that passes as an argument in this vein, an archive in state authority is an archive; without state authority, it is not an archive.

What I am suggesting is that the singular control over history and memory that is implied by this Derridean position has never existed, and that an etymology is not a history. Inventing the archive is not the same as reading the archive, with or against the grain: in the first, material is made to serve as archival evidence, called into being in the service of a question or set of questions; in the second, the material is already archival, only to be 'read' differently by different historians. 'The' colonial archive— where is that? When was that? The Invention of the Archive can now be a

---

[38] Derrida, 'Archive Fever', 9–10.

phrase that is recoverable from the enormous condescension of historiography: we invent an archive every time we have a question to answer, and then someone reinvents the archive in the service of a new question.

Viewed from this perspective, of course, historians are open to the charge of the old spectre of 'cherry-picking' as archives are used to confirm a bias, test a hypothesis, or used in the manner of consulting an appropriate oracle. Are we always sure of what we are looking for? Are we looking for Something that we suspect is there? Are we looking for Anything? For Everything? When do we think we know what our Archives might be? These are questions that lead in the direction of an enquiry into the nature and state of the discipline, if it is still a discipline, that we inhabit. Does anyone browse in an archive in the way that some historians were wont to do? What do we need to know before we know what we are looking to know?

Afterword

Is There a Discipline to This?

Our understanding of the lives and worlds of Indian historical thinking would be pretty poorly served if it did not include material on the social, political, and institutional landscapes in which historians operate, and the demands made upon them and the histories they write. This would require an account of the complexities of Indian historiographical production, the vicissitudes of the historical profession in a wider sense, and at the same time, the meanings of history in the public domain in India and outside, and the (diminished?) role of professional historians or histories in public arguments.

Historiography is usually written about as an internal tale of approaches, of intellectual choices or political commitments. An externalist and contextual approach would have to include the politics of the spaces and zones of engagement it inhabited. That would of course need to account for the banality of everyday academic life, an *Alltagsgeschichte* of machinations, of the awarding and sustaining of professorial chairs at universities, rigged jobs, collusive funding and collusive footnoting, the selective inclusion of subservient minorities, and many other such unsavoury episodes that are systemic problems of academic life. If we have indeed adopted a power/knowledge approach (whose discursive hegemony must seem at least partly ironic to the Foucauldians among us), the workings of institutions, their evolution, their functioning, and their histories, as well as the collective biographies of historians working in them, should be up for scrutiny. This, I think, is both in opposition to and a logical continuation of the identitarian arguments made for and against the speaking or writing voices of historians that this book has concerned itself with in large measure; for if we are not to reduce public utterances to the identitarian (or youdentitarian) identifications of the speaker or writer, a more contextualized understanding of how disciplines and institutions work is required. This understanding has to be more than a game of guessing victimhood affiliations from names or assumed origins of individuals.

For now, however, this is a programmatic statement rather than a history that has been or is being written. Academic disciplines claim the right of a self-regulating corporation, and the claiming of that autonomy is based on the right to self-regulate, itself derived from the feudal idea of being 'judged by one's peers'. Historians, to take our current disciplinary example, are a corporation for itself, though not in itself. Therefore, they are less and less accountable to anyone outside. That was perhaps precisely the point once, when universities emerged as distinctive institutions in the twelfth century—the need to maintain autonomy from the domains of feudalism (even as universities were largely modelled in their internal organization on feudal hierarchies), or from absolute monarchs and arbitrary laws; however, the need therefore to maintain robust self-criticism systems, not in some diluted Maoist sense, but in a better and more honest fashion, is ever greater and has not been observed, seriously reducing the weight the profession of historians can have as a body operating in the public. The social capital of historians is shrinking in value. In an analogy that we can draw from the world of companies and shares, the expectation of future value is seriously damaged by a perception that mismanagement of its own affairs has damaged a corporate entity. And in the world of markets and futures, this is what has become crucial for the profession of historians.

In the world outside academia, claims to history remain crucial in the public domain. Present-day Indian situations such as the vanishing of characters of historical importance from textbooks,[1] or the engineering of mob action around the alleged 'historical' misrepresentation in a film of a character that was fictional in the first place,[2] or of Indian editions of 'controversial' books being edited, censored, or banned, might be more obviously a caricature of history (and it is true that every time the Hindu right has had a smell of power they have attempted to edit or censor

---

[1] https://asia.nikkei.com/Politics/Hindu-nationalism-creeping-into-Indian-textbooks, accessed 28 December 2018.

[2] https://www.bbc.com/news/world-asia-india-42048512, accessed 28 December 2018.

historical texts), but the profession as a whole, which is a far larger entity than 'historians of India', no longer has any common standards to which to hold its own members, let alone to explain themselves to members of the public.

Meanwhile, historical framing and public controversy appear to collude over the necessity of avoiding 'insults to groups'. Groups seek legitimation by asking to be represented as part of the 'freedom struggle' or 'national movement' or even the 'Great Revolt of 1857'—'we were there too' becomes a model for political legitimation through history, with the 'we' projected back in time. History has a purpose as direct justification for present-day problems or solutions. States can base their actions on events allegedly associated with Vedic or Mughal or Maratha times and seek retrospective revenge or justification, on the basis of the assumption that the past is a guide to the future, and of course the present. The counterarguments do not for the most part attack this basic principle of arguing from historical (instrumentalized) narrative to present-day political imperative, arguing instead (from counter-instrumentalized 'history') that the past was not quite as depicted, and therefore the present and future were different too.

A persistent question lingers on about the role of history in the public domain and the role of historians as 'experts' who 'tell the truth'; another is the question of whether and when it was important for the right to attack this more or less widely held view of 'objectivity' as much as it was for the identitarian 'left' to do so. The right in India, being from a former colony and therefore able to claim victimhood generically, was of course able to draw on versions of PoCo and PoMo as they emerged (long before the 'white' identitarianism of the 2000s and 2010s), and even more so as it became an obligatory language of academic legitimacy that had resonances in the public domain outside academia. PoMo was useful to destabilize truth-claims, and PoCo was useful to sustain or to invent an indigenist narrative, versions of which were already available.

None of this challenged the dominance of an undifferentiated idea of nationalism in Indian historiographical production—the assumption that history would serve the 'nation-building' (or more accurately state-building) process remained untouched, because there has not been an anti-state or non-statist historiography of India. Historical thinking can therefore only provide different versions of nationalism and different fantasies of state power.

How does one historicize the present in historiographical terms? How does one look at the uses of history in the present? Does one examine the truth-claims of those uses? Does one instead or additionally look at what claims are being made with history? And does one intervene by destabilizing the truth-claims of the public uses of history, and/or by examining each claim for its mechanisms of exclusion, its political potential for danger? Have we to fight back against 30 odd years of resolute opposition to truth-as-'closure' and celebration of subjectivities as 'postcolonial' self-assertion? Who is this 'self' anyway?

Are we surprised then that we cannot hold a 'public' in general to standards of historical thinking that are recognizable in the profession, when the profession cannot recognize or agree on such standards? What is our view of whether or how we communicate with an audience outside of the profession itself? And given our own fragmentation into specializations, interest groups, self-perpetuating cliques, however, you wish to describe it, can we even talk to one another?

To what extent does one take one's public duties seriously? Does one stand forth (or pose) as 'public intellectual' or retreat to a quietism that protects self, income, and family? How do we deal with self-censorship by intellectuals—what should we stop saying so as not to endanger ourselves—before the law, before the regime, and its organizations of violence? How far does that go—do we start examining our names themselves to ask whether we can 'pass' as the mainstream (in India, appearance is an unreliable guide to religion or caste, but it serves as a shortcut: beards can be dispensed with, but what does someone from Shillong or Kohima who allegedly does not fit the general idea of what an 'Indian' looks like do as a defence mechanism)? There used to be an old adage, or perhaps a slogan: demand democracy where there is none, point out its limitations where democracy exists and point out the democratic critiques of forms of actually existing democracy. How would that translate into historical thinking when hard or soft teleologies of 'Mera Bharat Mahaan' (My India is Great') dominate public debates and silence other voices? And how would the accommodation of those other voices happen without descending into victimhood narratives that are allegedly empowering?

But perhaps the larger, and prior, question is: have we anything to say at all? As professionals? As we flail around with analogies, teleologies, genealogies, and slogans, perhaps we should figure out that the creation of appropriate and appropriable histories for often very instrumental political purposes will take place regardless of whether it is endorsed or not by 'the profession', which of course is an idealized creature that does not exist. The answer to the question of how far we resist this or collude in it might be the last remaining way of not abandoning our posts.

Index

For the benefit of digital users, indexed terms that span two pages (e.g., 52–53) may, on occasion, appear on only one of those pages.